Higher Ground

DUKE UNIVERSITY PRESS   Durham and London   2006

Higher Ground

Ethics and Leadership in the Modern University

NANNERL O. KEOHANE

© 2006 DUKE UNIVERSITY PRESS

All rights reserved.

Printed in the United States of America
on acid-free paper

Designed by C. H. Westmoreland

Typeset in ITC Stone by Keystone Typesetting, Inc.

Library of Congress Cataloging-in-Publication Data

Keohane, Nannerl O., 1940–

Higher ground : ethics and leadership in
the modern university / Nannerl O. Keohane.

p. cm.

Includes bibliographical references and index.

ISBN 0-8223-3786-X (cloth : alk. paper)

1. Education, Higher—Administration.

2. Education, Higher—Moral and ethical aspects.

3. Education, Higher—Aims and objectives.

I. Title.

LB2341.K39 2006

174'.9378—dc22   2005030739

Duke University Press gratefully acknowledges
the support of trustee emerita Dorothy Lewis Simpson
W'46 and W. Hunter Simpson, who have contributed
generously toward the production and distribution of
this book.

Contents

Acknowledgments

Each of these papers was written for a specific purpose over the past two decades. My editors at Duke University Press brought their considerable skills to bear in transforming a set of essays and speeches into a more coherent book, in a timely and efficient fashion.

In preparing the book for publication, we have not brought references up to date, nor have we extensively rewritten any paper. We have corrected a couple of errors of fact, and to avoid repetition have omitted several passages that appeared more than once in the different papers. The editors have also made some minor stylistic changes in each of the papers, to alleviate grammatical quirks or eccentricities, and make the book more readable. These people at the press, including especially Ken Wissoker, Courtney Berger, and Fred Kameny, have been very helpful all along the way, and it is a pleasure to express my gratitude to them.

Senior Vice President John Burness at Duke University first broached the idea of publishing these essays and speeches, and provided encouragement and support throughout.

Deborah Copeland in the President's Office kept track of all my Duke papers and helped shepherd the process from beginning to end. Paul Baerman, who provided assistance in speechwriting during my final years at Duke, suggested some of the prose in a few chapters here, particularly certain passages in the Atwell Lecture to the American Council of Education and the essay on "The Liberal Arts and the Role of Elite Higher Education." In each of these instances, the conception of the papers, and most of the prose, is my own. And apart from this, the responsibility for the authorship of all the papers is entirely mine.

Dorothy Lewis Simpson (W '46) and her husband W. Hunter Simpson graciously provided financial support for publication.

Dottie was on the search committee that brought me to Duke, and she and Hunter became our good friends over the years.

Fred Chappell was kind enough to grant permission to reproduce his poem "The Attending" at the end of the Introduction. I am grateful as well to several publishers who allowed us to reproduce other material; they are listed on the last page of this book.

My husband Robert O. Keohane helped me think through the arguments in many of these speeches and essays and provided useful comments on drafts. Even more important, his staunch and buoyant support for my work as a university administrator was essential in making it possible for me to do my job. And his continuing, deep involvement as a distinguished scholar ensured that I never lost sight of the major purpose of my work. As always, I am deeply grateful.

The book is dedicated to my father, James Arthur Overholser, who found his vocation as a teacher only late in life but pursued it with great joy. More informally, he taught me a great deal as I was growing up, and launched me as a leader in higher learning with a lovely invocation when I was inaugurated at Wellesley in 1981.

I know that he (and my mother) would have been proud of whatever I was able to accomplish as the president of two fine institutions, and would rightly have disclaimed any responsibility for the mistakes of judgment that occurred along the way.

Finally, I want to thank Duke University for the generous sabbatical support provided to me while I was working on this volume, and the Center for Advanced Study in the Behavioral Sciences for making available its uniquely hospitable environment for scholarly exploration and refreshment.

Princeton, New Jersey   September 2005

Introduction

The papers and speeches in this book are about governance in higher education. They are held together not by a discussion of techniques of administration or a comprehensive philosophy of education, but by a set of deep personal convictions about American colleges and universities and their role in society. These convictions were shaped by my experience as president of Wellesley College and Duke University, and my training and career as a political philosopher. As a political theorist, I studied reflections on power and community offered by philosophers across the centuries. As a president, I was responsible for many aspects of the governance of two institutions. These speeches and essays thus reflect a particular synthesis of theory and practice.

The convictions that provide common themes throughout the book include a belief in the durable, distinctive character of universities over time, as institutions that respond to deep human needs and aspirations. I regard colleges and universities as intergenerational partnerships in learning and discovery, with compelling moral purposes that include not only teaching and research but also service to society. Successful leadership in such institutions requires skills useful for leadership in any human organization, as well as an understanding of the distinctive character of academic life and a true spirit of collaboration. The papers reflect in several ways a commitment to diversity, and a serious concern about the implications of growing inequality both within and outside our institutions. And they include some guardedly optimistic speculation about the future of universities in our country and the world.

It is often noted that a few European universities are among the oldest human institutions still flourishing today. They have been replicated closely on other continents, and although there have been major changes, the core enterprise remains recognizable over all those centuries. Such continuity is remarkable among human organizations. This helps account for the conviction that universities will survive the challenges of our own day—challenges from new technologies, corporate alliances, government indifference, for-profit competitors, consumerist students, nomadic faculty members, and hostile publics. Some pundits have confidently predicted that the challenges will do us in entirely. But institutions like ours have dealt with worse things in the past, and I believe that they will continue far into the future.[1]

THE DISTINCTIVE GOALS OF HIGHER EDUCATION

Colleges and universities play a crucial part in determining whether humanity will indeed have a future, and what it will be like. Our institutions have significant moral purposes; we are not just collections of loosely affiliated persons with convergent or conflicting interests, but institutions that make a difference in the world through pursuing our basic goals. To understand this perspective, it is important to consider what a university is at its core, and how that core has evolved across the centuries. In the essay "The Mission of the Research University," I offer a definition: "The modern research university is a company of scholars engaged in discovering and sharing knowledge, with a responsibility to see that such knowledge is used to improve the human condition." I emphasize the fellowship here among students as well as faculty members, which I call "an intergenerational partnership in discovery and exploration."

Such a definition may appear hopelessly naïve. Most of us, most of the time, are not thinking about our campus as a "company of scholars engaged in discovering and sharing knowledge." Faculty members are often caught up in the irritating minutiae of department or committee meetings, grading, letters of recommendation, dealing with recalcitrant colleagues, bonehead administrators, and unresponsive students, juggling impossible demands of work and family. Undergraduates of the traditional age are much more likely to be thinking about athletics, sex, the agenda for the club they belong to, the newest irritation from their roommate or intrusion from the 'rents and plans for the weekend, as they sit through what may seem an incomprehensible or impossibly boring lecture, than

2

they are to be celebrating their place in an "intergenerational partnership." Graduate and professional students brood about when they will get a job, and how to get the attention of the mentors who are crucial to their success in doing so. Administrators worry about scarce resources, pressures from the state capital or the alumni body, faculty members who "just don't get it," fiercely competitive admissions and faculty recruitment, students who are into drugs or alcohol, and political activities on campus that bring down the wrath of the local populace or capture the attention of the national media.

Nonetheless, there is a basic truth in this definition that most of us would acknowledge, at least at certain points of our lives. When a prospective freshman chooses a college or university, and dreams about what it will be like, the prospect of a new level of intellectual challenge, and opportunities for mingling with other bright people of all ages committed to teaching and learning are among the things that will probably be on his mind, along with more mundane concerns. A student who commits to graduate work in a discipline that fascinates her will surely think about the new horizons she expects to be open to her and the contributions she will make to her chosen field, not just about doing well on the GRE. And a newly minted Ph.D. lucky enough to get a good job in a fine institution would not find the definition of a "company of scholars" far off the mark in what he hopes to find and enjoy in the life he has chosen.

Not only the faculty and students but all those engaged in making the university work are crucial to this enterprise, and "the benefits of advancing knowledge should extend to all its members." Our "partnership in discovery and exploration" should "include those who provide material support for the voyage."[2] This means job training and skills development, opportunities to attend lectures or take courses that will help them grow personally and professionally if they have the time and qualifications to do so. Workers on campuses at every level tell us that they take special pride in being part of a university, and identify with its successes—so long as they are paid a salary they regard as fair, have challenging work that they see as connected to the mission of the university, and are regarded by others with respect. Sadly, these conditions are too rarely met;

many campus workers see their role as "just another job," in which no one asks their views on how the enterprise could be improved, gives them a sense that their work contributes to the institution, or treats them with dignity. This is one of several ways in which contemporary social and economic inequalities have an invidious effect in higher education.

My definition of the university includes "discovering" and "sharing" knowledge, as well as using knowledge to "improve the human condition." The "sharing" was the original impetus for groups of clerics to band together and offer instruction for interested students in medieval times. Educating the young was also the prime motivation for the creation of the earliest universities in our own country, to train ministers, teachers, and lawyers for the new society.

From the outset, these institutions in America partook of the distinctive orientation of our people, at once idealistic and pragmatic, and were regarded as "improving the human condition." The "muddy commons and frame buildings" that were our earliest locations on this continent were crucial to the definition of civilization against the wilderness; these colleges were designed to contribute useful knowledge, by training citizens and professionals for a new world.[3] Many of these institutions were founded by religious groups, and the commitment to "improving the human condition" by educating clergy and laymen was very clear. The same was true in a different way for land-grant universities in the nineteenth century, where instruction in the "mechanical arts" to produce engineers, agronomists, and architects was a primary goal.

The focus on "discovery" as part of the mission of the university was a relative latecomer, both here and in Europe. Most of the great scientists and humanists for many centuries, as well as their lesser-known counterparts, the amateurs who pursued astronomy, botany, archaeology or history as avocations, were independent pioneers, not teachers or professors. In the schools founded by Greek scholars, including Plato's Academy, or in the academies of science common in Europe and America in the eighteenth century, some of these discoverers also formed part of a continuing "company of scholars." But colleges and universities taught primarily "received knowledge," familiar materials from a respected canon, sharing some of the surrounding society's suspicion for newfangled ideas rather than encouraging bold exploration. This separation between the "sharing" and "discovery" of knowledge was broken down in certain European universities, especially in Germany. By the late nineteenth century, it was also decisively breached in our own country. Both established and newer universities followed the Johns Hopkins, or Germanic, model, incorporating in the same institution the traditional liberal arts college and schools for professional training and advanced research.

As several of these papers emphasize, "the joys of pure research . . . can be profound." This exhilarating sense of discovery, along with the clear priority given to research accomplishments in the reward structures of higher education, explains why so many faculty members regard this as the most important aspect of their work. Research also contributes to "improving the human condition," in a directly utilitarian fashion—through medical research, applications of findings in the natural sciences, and developments in engineering. In less tangible but equally important ways, research on our campuses yields more effective legal systems and public policies, corporate management practices and global communications systems. Research in the humanities and the arts deepens our understanding of language and history, expands our awareness of what it is to be human, and enriches our lives in countless ways. It is thus not surprising that by the late twentieth century, "discovery" had become the primary purpose of the university in the minds of many people, including faculty members on research university campuses.

Research activities do not always conduce to building community, even when researchers work in teams. Tensions over scarce resources and concerns about proper credit for discovery separate scholars into their own cocoons rather than bringing them together to share information and learn from one another. What I call below the "fierce, focused curiosity" that marks the pure desire to *know*, to solve a problem that has worried people for centuries, makes people jealous of their time for research and resentful of other demands, including the "service to the institution" that helps make governance effective in research universities. But in laboratories with sufficient funding, and in those wonderful centers for advanced study that occasionally give scholars a break from their normal routines, the exchange of knowledge in the process of collective discovery can be profoundly rewarding and deeply enjoyable.

At the same time, the "sharing" part of our mission has grown more complex, more demanding, and potentially more exciting. New groups of students are seeking education, from immigrants to retired people; and new ways of sharing knowledge, through increasingly sophisticated forms of on-line learning, are being developed. Such new dimensions also bring new challenges, and create risks to the core enterprise of teaching and learning that should always be the heart of these complex and sometimes evanescent new endeavors.

One well-known way of picturing that core enterprise was President James A. Garfield's reference to Mark Hopkins, president of Williams College, sitting on one end of a log with a student sitting on the other.[4] All the fancy technologies, new devices for communication and presentation, should not obscure this fundamental relationship between teacher and student that defines our enterprise, whose radical simplicity is beautifully captured by the notion of the "log." It is surely true that teachers learn from their students, and that students learn a great deal from one another. And there is no doubt that when wisely used, new technologies for sharing knowledge vastly improve our capacities to teach and learn. But these truths should not be allowed to undermine the core responsibilities of the folks on both ends of that famous log.

Donald Kennedy's essay on the duties of faculty members, in addition to their rights, underscores this point.[5] It's important to be clear that students have duties as well. This point easily gets lost in our consumer culture, where students and their families are focused on how much they are paying for their time on campus, whether they will get into the grad school of their choice, and what kinds of jobs they hope to hold as a result. These concerns are understandable in an era of rising costs of higher education and intense competition for spaces in the most prestigious institutions. Some of the essays in this book deal with the dilemmas that this situation creates for us, and how we might go about addressing them. But the concerns should not overshadow the whole point of the education, which requires that students accept guidance from more experienced—and, we hope, wiser—members of the faculty, and put in long hours and hard work in order to grasp difficult material whose utility may not be immediately apparent.

Such commitments on the part of students also bring deep rewards, including one I often commended to first-year undergraduates at Duke at Opening Convocation (including my first in 1993). I used one of my favorite images from Michel de Montaigne's *Essais*: "We must establish a back shop (*arrière-boutique*) all our own, entirely free, in which to establish our real liberty and our principal retreat and solitude."[6] We all have such back rooms in our minds, and my counsel to the students was, "Think of your education first of all as a way of furnishing that back room of your mind."

This is the core concept of the university that animates these papers: a place where the important work of sharing and discovering knowledge can be carried on, supported, and expanded. The power of the concept depends upon the awareness that this is "some of the most exciting, rewarding, and deeply meaningful work done anywhere." I used this phrase in my Founder's Day Address at Duke in October 2003, and the spirit that it reflects surely permeates this book. And in that same speech, I went on to say: "If you ask why universities survive and flourish for centuries in many disparate cultures, despite incredible challenges and changes; why the students and teachers in Iraq are still dedicated to their enterprise amidst bombed out and looted classrooms; why girls and women in Afghanistan rushed to take advantage of the education that had so long been denied them—the answer has to be that universities are places where we pursue and nurture a fundamental human passion . . . [which is] as deep and hungry as any other human passion."[7]

THE MORAL PURPOSE AND PUBLIC RESPONSIBILITY OF COLLEGES AND UNIVERSITIES

The "moral purpose" of the university can be seen as a combination of all these features of our work, and more. We have an obligation to our predecessors and successors in our profession, as well as to our students and to one another—an obligation to keep the flame of knowledge burning, to do our best to stimulate and satisfy that "fundamental human passion" in our own time. This entails protecting the pursuit of truth when it leads to unpopular or unsavory results, and defending the freedom of speech of those who explore and define such difficult paths, against those within and outside the academy who may question the utility or veracity of those findings.

We also have an obligation to repay the debt we owe society for the resources provided to us from both public and private sources, by offering the best education we can to students in a variety of disciplines and professions, and by contributing the fruits of our discoveries to "improve the human condition." As I put it in my Address to the Faculty of Duke University in October 2002, "As a political philosopher, I see a loose kind of social contract here: it is in return for providing these services that universities are given public funds and public confidence. And in that sense, almost everything about our basic mission involves some form of public responsibility."[8]

One of the ways in which American higher education discharges our public responsibility has been through increasing access to education for people from all backgrounds. This has taken place in multiple ways. One of the earliest was the admission of women to several fine colleges established for their education in the late nineteenth century and then to a number of excellent universities, both as undergraduate and graduate students. During the twentieth century, Jews and blacks were admitted to institutions that had been closed to them, or where they had faced exclusionary quotas for many years. Increasing access has also involved the creation of institutions to serve people of varying ages and with different educational needs, including comprehensive universities, technical schools, and community colleges. Reaching out to students from abroad, and first-generation college students from immigrant families, has continued the tradition. The intentional accessibility of higher education in the United States has been one of the greatest strengths of both our system of higher education and our nation.[9]

Currently, however, we face a challenge in this area: the growing concentration of people of wealth and privilege in our élite institutions. This reverses a tendency that spans decades, and threatens to return our campuses to their nineteenth-century status: populated by children of the upper and upper middle classes, with a sprinkling of clerics thrown in for good measure. At a time when growing inequality in American life is a source of concern for many reasons, the possibility that our best colleges and universities will reinforce this trend rather than help to combat it is truly worrisome. In a democracy, educating leaders from many backgrounds, for many purposes, not just serving the children of the privileged, is a paramount public responsibility. We do not meet it by allowing our university system to become stratified on the grounds of social and economic class. Economic and class diversity, along with racial, religious, and gender diversity, has thus become a major topic of concern today.[10]

Diversity in higher education is a contested concept, prompting both passionate attacks and equally fierce defenses. Part of the problem stems from our lack of success, as educational leaders, in explaining just what diversity means in educational contexts, and why it is crucial to what we do. Educating students from many backgrounds is a key part of our public responsibility. But it is also a key part of what makes education work.

Diversity in education is not simply a matter of numbers. Bringing people of many backgrounds to campus is only the first step. If these students self-segregate, seeking out the company only of persons just like themselves, much of the educational purpose of diversity is defeated. As I point out in several of the papers in this book, nobody learns much by spending all their time in the company of people who share all their habits, perspectives, and beliefs. Instead, we learn from difference: historically, culturally, and through companionship. Majority students, at least as much as minority students, benefit from being educated in a diverse environment. Everyone is better prepared to live in a multicultural society and to provide leadership in that context. To fulfill our obligations to a democratic society, we must remain faithful to this commitment to diversity.

In terms of the moral purpose of the university, I also express concern about "the alarming tendency for inflated corporate compensation to spill over into higher education." This particular feature of "corporatization" holds that university CEOs and other se-

9

nior officials need to be paid salaries comparable to those in the corporate sector to reward them appropriately for their work, and keep them from jumping ship to some other job. Very few of us chose higher education for the financial rewards involved, and if we did, to use Humphrey Bogart's classic line in *Casablanca*, we were misled. I am well aware that the job of a university president is at least as complex and demanding as the job of any corporate CEO; but this does not, in my view, justify paying salaries that are anywhere near comparable. University leadership provides other kinds of rewards, and offers a different sort of prestige and recognition; and those who pay tuition or support our programs are doing so to help us accomplish our basic mission, not bolster our compensation.[11]

None of this is meant to imply that we should take a vow of poverty when we enter academic life. Indeed, I worry about prevailing levels of compensation for many people on our campuses—including part-time faculty members, lower-level administrators, staff employees in many areas. The work that these people do is crucial to the long-term success of our institutions, yet their salaries and wages are sometimes too meager to support their families unless they take a second job. My opposition to inflated salaries for people at the top is a reaction to the increasing gap between what those people are paid and what people in the trenches, in more ordinary jobs, can reasonably expect. On this dimension, contemporary corporations should worry as well. Excessive disparity between the salaries of those at the top and hard-working people further down the line stores up trouble for the future. It isolates the leaders from their followers, builds understandable resentment, and renders organizations more vulnerable to critics of our ethics and the way we use our funds.

Beyond this, I am convinced that it is part of our moral purpose to educate people who will, as citizens and as professionals in various fields, carry out their responsibilities with integrity, breadth of understanding, and compassion, as well as skill and commitment.[12] This is a tall order, and more controversial than my assertions in the preceding paragraphs. When many people hear this claim, they assume that it must entail indoctrination, instilling a particular moral doctrine in the classroom; but this is no part of what I have in mind.[13] Instead, I believe that universities should teach students to think clearly and carefully about ethical issues, just as they are trained in quantitative reasoning, aesthetic appreciation, or familiarity with history and culture. Amy Gutmann, writing about teaching professional ethics, says: "The valuable social purposes that universities serve—pushing forward the boundaries of human understanding; learning for leadership, citizenship, and living a good life—require us to conceive of the ethics of the academic profession as entailing both moral reasoning and moral conduct."[14]

The Kenan Institute for Ethics at Duke University provides a fine example of the "goodness of fit" between a thoughtful education in ethics and rigorous academic standards. The director of the institute, Elizabeth Kiss, and the political philosopher Peter Euben have recently defended ethical education for undergraduates as well as professional students with particular clarity in an essay on moral education in the modern university. As they put it: "While indoctrination clearly corrupts efforts to teach ethics, there are parallel dangers from the arguably more common professorial stance of moral detachment and ironic distance, which can convey to students the view that no value system is worth defending, reinforcing fashionable and uncritical forms of moral relativism and apathy."[15] We should also remember that for residential undergraduates, the entire college experience has formidable implications for their development as "whole persons," and often plays a major part in shaping their personal ethical beliefs, for good or ill.

Asserting that a good education builds character as well as training the mind would have been common wisdom in earlier centuries. I believe that it is time for us to recall this belief and adapt it for our times, confronting the numerous obstacles to accomplishing this goal in our complex and pluralistic society. In that spirit, I have often recalled Tocqueville's observation on the importance of education for ensuring that American society remain healthy and vigorous in the troubled times that he foresaw: "Educate then, at any rate, for the age of implicit self-sacrifice and instinctive virtues is already flitting far away from us, and the time is fast approaching when freedom, public peace, and social order itself will not be able to exist without education." For me, and I hope for my readers, that plea surely resonates today.[16]

CONTEMPORARY CHALLENGES

Yet how realistic is it to hope that any of these ambitious goals can be accomplished? Some contemporary observers assert that the university faces challenges that threaten to destroy it altogether. In a recent essay analyzing this phenomenon, Henry Steck identified the daunting number of threats that universities confront these days.[17] Several are hardly unprecedented: the pressures of large numbers of new students, opportunities and demands of new technologies, concerns about the sources and amounts of financial support, and the particular worries accompanying big-time athletics. Universities have grappled with similar problems in the past, and found creative ways of dealing with them; there is no reason to think that current leaders cannot do so as well.[18]

However, another set of challenges, less familiar than the ones above, is captured in the phrase "corporatization." It is these new factors that many observers have in mind when they make dire predictions about our future, especially as the new factors interact with and exacerbate more familiar ones. Steck's premise is "that the values of the market and the culture and the organizational style of corporate life are changing the university." The image he finds most appropriate is from "the classic film, *Invasion of the Body Snatchers*, a story of alien creatures who steal the soul and personality of individuals while retaining the identical and pleasant and amiable exterior."[19] Thus, where "once college presidents meant what they said when they spoke of excellence or providing opportunity, today such sentiments come across as advertising slogans, carefully crafted with the latest market research findings in mind." The books by respected authors that he cites in support of his position have titles like *The University in Ruins, Campus, Inc.*, and *The Knowledge Factory*.

This is strong stuff, and anyone who cares about higher education must reflect thoughtfully on Steck's charges. But what exactly is being claimed? As Steck himself points out, universities have long collaborated with the business sector and had significant ties to the corporate world. Thus, "the linkage between business interests and the university as a social institution . . . is rooted deep in the modern history of the American university." According to Steck and other observers, what has changed is that the corporate culture has permeated and transformed the university itself. Administrators behave like corporate executives and treat faculty members as employees; faculty members in turn increasingly think of themselves as "entrepreneurs with skills and products to sell." We "look to the corporate sector for operational guidelines" and think about our institutions as "businesses retailing and wholesaling a product." And more and more, it is said, we regard corporations themselves as partners, "sharing important decision-making" with them and allowing their priorities to determine our own.[20]

This particular set of challenges receives little attention in this collection. A cynical reader might assume that this is because my colleagues and I didn't recognize the problem during my years as a university president, or even that I embodied it, so that all my smooth prose about "excellence or providing opportunity" is just so much evidence that body snatchers are at work. I would argue, instead, that universities like Duke are more resilient than the critics allow. The corporate pressures outlined above have so far been kept within reasonable limits, and not permitted to deform or denature the core enterprise. It's not that we are unaware of the problem, or remain untouched by these complex and somewhat novel forces. We feel the pressures these critics worry about, and no doubt there are times when we go further in the direction of "commercialization" than they would find appropriate. But for the most part, the distinctive character of the university has been sufficiently powerful and flexible to allow us to deal with these challenges by using the same kinds of instruments that have proved their value to faculty members and administrators in the past.

I am well aware that this has been possible in part because Duke (and institutions like Duke) enjoy a degree of financial security and broad-based support that is the envy of many other institutions. We can resist the temptation to accept lucrative partnerships or questionable sources of support that are much harder to turn down if your organization is facing severe financial pressures. We also have the tradition and the privilege of choosing, for our senior administrators and trustees, people who "get it" about universities, including many who are themselves respected academics.

Not reflected in these papers, however, are the hours we spend, as administrators, faculty leaders, and trustees, figuring out how to walk the fine line between rejecting corporate support and being dominated by corporate partners. We are very conscious of this problem, but have had the good fortune to be able in most instances to define our part of the bargain, in clinical research, medical and engineering partnerships, and support for research and policy development on the environment, institutional property issues, health care, and other major social problems. Nor do the papers mention the hours we spent dealing with threats from the "commercialization" of big-time athletics, on a campus where athletics rightly hold a very significant place in the hearts of students, faculty, and staff as well as alumni of all ages. We talked about what kinds of commercial messages we would allow, and in what contexts; about student-athlete admissions and time commitments; about coaches' salaries and lucrative TV and pre-season appearances; and about how the Duke "brand" might be used or abused.

In one of my annual reports to the faculty of the university, in October 1997, I mused about the similarities and differences between corporations and research universities. I began by stressing the differences: no simple "bottom line," no shareholders, a truly weird pricing structure that in many institutions covers no more than three-quarters of the cost of the education we provide, no clear-cut "product," and distinctive difficulties with improving "productivity." However, I went on to note that universities can learn from corporations in the area of strategic planning, through "thinking in bold, hard-hitting and visionary terms about their future." I pondered some of the challenges that Duke is likely to face in the years ahead, and suggested how we might rethink our enterprise to make it more likely to be successful in the climate that we faced. But although the speech points out some lessons that we might learn from corporate strategic thinking—lessons that I have no doubt are valuable and not in any sense antithetical to our mission—it ends by reaffirming what I called the "Madisonian model" of checks and balances as the appropriate governance structure for the university, with significant faculty participation, not the corporate or bureaucratic model as such.[21]

For the most part, however, the challenges to higher education identified in the pages that follow are not much related to "corporatization." Instead, I worry about access to education in a world of rising costs and increasing economic inequalities, and about finding ways to keep those costs under some kind of control. I ponder the impact of information technologies on our core mission, how we can use them boldly and imaginatively while avoiding their potential pitfalls. I express concerns about threats to academic freedom and appropriate expressions of opinion on campus. I consider the "uses of diversity" and how we can take best educational advantage of our increasingly pluralistic campuses. And I explore the challenges and long-term implications of becoming more "global" institutions and at the same time carrying out our responsibilities to the cities and towns that are our institutional homes.

THE RISING COSTS OF HIGHER EDUCATION

In the 2003 Address to the Faculty, I noted that critics have surely been wrong in predicting that traditional universities will succumb to the competition from on-line counterparts ("cyber U") and rapidly follow the dinosaurs into extinction. But I go on to say that even though this prediction was wide of the mark, "instead of just celebrating that fact and moving on unthinkingly, we should ask why this is true, and even more important, ask the next question: if it isn't cyberspace education in the present crude, imperfect form that requires us to think in novel ways in order to survive and flourish, then what will it be?"

The three problems that I go on to discuss in the speech are "the inexorably rising costs of doing business as usual; challenges in undergraduate education, and threats to academic freedom." Quite a few of the papers included in this book touch on issues of undergraduate education.[22] On threats to academic freedom, see especially the excerpt "Threats to Academic Freedom" and "When Should a College President Use the Bully Pulpit?" In the next few pages, I want to summarize my thoughts about the "costs of doing business as usual," and add some reflections to those outlined in the papers that follow.

My concerns have to do with the peculiar economics of an ambitious research university. In an institution like Duke, the most powerful pressures are always towards greater expenditures: to meet the needs of faculty members engaged in expensive research operations through new buildings and laboratories; to create facilities and services that allow us to compete for and retain those faculty members in a highly competitive environment, including state-of-the-art libraries and cutting-edge technologies; to provide the environment for residential education that allows us to appeal to the best undergraduate students, which involves a different set of expensive facilities and services, including student centers, recreational and athletics facilities, computer support services, residence halls and dining facilities, counseling systems, and other perquisites that students and their families have come to expect. Unlike virtually every other complex economic enterprise, we are rewarded for spending more money, not for cutting costs. And as many observers have pointed out, the appetite for resources on a top-notch university campus is omnivorous and never satisfied.

So what's the problem? Administrators and trustees in every institution have for years embarked on cost-cutting measures in administrative services, constraining faculty and staff growth, holding salaries constant. These measures may not seem like much to the outside world, but they are very apparent to those on campus and are never easy to implement, given the complex governance structure of our institutions. Moreover, our prices don't even cover the full costs of the education we provide, so that every student, even those who pay the full "ticket price," receives some kind of subsidy. Instead of responding "rationally" by turning to lower-cost competitors, the students we want are as eager to get into top-notch institutions as we are to have them. There are far more well-qualified applicants for most of our programs than we can accommodate without diluting the quality of the experience; and although we hear a lot of grousing about our prices, there are plenty of families who seem to be willing, even eager, to pay for what we provide. Why then should we be concerned? And if we are, what more can we do, short of radically revising the entire structure of our institutions?[23]

I do not favor radically revising our whole structure; but I believe that there is ample cause for concern. As I said in that 2003 address, "I worry that we may be lulled into a sense of false confidence by the fact that our admissions statistics keep improving, and there seems to be no real limit to our ability to charge prices that rise steadily above inflation . . . Just as anyone with a sense of history knew that the 'new economy' of the 1990s could not possibly be sustained forever . . . so anyone who has been through Econ 101 knows that we can't just keep increasing our costs indefinitely."

One of the major problems with indefinitely rising costs in a time of shrinking government support is that the character of our student bodies, and thus of higher education in America, is in danger of being fundamentally altered. As I argued earlier in this introduction, that would be a very significant loss, reversing decades of efforts to make higher education affordable to bright, eager students from all kinds of economic backgrounds. But this historic commitment is being significantly eroded; "funds for aid for children of the poorest families are becoming scarcer," both from the federal government and from other sources. "More of the funds available for aid on many campuses are being channeled to attract talented students to a particular college, rather than to make it possible for underprivileged kids to attend any college at all."[24]

Campus leaders argue as eloquently as they can that the cost should not be borne entirely by students and their families, especially when their financial situation makes it difficult or impossible to pay what we charge. Education is a social good that provides major advantages for everyone, not just those who benefit directly, and our society should take significant responsibility for funding it, through both state and federal resources. But this argument more and more falls on deaf ears. Ignoring this truth is very shortsighted; and the resulting shift of responsibility to the increasingly strapped institutions themselves means that only a few of us will, in the foreseeable future, be able to offer the kind of financial aid that will truly allow students from any background to benefit from what we offer.

So there is good reason to worry about our steadily rising costs. But what can we do, besides assert as eloquently as we can the importance of our services, and spend ever-increasing amounts of time raising funds from generous and farsighted supporters? Proposed solutions include using information technology more creatively as it becomes more cost-effective and powerful. We should rethink the ancient system of having faculty members stand in front of student audiences and deliver lectures that could just as easily be read on line. Some skilful professors use the lecture system brilliantly; they deliver lectures with charisma and panache, and include students in discussion even in large lecture halls. Reading material on line is no substitute for this experience, and it should not be expected to replace it. Not all professors are charismatic, however, nor can they all draw large numbers of students meaningfully into discussion and response. Other ways of interacting directly with students, through small-group discussions with faculty members of the material provided on line, responses to students' individual questions and written work, and more informal encounters outside the classroom would improve teaching and learning significantly.

However, such an approach is unlikely to save money. If it is designed to serve students' needs effectively, it takes even more faculty time than the current system. Unless we are willing to accept a significant change for the worse in the student-faculty ratio— which would be a serious setback in our educational system—it's not clear how using technology in this way will help to control costs. The same is true for a number of other "technology fixes" such as more efficient administrative information systems, which may indeed improve the services we provide. The problem is that most of them require rather than conserve resources, to pay not only for the systems but also for the talented people who can support them and teach others to use them.

A more promising strategy, in terms of improving education while also reducing costs, is much more extensive use of inter-institutional collaboration. Universities have historically had the luxury of being "full-service" providers; apart from successful library consortia, and a handful of joint programs like the Five Colleges of the Connecticut Valley in New England, serious collaboration has been rare. I argue in several of these essays that this needs to change. There are multiple ways in which we can benefit from significant new divisions of labor among our institutions. Collaboration both with our physical neighbors and through virtual linkages will make it possible to offer a wider range of courses for students and provide collegial ties for faculty members in small departments, without having to produce everything on our own campus.

This proposal faces a number of significant obstacles. The most stubborn is the belief on the part of many faculty members (and some administrators) that nobody else can do whatever I do as well as I can, whether it's teaching Swahili or providing library services. Antitrust laws designed to prevent corporate monopolies have been used several times against institutions of higher education, and the fear of this prevents universities from considering agreements that most people would judge to be clearly in the public interest.[25] Collaboration means meshing calendars and schedules (no mean task on any campus) and often accepting some travel time to a neighboring institution. This in turn requires addressing parking and transportation issues (everyone's least favorite topic) and learning new technological skills to communicate more successfully.

Collaboration requires taking action jointly with your competitors for faculty and students, even in some cases your bitter athletics rivals. This was in the minds of many people at Duke and UNC–Chapel Hill when we launched a number of substantial collaborative programs. As I put it in a speech on our neighboring campus: "It is as if the families of Romeo and Juliet, in addition to fighting each other on sight when discovered on Franklin Street or in front of Duke Chapel, were also partners in the thriving law firm of Montague and Capulet on the side."[26] But as we discovered, the rewards can be significant, in enhanced collegiality for faculty and graduate students, especially in small departments; the range of options available to students in terms of both courses and extracurricular experiences; and potentially significant cost reductions through cutting back on certain programs and expecting students to meet their needs on other campuses.

Cutting programs is never easy. As I noted in my Address to the

Faculty in 1997, "When a president or provost talks about abolishing programs, the tendency of many faculty members is both to reach for their wallets and to raise the flag of academic freedom." But unless some campus programs are cut back or phased out, the economic and educational benefits will never be realized. Like all significant change on campus, this collaborative course requires committed, persistent, visionary leadership at the top.

THE CHARACTERISTICS OF ACADEMIC LEADERSHIP

In "Politics as a Vocation," Max Weber described politics as "a strong and slow boring of hard boards [which] takes both passion and perspective."[27] That lecture was delivered at Munich University in 1918, with a companion lecture, "Science as a Vocation." Taken together, these two brilliant essays provide an excellent perspective on why academic leadership is important, and how difficult it is for those who are by vocation scientists and scholars to understand it or exercise it successfully.

Weber makes clear that the work of scholarship must be highly focused and supremely intense. "Whoever lacks the capacity to put on blinders, so to speak, and to come up to the idea that the fate of his soul depends on whether or not he makes the correct conjecture at this passage of this manuscript may as well stay away from science. . . . Without this strange intoxication, ridiculed by every outsider; without this passion . . . you have *no* calling for science and you should do something else."[28] Both vocations, therefore, require passion: "for nothing is worthy of man as man unless he can pursue it with passionate devotion." But the means and the mental approaches are quite different.

Towards the end of "Science as a Vocation" Weber distinguishes between political science and practical politics. In a political meeting, he pointed out, the "words one uses . . . are not means of scientific analysis but means of canvassing votes and winning over others. They are not plowshares to loosen the soil of contemplative thought; they are swords against the enemies."[29] Only in rare instances do university presidents think of their arguments as "swords against the enemies." Such an approach normally undermines our efforts and makes it impossible to succeed. But it is equally true that if decisions are to be made and action taken, the ideas of a leader cannot simply be "plowshares to loosen the soil of contemplative thought." They must be designed to plant seeds for growth, cultivate those seeds, and move towards harvest.

Successful leadership requires intensity and focus, but of a very different kind than the mindset of the scientist. Leadership requires both breadth and depth, and depends upon a particular form of good judgment.[30] This perspective encompasses multiple possibilities; it is goal-oriented, but also needs peripheral vision that is alert to where the next challenges are coming from, not the fierce, laser-like focus of the scholar. Both activities require patience and persistence; but the obstacles that confront practitioners of each encounter are quite different, and so are the ways of measuring success.

The job of a university president has a number of peculiarities that thoughtful practitioners have mused about across the years. As Bart Giamatti put it in introducing his reflections on the job: "Being president of a university is no way for an adult to make a living. . . . It is to hold a mid-nineteenth-century ecclesiastical position on top of a late-twentieth-century corporation."[31] Given the highly traditional, distinctive culture of the academy, it is difficult for men and women trained in other professions to succeed in these posts. A leader who has excelled in a career with different mores and expectations inevitably finds it hard to understand the particular requirements of leadership in higher education. Some successfully make this transition; but it is far easier for those who have spent their working lives as members of faculties to "speak the language" and grasp the motives behind what otherwise may seem incomprehensible proposals or objections. These leaders are also familiar with the deliberate pace at which action on campus is normally conducted.[32]

These men and women face a different challenge, however, as they move into university administration: how to leave behind the skills of the scholar, and adopt those essential to leaders of complex organizations. This was one of the most difficult aspects of my job at first. I continued to think of myself as a member of the faculty when I moved directly into the presidency of my alma mater. As I took the job, I was as delighted by the news that Wellesley was simultaneously promoting me to full professor as I was by the presidency. I assumed that the skills I had acquired in becoming an associate professor at Stanford would serve me well in my new post. But even in a small, collegial environment like Wellesley, it was obvious that I had crossed some deep divide in becoming an administrator, and that the faculty could no longer, and with reason, consider me one of them.[33] And it became equally clear that many of the skills of a successful faculty member would not carry me very far in my new position.

My colleagues in political philosophy, somewhat bemused by my decision to move to the president's office, wondered why I would leave the sunlit uplands of scholarship for Plato's Cave. Why would I spend my days helping people sort through shadowy reflections of reality rather than directly contemplating the Forms of truth?[34] Although I half-feared when I accepted the job that it might feel this way, I soon realized that this familiar image is way off the mark, as far as the university presidency is concerned. Administration requires as much mental acuity as scholarship, but of a different kind; and the issues one deals with are anything but shadowy.

Another of Plato's images, however, proved useful to me in envisioning and explaining to others what academic leadership is all about. Plato describes leadership as "cybernetics," and stresses skills of navigation.[35] This image of the navigator is closer to the mark in describing much of the president's job than other familiar analogies, each of which nonetheless rings true in particular contexts—including the jobs of mayor, preacher, negotiator, coach, and CEO. I used nautical metaphors in my first Annual Report to the Faculty of Duke in March 1994, to introduce the topic of strategic planning. The substance of that speech was closely bound to that particular purpose, so it is not included here. But the points about leadership are helpful as a background for much that follows.

In that address, I noted that Duke had "as an institution, a general sense of direction," and "a rough sense of the sources and character" of the strengths we wanted to protect and advance. There was an element of "saying can make it so" in this expression of faith. Giving voice to inchoate realities and calling them by appropriate names is one of the main instruments that a leader can use effectively. But I was (and am) convinced that there was a shared general understanding about where Duke needed to go if we were to realize our ambitions to become an even better university.

In the rest of the speech, I provided some examples of the goals we should keep in mind and the types of activities we would surely need to undertake as a university in the future. Becoming more precise about that direction, and how we were going to get there, was the whole point of the strategic planning exercise in which I was trying to enlist the faculty's involvement and support. And so I judged that it was a good idea to assume this shared understanding, rather than either question it or attempt to put it into too detailed a form. I went on to say: "Thus we are in the position of a group of adventurers linked by institutional affiliation, all in the same boat, as the saying goes, generally agreed on our destination. We know that there will be unforeseen storms and currents—we may be buffeted about, blown off course, becalmed; there will be problems with logistics in the galley, and arguments about how to get back on course at the helm. We also know that there is no Loran system cueing us in to precisely our location on this globe at every moment of our trip and homing us in to our destination. There are only compasses, and rough maps indicating generally the direction in which our destination lies. But we are better off relying on these guides than just setting out and trusting our luck to wind up someplace interesting."

I noted that in one of our planning discussions Duke had been compared to a large ship, "big and cumbersome and hard to move even when one knows the direction in which one wants to go." I suggested that instead "Duke might better be compared to a flotilla made up of several schools of different sizes, all generally agreed on the destination, each with its own resources and some degree of independence in charting the course." And in that context, I reflected on the role of the president: "Captaining a flotilla is complex in many ways, not least because it is hard to get everyone on board at the same time. Nonetheless, there are many advantages in a flotilla rather than a cumbersome barge or even a streamlined cruise ship—advantages of deftness, imagination, variety. And if we are to be a collection of enterprises, I like this metaphor better than . . . 'each tub on its own bottom.' Much better to be a group of boats going somewhere together, however haphazardly, than a stolid set of tubs firmly positioned on their bottoms."

And indeed, as I think back on my years in the president's office at Duke, the admiral of a flotilla seems about as good a description as one might find of what the job was really like. Each of the other "ships" in a significantly decentralized university has its own captain, a dean who commands a good deal of autonomy in many respects, including control of resources. Yet it was important that we all hang together, since the Duke name and the concept of the university, as well as its traditions and alumni loyalties, were much more powerful for a variety of key purposes than those of any of the schools individually. And there were many things that the central administration could do more efficiently and effectively than allowing each ship to have a full range of services and matériel. Thus, the president and her officers had a good deal of scope in setting the course, mediating disputes, responding to proposals and demands, creating basic parameters, deploying a few key sources of financial support, and providing aid and comfort to all concerned.

Nonetheless, there are always tensions in such a structure, between the central administration and the schools, between the dean's office and the departments or units of the schools, even between the department chairs and faculty members. The role of the faculty in a top-notch university is crucial in successful governance; this requires a distinctive approach to solving problems and developing strategies, compared to any other enterprise. As George Keller put it in a recent essay: "To govern a leading academic institution today is to deal heavily with gifted, avant-garde intellectual entrepreneurs who cling to medieval notions of community control over their own activities while wanting to help run a multimillion-dollar organization that has become a central institution in modern society."[36]

In such a setting, collaboration is essential—but so is leadership. A faculty critic of "the administration" at Duke once complained in a campus publication that "the president thinks it's her job to set the agenda" for the university. I pled guilty as charged. Setting the agenda is one of the main things a president is for. The crucial point, as I noted in one of my first essays on higher education, is that collaboration and leadership are not in conflict, but mutually reinforcing.[37]

In a later essay on this same topic, I discussed "the modern campus as a political system." I explored a model that has more in common with the Madisonian system of checks and balances than with the Hamiltonian model of a very strong presidency, or a more democratic Jeffersonian system. But I recognized that a Madisonian system can lead to stalemate and make it difficult to take action of any kind. So I concluded with these words: "To make our campus governance systems work effectively, we need both Madison and Hamilton. Presidents must be willing and able to lead, to inspire, to make tough choices, to bring others onto common ground, to envision. Given the challenges we face, the tendency on many campuses is to choose experienced managers to solve corporate problems. But if presidents lack qualities of courageous leadership and a deep understanding of the academy, the system is tilted out of balance."[38]

WHAT MIGHT THE FUTURE HOLD?

No less an authority than Clark Kerr recently described the future of higher education as "a road filled with potholes, surrounded by bandits, and leading to no clear ultimate destination."[39] As he puts it, compared with the 1960s, "having a clear view of the future is now much more difficult, perhaps impossible. We live in an age of too many discontinuities, too many variables, too many uncertainties, as almost any university president today can certify."[40]

Despite such precautions, in several of the papers in this book I muse about the likely situation of universities in the next few decades. Among the common themes is that universities will continue to have a physical identity, with many of our activities taking place on a campus, rather than becoming completely "virtual." Depending solely on networks and computer linkages for the transmission of knowledge would not be in any way impossible; the feasibility of the virtual campus is now beyond question.[41] But as I said in the Stanford Centennial Address on the University in the Twenty-first Century: "it remains true that the reasons why people come together to learn in the intensified atmosphere of the university campus transcend the mechanisms by which knowledge is stored and transmitted."

It is clear also that in the years ahead, education will become an increasingly important goal for people across the lifespan. Computer linkages provide wondrous opportunities for burnishing professional skills or exploring new fields at any age. But those in later life who have time, money, and interest in educational experiences often crave the opportunity to interact with teachers and other learners and to visit new places, not just to learn in cyberspace.

The advantages of computer linkages in sharing knowledge are incontrovertible; these linkages offer astounding opportunities to interested scholars around the globe. The world's major libraries are increasingly available to anyone with access to the Internet. Computer discs in ordinary personal computers allow us to tour the great museums of the world, roam around famous ruins, turn over the artifacts, learn more about the society and culture of almost any region through visits in cyberspace. MIT makes its syllabi and course materials available to eager students around the globe. These steps enhance our ability to teach and learn in countless ways, and fortunately, there will be many more such enterprises in the years ahead.[42]

However, the "brave new world" of information technology, like the one Miranda marveled at in Shakepeare's *Tempest*, is not without its pitfalls. As I point out elsewhere in this book, "ironically, the wonders of email and teleconferences and satellite hookups may make it *less* likely that people in the future will actually assemble . . . Why risk airline cancellations and jet lag if you can sit in your own study and communicate with your counterparts in Florence or Tokyo?"[43] But there are significant differences between communicating in cyberspace and being in the same place. These have to do not only with the different quality of the "relationships" engendered when people never meet face to face and share a meal, but also with the absence of the immersion in sights and sounds and smells that make cyberspace learning about nationality and culture inevitably thin by comparison with the "real world."

Computers may soon be able to translate seamlessly from one language to another, obviating the learning of another language for research in many disciplines. But despite its advantages, this will be a mixed blessing. Learning a language is an important route to learning about the varied ways of looking at the world experienced by members of our species. If everything that we in the United States need to know can always be retrieved in English, our tendency towards narrow chauvinism will be reinforced, and a rich source of information about human difference will be lost for many people.

Some of the most ambitious schemes to deliver education entirely across cyberspace have faltered and been dramatically rethought and downgraded. No doubt capacities will continue to be improved; but even the best of these schemes will be unlikely to displace campus education completely. Campuses have at the same time become more sophisticated and complex in the experiences they provide for students and for faculty members with each passing year.

Thus, even with the incredible opportunities opened up by computers these days there seems no reason to revise my earlier prediction about the durable importance of "place." Several of these essays and speeches emphasize its continuing importance in a university education, for reasons ranging from the nostalgic to the practical. As I point out, despite its drawbacks, "the impulses towards parochialism in the human spirit are not all bad. They are also a source of much that is good in our lives and universities." As Virginia Woolf, a deeply committed internationalist and critic of patriotic zeal, noted in *Three Guineas*, the sense of place is a durable emotion that retains its power in our consciousness long after "reason has had its say."[44] Furthermore, even as our world becomes more globally interconnected, we will still need "manageable political and economic units . . . nobody can live purely globally."[45]

Undergraduate residential education, particularly, will continue to be a robust part of the mission of universities in the years ahead. This role stems from the particular quality of the experience, which has as much to do with what happens outside the classroom in the interchanges among students, faculty, and others as it does in the quality of the instruction provided. For many of us undergraduate education is "an important rite of passage, a way of developing and maturing that depends precisely on the context, the whole environment, the interplay of different activities in a very personal and direct experience. It is not possible to replicate that experience in cyberspace."[46] For other parts of the university, a deft combination of physical place and cyberspace is the appropriate goal. Successful institutions in the twenty-first century will be those that find creative ways of bringing these two types of "space" into productive and rewarding combinations.

What will people learn in those two types of space? Another common theme in these papers is the indefinite expansion of knowledge, as we learn more in virtually every discipline. The old image of the "storehouse of knowledge . . . neatly packaged by categories and imparted in measurable bits through the educational process" no longer serves us well. Instead, "we should think of education as an activity, a dialogue." Research is increasingly carried on with powerful tools of interdisciplinary exploration, and occurs in fields that did not even exist twenty years ago. In the coming years, we will "recover more from the past, as our ability to decipher the records of millennia is enhanced." And we will extend our knowledge "of what we now call nature, by ventures in all the sciences of which we only dream, including ventures far beyond our planet."[47]

In such a world, deciding what constitutes the best form of education for people at all levels of the university will be an increasingly complex challenge. We will have "to think more carefully about what education really needs to accomplish, at every stage." We will also need to grapple more directly with questions about how knowledge will be used, and face the possibilities of significant abuses that could actually worsen the human condition. But "if we are careful to use science and technology responsibly—and I know that this a big 'if'—we can expect to improve and lengthen human life, at the same time that we learn how to live more sensibly together on this earth."[48]

A number of other speculations about the future of the university appear in these papers. There are also many questions that I did not address. And several aspects of the world today that were absent or obscure ten or twenty years ago have important implications for our institutions in the years ahead. On at least one topic, my statements have rapidly been overtaken by recent events. That is the issue of how institutions of higher education in the United States are positioned in the world.

In the period in which these essays and speeches were written, American higher education was the envy of the world, one of the few undisputed success stories in our society. Students flocked to our campuses from around the globe, and the leaders of many countries had been educated at least in part in the United States. We grappled with questions about the imbalance between the interest in science, engineering, and mathematics among students from the United States and the interest among students abroad, since in many universities a very high proportion of students in these fields were from other countries. Yet despite suspicions about these "outsiders" expressed by some observers, we continued to enjoy the rewards of a powerful interest in American universities by students from almost every country, and became dependent on that interest in our laboratories, our research grants, and our teaching programs. We worried about the complacent isolation and apparent arrogance of American universities, since most of us expressed little interest in nascent organizations and consortia of universities around the world; but few of us did anything to tackle this problem directly.[49]

Of course we were not totally cut off from the rest of the world. Scholars from the United States in all disciplines regularly communicate with colleagues in other countries and attend conferences abroad. Study abroad is a thriving part of the baccalaureate program on many campuses, attracting a large number of students every year. But we suffered from complacency in several respects. The status of English as the contemporary lingua franca for scholarly papers, conferences, and electronic communication makes it easy to assume that others will adapt their behavior and requirements to ours, and that we have little or no adaptation of our own to worry about. The advantages of our distinctive system of higher education, coupled with the difficulties that universities in other parts of the world face in trying to match our success, have deepened our complacency.

This last situation is now changing, with bewildering speed. Two largely independent factors have converged in the first decade of the twenty-first century to alter this landscape profoundly. The first is the climate in the United States in the aftermath of 9/11, and the increasing concerns about security and terrorism on our soil. Significant barriers have been erected against entry by students and faculty members from other countries; they face difficulties in securing visas, uncertainty over their ability to return to the United States if they go home to visit or for a family emergency, and a maze of other bureaucratic complexities. Equally discouraging is the suspicion and mistrust that people from abroad may now face once they arrive, whether undergoing airport security procedures or shopping in supermarkets.

It is possible to argue that all of this is necessary from the point of view of domestic security. It is equally possible to argue that we have indulged in overkill and that less stringent barriers would achieve our goals. But no one could deny that this situation has implications for the ability of American institutions to recruit and interact with scholars from abroad. The *Chronicle of Higher Education* noted in November 2004: "A survey of major graduate institutions, conducted by the Council of Graduate Schools, found a 6-percent decline in new foreign enrollments this fall, the third year in a row with a substantial drop."[50]

Fortunately, this tide may be receding.[51] Under the leadership of Secretary of State Condoleeza Rice, authorities in Washington are beginning to recognize the impact of some of these policies on admitting visitors and are liberalizing access to student and faculty visas in a number of countries. But much of the damage has already been done, in terms of expectations about when and where students from abroad will be able to enroll. And the tensions around terrorism may well be only in remission at this time, ready to reappear with the next occurrence on our soil.

The second factor is the increasing quality of institutions in other countries, the result of years of deliberately emulating American higher education, combined with the distinctive strengths that other systems can provide. Universities in Great Britain, Canada, Australia, and New Zealand are engaged in intensive and successful recruitment of students from Asia especially, students who in earlier years would have been likely to choose a university in the United States. Universities in the home countries of these students, including particularly China but also Japan and India, are at the same time improving their own quality and attractiveness so that their students will not have to travel abroad for their education.[52]

These two factors taken together have substantially reduced the number of students applying for positions in American universities. We face a number of challenges as a result: sustaining the work in laboratories and disciplines that has depended on students from abroad, and preparing more American students in these disciplines; ameliorating obstacles that are not essential to national security but that are a burden to students from abroad; adjusting campus budgets that have depended on enrolling a large number of these students; and taking fuller advantage of new communications technologies to make the benefits of American higher education available to more people around the world.

However, from any perspective other than a narrow focus on the immediate interests of universities in the United States, the increasing quality of universities around the world is clearly a positive factor. We should celebrate this rather than only bemoan its implications for our own campuses. The improving capacities of universities abroad also make possible significant new collaborations between universities on different continents. Exploring such possibilities has been on the agenda for a number of institutions in recent years.

Stepping back in this way from our concerns about the specific challenges that confront higher education in the United States these days, we may draw a few more balanced conclusions about universities around the world in the early years of the twenty-first century. It is an exciting time to be engaged in higher education, and there is much important work to be done. There cannot have been a time when education was more crucial to our future on this planet, given the interconnections of our societies, the tensions within and among them, the possibilities and challenges of new technologies and discoveries, the complexities of leadership in every area—political, economic, cultural, environmental.

At such a time, it helps to renew our acquaintance with those who have spoken wisely in the past. As president of Wellesley and Duke, I was occasionally asked which of the major political theorists were most helpful for my work. The answer: Aristotle, Machiavelli, Rousseau, and Weber. It's a rather motley set, not necessarily the names that first come to mind as resources for an active leader in higher education. But in practice, these were the authors who proved most valuable, either as foils or as sources of inspiration, while I practiced my craft. Taken together, they offer a number of crucial insights: on the importance of associations to human flourishing; the decisions that have to be made by those in power, which must sometimes reflect the lesser of two evils rather than the greater good; the importance of rhetoric and articulating goals; the necessity of both passionate commitment and cool detachment for success in leadership; and how selfish individual pursuits can be brought together for common purposes.

I have also found several books on higher education inspiring across the years, from John Henry Newman's *The Idea of a University* to the present. Some are cited in notes to the papers that follow. In addition to those mentioned in this Introduction, they include George Keller's *Academic Strategy*, *Leadership and Ambiguity* by Cohen and March, Jaroslav Pelikan's *The Idea of the University Reexamined*, Charles Anderson's *Prescribing the Life of the Mind*, and several books on governance in higher education by Richard P. Chait.

Among these I would surely include a collection of addresses given by senior scholars each year to first-year undergraduates at the University of Chicago, called *The Aims of Education*. There are many fine and thought-provoking speeches in this book. I am especially fond of one delivered by Hanna H. Gray in 1987. In her address Professor Gray points out that "ultimately an ideal of education—what it should be about, what it should be for, how its worth should be assessed—is a statement about the future and the ideals one would wish to see realized in that future; a statement about human purpose and possibility, about the nature of human society, its needs and aspiration; about the character and direction of civilization; a statement, too, about the past, its models and meanings, the lessons it provides to be perpetuated or discarded."[53] These stirring words remind us that our work is more important than any particular discussion of curricular reform, budget stringency, campus services, or admissions standards. It is incumbent on us to think clearly about how to accomplish our work in ways that remain true to our historic strengths.

In the first major speech I gave after 9/11, the Faculty Address of 25 October 2001, I discussed the contributions of various campus disciplines to our understanding of that event. I reflected especially on the humanities and the social sciences, and urged my colleagues "to bring to bear our best possible collective thinking on issues that are crucial to our lives." I noted that the humanities (including those pursuits we call "the arts") were particularly valuable in the immediate aftermath of the attack. Our need for solace and comfort led many of us to music, literature, poetry, or art, and also to search for patterns in history that might help us put this terrible event into perspective. I then noted the particular importance of the social sciences in helping us to understand what had happened and how to avert new disasters.

The speech concluded with a poem called "The Attending" by the poet laureate of North Carolina, a Duke graduate, Fred Chappell.[54] It is an appropriate conclusion to this introductory essay, and a prelude to the papers that follow.

> Let us, in this time of bitterest lament,
>   Go awhile apart and meditate
>   And reverently attend the ancestral choir
>   Or prophet, sages, founders of the state,
> Who lend us strength and solace when the world is rent
>   And everywhere besieged with fire.
> Let us linger, as we may, within the grove
>   And hear those voices in the heat of day
>   Speak like gentle winds stirring the silence
>   Softly in their never-ceasing play
> Of loving variations on the theme of love
>   And weary descant against violence.
> For we are nothing without the ones who came before,
>   They who with palette, loom and graceful pen
>   And sculpted stone, with treatise and debate
>   Built our world and built it up again
> When it was brought to rubble by incendiary war
>   And the towering, sword-blade flames of hate.

And let us join with them in spirit by going to
    Their words and deeds that make our history
    A matter of some pride, if we will know
    The best of it, forgoing vanity
And boast and doing calmly what we ought to do
    As they did then, a world ago.

PART I   Articles and Speeches

Collaboration and Leadership

Create, communicate, collaborate. These are directives I applaud, virtues I admire, strategies that are promising in many ways. But are they compatible with whatever it is that Clark Kerr (see his recent book, *Presidents Make a Difference: Strengthening Leadership in Colleges and Universities*)[1] and others are telling us we ought to do more of—not just college presidents, but all people who have administrative responsibilities with the opportunity for leadership, setting goals, telling other people what to do?

The current advice from many of the best-respected authorities in our field, including Kerr, is that we should be bolder, more effective as leaders, and should support those presidents, deans, directors, and others who are attempting to exercise leadership in the academy. If you believe that this advice is good and timely, as I do, where does that leave you on the subject of the conference? Can one be a leader, and a collaborator as well? Or are the two fundamentally opposed to one another?

Common wisdom on this kind of issue holds that collaboration and leadership are not easily compatible. To lead means to be out front, to push forward. It means having others behind following you; it means being visible because you are giving orders and setting the pace. To collaborate means to labor with others, to cooperate, to work as part of a team. Instead of being out front by yourself, collaboration means blending yourself into a group to move more effectively together. The two might almost be taken to be opposites, in fact.

AN ESSENTIAL RELATION

My main purpose is to argue that collaboration and leadership are not opposites, but essentially related; that good leadership requires a kind of collaboration, and that creative collaborative work is the best route towards bold and effective leadership. But I do not wish to reach that conclusion too soon. As a student of political theory and political ideas, I do not think it is an obvious conclusion, and there are some good arguments against it that have to be dealt with along the way. And as an educator in a position of leadership, I do not underestimate the obstacles to achieving the goals that I propose to sketch out for you.

First, therefore, I want to say something more systematic about leadership—how we might define it, what it looks like, what it requires. In doing so, I'll try to indicate why leadership may seem at odds with collaboration, given what we conventionally expect leaders to be like, and to do. And finally, I'll sketch out another way of interpreting leadership which I find more promising, one which is fully compatible with creative, communicative collaboration.

DEFINING LEADERSHIP

In discussing leadership today, I am thinking of the kinds of responsibilities and pieces of authority that many of us exercise as part of our day-to-day work. Although most of my examples will be taken from studies of college presidencies, since these are just now in vogue and easily available, what I have to say is certainly not limited to the office of the president. Deans, directors of admission or financial aid, heads of offices, and staffs of any kind in an educational institution—indeed anyone with the responsibility to state purposes and set goals for a school or college in any setting or portion of its work—can be a leader in the sense I have in mind.

It is also important to be clear that in talking about leaders, I'm talking about real human individuals doing things. We sometimes appear to have other meanings in mind. For instance, we sometimes speak of "institutional leadership," by saying that a college or a country is a "leader in its field." But I have always found that when you look closely, this assertion is really a statement about people doing things.

Suppose, for example, we say that an institution is taking a leadership position on some crucial issue like financial aid or athletic standards. This turns out, in my experience, to mean that some particular person in the institution, or more often several people, are taking stands and speaking for the college as they do so. We can also say that a college or a school is "a leader in its field" if it is doing really well, attracting students, winning prizes, retaining strong faculty, or whatever else. What we really mean by this expression is that the school or college is outdistancing the competition, doing better than the others. And again, this winning outcome usually turns out to depend on some human actions taken by the people in the institution, who do things that put their school or college right out front.

Since, when we think about it, we usually ascribe leadership to human beings, and think about individuals as leaders, it is easy to assume that whatever defines leadership is some kind of quality that an individual either has or lacks: some indescribable but potent personal charisma that makes people follow someone, that gives an air of authority. You either have it or you don't: it helps to be tall, middle-aged, white, and male, perhaps, but it's mainly a matter of personal style and presence that makes people want to follow you, and this is what makes a leader.

At Swarthmore, one of our colleagues was a distinguished professor of history named James Field. I well recall an incident when there had been a good deal of discussion about students sprawling about on the carpets of the brand-new library instead of sitting properly at the desks where they belonged. This example may seem unreal to you, since of course carpets are a perfectly comfortable and familiar place to read these days, and nobody would dream of asking students to do anything else. But in those days, in the mid-sixties, it seemed worthy of remark, and Jim Field managed to get some of the students to stop sprawling on the carpet and return to their desks. Another professor, watching this, said with some amazement that he had tried to accomplish this goal for months without success. Jim Field turned to him, his military demeanor and hauteur evident on his countenance, and said simply, "You don't have the bouquet."

Whatever that indefinable bouquet may be, we often think of leadership as a personal attribute that some people have, and others simply lack. Yet, although a compelling personality and an attractive or attention-getting style may help someone make his or her mark as a leader, we all know people who are effective leaders in a low-key way, and other people who have all the dash and smash and turn out not to be worth following. The essential things about leadership, in my judgment, turn out to have more to do with what you do and how you do it, rather than the way you look or impress or attract people.

WHAT DO LEADERS DO?

If we try to draw up a list of what it is that leaders do, it is easy to see why leadership may seem to fit ill with collaboration. When we describe the job of a leader, we often stress the personal responsibility, the individual focus and weight, or even the loneliness of the job.

To support this point, let me turn to one of the great reservoirs of evidence on modern mores and practices, the cartoon pages of the *New Yorker*. Jokes in this journal will doubtless be a gold mine for future historians of our society, if they can understand some of the finer and more transient points of humor that are very much bound to the current scene. Among the most prominent kinds of *New Yorker* jokes are people at cocktail parties, discussing or exemplifying the latest fad, and people in shabby rooms inhabited by mangy cats and apoplectic-looking dogs, discussing some major point of metaphysics. There are also a lot of jokes about leadership as well—about kings or chairmen of the board. Apparently the audience of the magazine includes a lot of leaders, as well as denizens of cocktail parties, if not of shabby rooms.

Two recent cartoons can serve as examples: a king on a balcony musing, "Perhaps I should go among the people and discover what they are thinking and concerned about. On second thought, what the hell!" and a king in a throne room, pacing, "Forget the self-doubts, and reign!"

These two cartoons illustrate beautifully the sense that leadership is a lonely occupation, a highly individual practice. It is fascinating that the old-fashioned king is still so often chosen as a symbol of authority in a world where monarchs are very rare, and those that exist have in fact less power than most other people—but the fact that kings are still our symbols of authority confirms the sense that leadership is lonely, monarchical, set apart. The symbols of service are the crown and scepter, the leader is upon a throne, set apart by dress and status, and expected to perform more or less inscrutably.

Much of the meaning of this lonely, symbolic individuality of the leader is incorporated in the meaning of the word *decide*, a central word for leadership. The word itself has semantic roots that mean to cut, to cut off—and this has at least a double meaning here. In deciding where to cut the issue, you cut off some people and cut others in.

Choosing among alternatives, coming down on one side or another of a problem, is essential here. By the time something comes to a leader's desk as a problem, there are arguments—usually good arguments—on both sides. By endorsing alternative X, you exclude and fail to satisfy those who support alternative Y. You'll probably fail to satisfy either contingent altogether, and the process of decision will thus inevitably make people unhappy with the leader. So deciding how to cut the issue, how to divide the goodies, cuts you off to some extent from all those involved in the question.

This is one of the reasons we are so often told that you can't be a good leader and expect everybody to like you. Another *New Yorker* cartoon shows a mob outside a palace window with pitchforks and hoes, and the queen drawing back the curtain and saying to the king: "It's the multitude, and they are *not* singing 'For he's a jolly good fellow!'"

In addition to the process of decision, which has its components of estrangement and loneliness, leaders also do other things that tend to cut them off. They exercise authority—they tell other people what to do, offering rewards and sanctions, figuring out how to motivate, coerce, or cajole other people to get things done. Being in authority means keeping your distance from those who are supposed to obey you, keeping some aura of mystery or higher status to lend credibility to your words, so that people will have irrational as well as rational motives for doing what they say.

DIGNIFIED RESERVE

The best prototype of this model of authority is the Wizard of Oz, who discovered that people were much more likely to obey his sensible suggestions for their welfare if he cloaked himself with mystery, blue smoke and mirrors, sounds of thunder, and rushing wind. When he was unmasked as just an ordinary salesman far from home, his authority totally disappeared, even though his ideas remained very sensible. Leaders are often exhorted to retain an aura of mystery, perhaps not quite as exaggerated as the Wizard, but definitely borrowing some leaves from the same book, with ceremonial attire, perks, and status symbols, and an air of dignified reserve.

Now there is no doubt that leadership can sometimes be a lonely occupation. Nor is there any doubt that an office such as that of a president, chairman, or director confers some aura of authority that helps enable ordinary human beings to induce other human beings to help get things done. I am not, in other words, denying that there is an essential core of truth in these familiar points. I do think, however, that the loneliness and distance, the reserve and mystery, can easily be overemphasized, and that if models of leadership overemphasize these things they tend to cut off their practitioners quite artificially from other sources of strength as well as other models of leadership.

THE MACHIAVELLIAN–ST. SIMEON MODEL

As my example of a model of leadership that overstresses separation and artificial mystery, let me take the one set forward in a book that I have found fascinating and instructive, although occasionally perverse: James L. Fisher's recent book *Power of the Presidency*.[2] Fisher is writing specifically about college presidencies, from his own experience in the job, and the book is of special interest to those of us who share that role—but also, I would imagine, to anyone else who is attempting to figure out how a college president does what he (or sometimes she) is doing.

In Fisher's view, it is very important to a successful presidency to cultivate an aura of genial reserve, to keep your distance from the common folk, and to keep people guessing about what you are really like and what you really want to accomplish. Reveal your emotions and your strategies only to your spouse and most trusted assistant, he advises; for everyone else, keep up a façade that keeps them guessing. If you don't personally have charisma, cultivate it, learn how to have it; avoid situations where you might be unmasked, such as question-and-answer sessions after a speech, where you might slip up and say something foolish or unprepared. Attend lots of social functions in connection with your job, but come late and leave early so they'll want more of your company and prize it for its rarity. Make the most of the trappings of office—the cap, gown, chain and medal, mace carried by an underling.

The model of the presidency that Fisher has in mind is best captured by his favorite image: St. Simeon the Stylite. In case your hagiography needs brushing up, let me remind you that St. Simeon was an early Christian ascetic who showed his devotion to his principles by climbing up to a platform placed sixty feet atop a pole, and staying there for twenty years, preaching to the multitudes who gathered curiously or reverently below.

Fisher advises college presidents to think of themselves as on a platform, like Simeon; to sit gracefully and almost carelessly, accessible to those who come to petition or watch, but never to get down off the platform and mingle with the crowds.

Now whatever else one might try to do or be atop a pole like St. Simeon's, it would clearly make collaboration very difficult. You can't easily form coalitions, cooperate, and work side by side if you are sitting sixty feet up in the air, either literally or allegorically. If Fisher is right about what it takes to be a successful leader, at least in this particular presidential role, then collaboration appears to be pretty effectively ruled out.

Fisher's book is full of good advice for using power, and his perceptions of the opportunities and pitfalls facing a college president are often shrewd. In one chapter especially, however, he uses some quotations to support part of his theory of leadership that made me pause. He cites such well-known sages as Machiavelli: "All men are motivated by self-interest: man should play his friends as pawns on a chessboard, one against the other"—or Eric Hoffer: "Our sense of power is more vivid when we break a man's spirit than when we win his heart"—or Henry Kissinger: "Power is the great aphrodisiac"—or Albert Camus: "We can't do without dominating others or being served. . . . Even the man on the bottom rung still has his wife or his children; if he's a bachelor, his dog. The essential thing, in sum, is being able to get angry without the other person being able to answer back."[3]

I would ask you, by the way, to pause on the heavily masculine flavor of all those pithy axioms; and at the end of my speech I will have a few things to say generally about this point.

Fisher is in good company with his Machiavelli cum St. Simeon model of leadership: distant, ruthless, self-interested, strategically cunning, cold, and isolated. For a lot of people, such a model will ring true even if it is slightly shocking, just as Machiavelli's *The Prince* affected its readers 450 years ago.

But is Fisher, any more than his famous Florentine precursor, right in what he says? As you will have gathered, I think his model is thought-provoking and memorable, but ultimately misleading. As I see it, the demands and ceremonial accretions of the office will do quite enough to create distance and reserve, and the work of a good leader, even—or perhaps especially—a college president, should be directed not towards increasing that distance and reserve, but towards trying to reduce or compensate for its effects.

Similarly, attempting to get your job done will inevitably lead you to think strategically, to assess your chances with other people, to figure out how to get where you want to be. And in a hierarchy— and an educational bureaucracy, like any other, is inevitably a hierarchy—you will always find that relationships are colored to some extent by some version of domination and obedience. But since these things will happen anyway, as a thoughtful leader you should bend your efforts towards reaching out in other directions as well, and try to extend and broaden your work instead of hunkering down and emphasizing the cold strategy, the narrow self-interest, the zero-sum game, I-win-you-lose sensations of the job. These things, like distance, will come unbidden; a strong leader should think not about multiplying them but modifying them.

Thus if you want to be an effective leader, in my book you ought to bend your efforts to finding ways to reach out to other people and work with them as colleagues, despite and across that distance that you cannot ever completely close. The distance will be there anyway; instead of placing your platform on top of a pole to exaggerate its effects, I would argue that you should be looking carefully for common ground.

WHERE CAN WE LOOK FOR OTHER MODELS?

Among the works that have recently been written on the subject of leadership, two in particular seem to offer some alternative models to that provided by Fisher: *Leadership and Ambiguity* by Cohen and March, and George Keller's book *Academic Strategy*.

Both these books are about leaders who are very conscious of strategy, but also stress the importance of participation and sensitivity to colleagues. Cohen and March describe the American educational institution today as an "organized anarchy," and counsel the would-be leader to recognize with humor and equanimity the limits on her power. They point out that many of the problems that present themselves to a leader for solution become "garbage cans" for all the other unresolved problems and frustrations that are lurking around the institution. All the leader can do is attempt to provide enough garbage cans to handle these impulses, and work unobtrusively behind the scenes to accomplish goals.

Cohen and March also advise a leader to stop seeking "symbolic confirmation" of his significance as a leader or falling into what they call the "esteem trap." Instead, they counsel leaders to look for opportunities to "exchange status for substance" in order to get things done.[4]

George Keller quotes Machiavelli with approval in his manual for strategists, but his Machiavellian model is much more participatory than Fisher's. According to Keller, "Strategic planning is *people* acting decisively and roughly in concert to carry out a strategy they have helped devise." Thus strategy making "must be participatory," so that "most of the key people" can "be on board the strategy train when it leaves the station."[5]

It is important to notice, however, that for these advisers, participation and collaboration are *instrumental in obtaining a leader's goals*. They advise the would-be leader to pay attention to the needs and purposes of other people to advance his own *ends*; they leave the impression that if human nature and institutional structure were otherwise, it would be much neater and more satisfactory for

45

the leader simply to pursue his own rational policy goals single-mindedly and single-handedly, without bothering with all this participation stuff. Collaboration and participation are thus seen more as necessary evils than as good in themselves.

My own argument, however, depends on seeing collaboration and communication as essential to effective leadership, as an integral part of what it means to be a leader—not just a more sophisticated form of strategy embarked upon by the single-minded leader in an effort to obtain individual ends. In the last section of this talk, therefore, I will sketch out some of the ways in which I believe this to be true.

LEADERSHIP AS PROBLEM SOLVING

If we pay attention to what leaders actually do in educational institutions nowadays, I would argue that we will see three kinds of behavior: leadership as problem solving, as making things happen, and as taking a stand. My claim is that to be effective, each of these kinds of action requires working in genuine collaboration with other people, not just using them as a means to your own ends.

In the current climate, much of the leadership of an institution will inevitably be tied up with problem solving: using scarce resources wisely, attempting to make limited opportunities go a long way, serving conflicting interests, and finding the best way out of a knotty situation. This may seem like the least glamorous and heady part of leadership, but realistically, it's what we are all doing most of the time. What does it have to do with collaboration?

If you conceptualize problem solving on the model of a jigsaw puzzle or a Rubik's cube, it might seem that the role of a problem-solving leader is to sit back and think through all the angles, juggle all the pieces until they fall harmoniously into place—a very rational, and eminently solitary enterprise. And yet we all know that the problems we face in institutions are very rarely of that sort.

Institutional problems that come up for solution are seldom the kind that have one best solution, to be discovered by dint of rationality; instead, there are multiple imperfect solutions competing for attention, and perhaps a few slightly less imperfect solutions lurking about somewhere waiting to be discovered by the diligent leader. The better solutions are far more likely to be found if you get some other people to help you look than if you insist on finding them on your own.

Aristotle said it first, as usual: Many heads are better than one in solving problems. Getting together all the people who have a stake in a solution around a table to talk out a problem—and some who have no stake but just a large dose of common sense—is often one of the best roads to a solution. And even if a solution does not immediately emerge, the process of having asked people for their views, and genuinely listened, may help rub off some of the excess freight of tensions or frustrations that the problem is carrying, and make it easier to solve.

So the successful problem-solving leader is almost certainly accustomed to collaboration: to working with other people to get at the facts, to understand the stakes, to try solutions on for size, and to foresee possible obstacles to any plan.

A leader who tries to solve problems without collaborating in this way risks either getting hopelessly bogged down in trivia as she attempts to assemble all the facts herself, or else striking out on a narrow but superficially appealing course of action that turns out to create far more problems than it solves.

LEADERSHIP AS MAKING THINGS HAPPEN

Although much of our work as leaders these days must be done in problem solving, there is still room for the second kind of leadership: making things happen. This is a more familiar kind of leaderly activity: achieving an end, making a difference, bringing about change, instead of just conserving the status quo or fighting fires. It might seem that this is a more individual activity, and that collaboration would be less essential here.

But I would argue that collaboration is at least as important in making things happen as it is in solving problems. Making things happen boils down to getting other people to do things to achieve your end: in energizing other people, harnessing their energies, directing their attention. To do this effectively, you have to really pay attention to what *they* want, instead of only to where you want to wind up. You have to ask people what they think is important and how they assess your goals, and you have to really *listen* to what they tell you if you are to persuade them to come on board with you.

Making things happen means building coalitions, forming alliances, compromising to get further, and working with other people whose purposes converge with yours to reach some common goals. Of course there must also be elements of strategy, and some degree of calculation; but if you only strategize and calculate, you are unlikely to motivate people to want to help you reach your goals. For the best way to motivate them to help you reach your goals is to have them understand why their own goals are encompassed there as well. They can never arrive at that position unless you have shaped your purpose so that their own purposes are truly taken into account.

The problem for the Machiavellian who sees other people only as pawns in his own chess game is that human beings rarely behave this way. They are much more likely to get up and wander off in their own directions in the manner of the games played by Alice behind the looking glass—which makes a fool of you and a mess of all your carefully plotted strategy.

Thus, it's not only that collaboration is an effective strategy for getting where you want to be, but that human institutions require the joining of minds and energies, the pooling of knowledge and strength, and the dovetailing of purposes, to get anywhere at all. There just aren't any reasonable goals in institutions that can be accomplished single-handedly, without communicating or taking into account what other people want to do; which is, at bottom, what institutions are all about. They are collections of people with purposes of their own, and the effective leader combines and channels various purposes to achieve a shared goal.

You may recall that earlier in my talk, I pointed out the heavily masculine flavor of those quotes from Machiavelli, Eric Hoffer, Henry Kissinger, and Albert Camus. I do not for a moment think that all male leaders approach leadership in quite this way—a kind of dominance game, in which the goal is to break someone's spirit to prove that you're on top. However, it has certainly been true, as Fisher's quotes make clear, that this has been one way of exercising authority, which has tended to permeate our thinking about authority across the board.

To speculate about there being something particularly masculine about this way of exercising power, whether linked to male hormones, military experience, or popular culture, would take me far afield from my subject today. Certainly we can all think about prominent women leaders who appear to follow exactly this same creed. I do find it fascinating, however, that some of the descriptions of leadership and authority provided these days by feminist political theorists are stressing collaborative power, power as "empowering other people," as making possible genuinely collective action, respectful of and sensitive to the needs and purposes of each collaborating person. And it is not accidental that my own approach to leadership takes a leaf from this same book.

And this approach to leadership—which depends heavily on creativity, communication, and collaboration—is fundamentally at odds with the zero-sum-game dominance and isolation model set forth in Fisher's quotes. To say that one is masculine and the other feminine would be wrongheaded and exaggerated; but it is true that some of the perspectives from feminist epistemology and feminine experience that have hitherto had little influence on our conceptions of leadership are now beginning to be heard. And these voices lend strength to other ways of saying the same things—from certain Asian cultures, from the teachings of the Quakers, and other sources of thinking about leadership that have tended to get buried under the dominance of the Machiavellian model.

LEADERSHIP AS TAKING A STAND

Even if you have been persuaded by what I have said so far about the consonance between leadership and collaboration, in the areas of problem solving or making things happen, you may find it odd to think of collaboration as having anything to do with the final sort of leadership I've named: taking a stand.

Taking a stand sounds like the most lonely and solitary way of leading; by definition, it means staking out your own ground and standing up for what you believe in, in the face of hostility and opposition. Taking a stand in a crowd is unnecessary at best and foolish at worst; it's when the crowd's against him that the leader takes a stand.

True, up to a point. It is easy to overstate the solitariness of the leader who is taking a stand, and easy to overlook the importance of the relation between that leader and his or her followers. If it makes no sense to take a stand in the middle of a crowd, it makes equally little sense to take a stand off by yourself where no one can see you. If you want to be counted for your beliefs, you almost certainly hope to persuade others to share them, to come over to your side and join in your stand. And even if your hopes of this are slim, at the very least your stand must be couched and presented in terms that your followers can understand.

So in deciding to take a stand, an effective leader will be sure to communicate creatively: to tell her associates and subordinates why she believes it is important to hold the line on this principle, or to come down firmly on that side of a thorny question. If the associates find the position hard to understand, or the principle hopelessly quixotic, the leader may still wish to stand her ground, but any hope of leading others to share the same view will be lost.

The leader who stands alone too often, too far out in front, risks losing that crucial symbiosis with his followers that is essential to leadership. He also risks a kind of infatuation with his own moral superiority, a deep dose of self-righteousness that may blind him to the arguments for other stands in the same situation, and lead him to have contempt for those who disagree with him.

Thus it is important to choose your stands wisely and, before you take a stand, to know how it will be interpreted and whom you might hope to induce to join you. Even the decision on when and how to take a stand, therefore, has an element of collaboration, although in the end it must be a personal, moral choice.

On this, as on so many things that have to do with leadership, some of the wisest counsel I know is contained in a speech by Max Weber, entitled "Politics as a Vocation."[6] Weber gave this speech at the University of Munich in 1918—clearly an agonizing time for a German leader to be counseling students on politics. He attempted to sketch out those qualities and attitudes most necessary for successful leadership, to assist his listeners in determining whether they had the vocation or calling to be leaders.

According to Weber, a good leader must have both a passionate commitment to some ends or ultimate purposes that he tries to serve, and a sense of responsibility or proportion that allows him to know his own limits and even the imperfect and partial status of those ends or purposes. "Politics," says Max Weber, "is a strong and slow boring of hard boards. It takes both passion and perspective." These two attitudes are difficult to hold in balance, but doing so, says Weber, is essential to good leadership.

The passionate commitment to purposes and ends that makes up one part of a good leader in Weber's formula is undoubtedly a very individual component in which collaboration has little role. However, the great virtue of Weber's model is his insight that passionate commitment must be balanced by a sense of responsibility and proportion that depends on a willingness to listen to others, humility, and a sense of humor. And this, I would argue, can only come finally from regarding one's followers as genuine colleagues in a common enterprise, as co-laborers in the same vineyard, to accomplish common goals.

The University in the Twenty-first Century

Centennial Celebration Panel, Stanford University, 15 May 1987

Stanford University sets formidable tasks for people who care about it: first the biggest fund-raising campaign in the history of the world, $1.1 billion, and now this glittering centennial bash, rivaling the one in Cambridge last fall that it took Harvard 350 years to plan.

At Harvard's 350th, the new president of Yale, Benno Schmidt, spoke of Harvard "quietly and modestly entering its 351st year."

I'm glad to be here helping Stanford quietly and modestly enter its 101st year, or its 97th year, however you count these things. This university has accomplished great things over the last century.

Of course, Stanford had the advantage of a modern start. From the beginning, Stanford could do things that it took eastern universities centuries to become bold enough to do. For example: co-education from the very first; a concentration on the most advanced research and teaching in science and technology; an opening to the Pacific; and a set of specialized research institutes. There are also things that even with all those centuries behind them, the eastern universities haven't managed to bring off, such as the California climate, the world's best tennis, a competitive football team, and a wonderfully infamous band.

For all these reasons, Stanford in its first century has become a truly world-class university, one of the few undoubted success stories in this business. But my assignment here today is not to praise Stanford for its past accomplishments, but to help us consider what this university and other American institutions of higher education will be doing in the twenty-first century.

I'm normally allergic to such exercises. Our record of forecasting, if you look back at the past, is ludicrous. We have few good tools for such purposes, and our predictions for the future, even over ten or twenty years, are often pitifully different from what actually happens.

Furthermore, the pace of change over the last few decades has accelerated almost exponentially, and this makes it even harder to look down the years to come with any confidence.

At a time like this, however, the exercise of forecasting has more purpose than it might in ordinary dailyness. A centennial celebration calls our attention to the passage of time, to those demarcations and boundaries along the way that this institution has taken through the years. It is natural to turn next in the other direction, to attempt to peer forward over the years and speculate about what the future holds.

If we are fortunate in our choices, we can make some difference for good in the course that lies ahead. We can at least hope to foresee, and thus have a better chance of avoiding, some possible detours or pitfalls. And even in the worst case, predictions give us the comforting illusion of control, which can yield its own benefits in confidence and readiness to face the future.

I was in New Orleans a few weeks ago for a meeting, and as is my custom (it seems to be a custom that peculiarly afflicts college and university presidents), I was getting ready for my early morning run. As part of my warm-up, I was leaning hard against the three-story high columns of my hotel, stretching my calves and tendons. A couple of workmen walked by and smiled benignly at my strenuous efforts, and one of them said "Ain't never gonna push that thing over." And I said, "I could use some help!"

That's the way I feel about this exercise: we're never gonna be able to predict the future, but our only chance of even coming close is with some help. None of us is an expert in the future, none of us has a crystal ball; but each of us has experience, imagination, and evidence of trendlines that we can draw upon to strengthen our joint ability to predict and plan.

THE UNIVERSITY AS COMMUNITY

My first prediction is that education in the twenty-first century will continue to be centered around a campus, with a physical identity and a core community of teachers, learners, and researchers in a common task.

This might seem an obvious prediction. In fact, it may be the boldest one of all. Consider the mechanisms for transmitting and storing knowledge which will almost certainly be available to us in the twenty-first century. The old familiar Gutenberg Express which takes books, journals, and readers back and forth from Stanford to Cal's libraries each day will be superseded very soon by instant computerized communication.

Our libraries, offices, and laboratories will be linked by networks that provide access for any scholar to the full range of work stored and ongoing on any other campus. It will become unusual and pleasurable to handle books and manuscripts, since the workaday transmission of knowledge will be almost entirely electronic.

Given these possibilities for instant communication from any scholar's work station to any other in the world, it might seem that the campus, the libraries, the classrooms will be superfluous. Why not just have people stay at home and plug into the world of knowledge on their own?

I do not think this will happen, not because it would be physically impossible, but because the reasons why people come together to learn in the intensified atmosphere of the university campus transcend the mechanisms by which knowledge is stored and transmitted.

People come together to converse and argue, to stimulate and inspire each other, to create an environment of discourse and dialogue essential to the very creation of knowledge. They have done so for many centuries, and I predict that they will continue to do so in the twenty-first.

There is an old image of the core activity of the university, coined at Williams College, the image of "Mark Hopkins on one end of a log and a student on another." All that is really needed for education is a great teacher and a ready student.

Over the decades, we have become convinced that the discourse between the two can be enhanced by providing sophisticated paraphernalia to replace the log: books, computers, laboratories, paintings. Today, it becomes more likely that it is Mark Hopkins on one end of an ether-net or token ring and the student on the other.

There is little doubt that the paraphernalia will become even more sophisticated in the twenty-first century, and will include instruments of knowledge of which we cannot now even form a concept. But the essential relationship of teacher and student, of discourse in which both explore together, will not be superseded.

THE STOREHOUSE OF KNOWLEDGE

Not only will the instruments by which knowledge is communicated be more sophisticated in the twenty-first century: knowledge itself will become more complex. If things continue as they are moving now, and have moved for decades, there will be an indefinite burgeoning of knowledge.

We will recover more from the past, as our ability to decipher the records of millennia is enhanced. We will learn more about civilizations and species as we discover lost manuscripts, new fossil records, buried cities, along with more sophisticated dating and interpretive techniques. And we will expand our knowledge of what we now call "nature" by ventures in all the sciences of which we can now only dream, including ventures far beyond our planet, perhaps literally into new dimensions in space and time. And perhaps most breathtaking of all, we can reasonably expect the next decades to be a period of unprecedented flourishing for the human sciences and the sciences of society. We should know far more about ourselves, about the way individuals and nations, economies and polities work, how they might cooperate and prosper, in the twenty-first century than we do today.

What will this mean for the education of ordinary undergraduates in the twenty-first century? Will they be required to learn all these new things, in addition to knowing everything we now expect people to learn? How could anyone possibly learn so much?

My second prediction is that there will be an inverse relationship between this indefinite burgeoning of knowledge and the standard for how much detailed knowledge needs to be imparted in a good undergraduate education.

In tomorrow's world, the old image of "the storehouse of knowledge," in which knowledge is neatly packaged by categories and imparted in measurable bits through the educational process, will be irrelevant. Instead, we need to think of education as an activity, a dialogue. The goal is to teach people how to think, and where to find the answers to their questions, and to stimulate and fix the native curiosity that leads them to want to know.

This tendency, of course, has been with us for many years; it will intensify over the next few decades. Education will be less *ergo-centric* and more *logocentric*: that is, it will be focused more on structures of knowing and reasoning, less directed towards teaching people trade skills, specific kinds of technical knowledge that will be used directly in their jobs. Learning in careers, imbibing technical knowledge, will happen every day for the professionals and skilled workers of the future.

SERVING SOCIETY'S NEEDS

My third prediction is that the university of the future will be more diverse in its composition than the university of today. There will be more people of different ages, races, and nationalities in the student body, and the faculties will be more diverse as well.

Demographics alone would lead to such a prediction, given the number of children of varied ethnic backgrounds now being born in our country and the world, and the growing number of people of retirement age. But it will not only be the force of demographics: the tendency to reach out to people of different ages and races and nationalities to provide a multicultural and balanced student body has been with us for some time, and there are good reasons to think it will continue.

As more people of different ethnic backgrounds attend our universities, their impact on our curricula and definition of our mission will be profound. We can expect that the old familiar emphasis on western culture will be supplanted by a much wider notion of "culture" itself, and an awareness of the complex patterns through which cultures in the past and present influence one another.

To assert that there will be more women on the faculties and staffs of our universities in the coming century might seem one of the more utopian of my predictions, since this is a change that has been occurring only with a glacial slowness across recent decades. Nonetheless, I make it with some confidence, given the tight market for talented faculty members that we can forecast for the 1990s. There are many women who would make strong teachers and college administrators, and higher education, like all other industries, will have to compete in a tough market to attract the best and brightest young people.

The greatest change in the composition of our student body may well come along the lines of age. The concept of preparation for life in its early stages, and greater readiness and flexibility for knowing in the younger human brain will remain with us, barring unlikely (though not impossible) alterations in these things. Nonetheless, the university campus of tomorrow will have more learners of different ages, not because they will have failed to be educated the first time round, but because mid-career and older people will have incentives and time for a second or third round of formal education.

The notion of a person starting out on a particular career at twenty-two, and climbing the well-defined ladder for that job until he or she gets the gold watch by retiring at sixty-five, will yield to flexibility across the life span, as people move from one kind of career to another, experiencing different kinds of self-fulfillment across the years.

Such career changes will be punctuated by renewed opportunities for formal education, which will bring intellectual refreshment and a reawakening of curiosity. And in the last years of a healthy life span, which may be extended by some significant amount in the twenty-first century, there will be other motivations for learning things that one always wished to know, along with the leisure for pursuing them.

This will be true, of course, only for those members of our society who have the talents and resources that make such extended education possible. One of those questions about which I am least certain of my ability to predict the future is how open the universities of tomorrow will be to people of different classes and financial backgrounds.

If educators and political leaders around the world act wisely, we will make sure that universities of tomorrow are more open than they are today. But our predecessors through the centuries have done a dismal job on this score, so the outlook is not encouraging. If the world's universities continue to be disproportionately accessible to people from advantaged backgrounds who can pay their way, we will have failed to meet our responsibilities for social justice and equity, and even more sobering, will have made more likely an international struggle of the haves and have-nots of the most devastating sort.

To mention the class biases of our universities raises the final question of how the university of the future will be financed and governed.

We cannot know how universities tomorrow *will* be financed and governed, but we have a pretty good idea of how they *ought* to be, based on centuries of experience. The governance of private universities such as Stanford should be left in the hands of faculty, trustees, administrators, and students, all contributing their particular expertise and vision. There must also be strong state-supported universities, and the healthy competition between public and private institutions, which has distinguished American universities across the years, must be fostered in the future.

Yet the financing of all kinds of American institutions will be more variegated in the future, as the line between "public" and "private" funding blurs. "Public" universities will reach out ever more aggressively for "private" support from alumni, corporations, and foundations. "Private" universities will need to receive comparably generous support from the "public" realm, in the form of student financial aid, grants for scholarly research, and sophisticated equipment.

This blending of private and public money for all the institutions in our diverse mosaic of American higher education will make visible one of its greatest strengths, a strength which has something of the paradoxical about it.

Education of all kinds is a fundamental political good in a republic of this sort, as it has been since the days of Jefferson. Yet education must remain free and open, not dominated by narrow public purposes, if it is to serve its basic mission: educating citizens, searching for knowledge, and speaking truth to power. Only if this paradox of a political good protected from political control is sustained by all of us who care about American higher education can we look forward with confidence to Stanford's sesquicentennial.

The Mission of the Research University

University faculties and administrators are notoriously dubious about mission statements. How can something as pluralistic, as multifaceted, as wondrously complex as a modern university have a clear-cut mission? The term is redolent of narrower and more intensely single-minded human ventures such as crusades or temperance movements. Yet among modern institutions, those that are keenest on mission statements are businesses. Dignified statements of institutional goals, embellished with the corporate logo, are commonly used to encourage the faithful within the firm and to communicate to potential customers an adherence to worthy purposes. The robust rhetorical tone of such messages sits poorly with the inherent skepticism and stubborn individualism of members of a university.

Universities are composed of large numbers of individuals pursuing many purposes. Some of those individuals (particularly the tenured faculty) enjoy a high degree of autonomy in defining their goals and measuring success. It is all very well for presidents or boards to issue hortatory statements; it is much more difficult to chart a course and arrange the incentive structure of such a complex institution so as to encourage semiautonomous actors to converge around common goals.

A mission statement that is sufficiently bland to encompass everyone's conception of his or her role in the university is of little use to anyone. A statement that has more substantive content risks threatening or ignoring the goals of some members of the university who have sufficient power to set their own direction. It is easier to celebrate variety than to be selective. To say that there are certain purposes that are definitive of our sorts of institutions, and that these should govern our choices when choices must be made, means taking a stand on some of the key questions that we delight in endlessly debating.

Yet at a time when universities are under attack for failing in their basic purposes and falling away from their historic character, it is of singular importance that we explain clearly and forcefully why our work is crucial, and what it is we are doing that matters so much to the world. It is also a time of internal uncertainty, in which all of us on campus can benefit from a joint discussion of our purposes. We should recognize that there is no single perfect definition; the elegant crafting of abstractions is only one part of this endeavor. The most important aspect is the dialogue, the process, the give and take that comes from thinking seriously about what you are doing in the company of others who are engaged in the same enterprise.

In the concluding paragraphs of *Political Parties*, Roberto Michels tells the story of a farmer who confided to his sons on his deathbed that there was treasure buried in his fields.[1] The sons could hardly wait till the funeral festivities were over to begin the search. They found no box of buried treasure, but in digging up the fields so assiduously they rendered them more fertile, and the farm increased in value manyfold. We may hope, in the vigorous dialogue of arguing about our mission, to come up with at least a modest statement that we are willing to present to the world. But the real treasure is in the activity, the exercise itself, and the enrichment of common understanding of our purposes.

AN INITIAL STATEMENT OF OUR MISSION

In 1965, on the verge of some especially profound changes in higher education, President James A. Perkins of Cornell University delivered the Stafford Little Lectures at Princeton University on "The University in Transition." He listed as the "three great missions" of the university the acquisition, transmission, and application of knowledge. These were his terms for the familiar goals of research, teaching, and public service.[2]

Perkins pointed out that modern American research universities are a hybrid of two earlier traditions, with a peculiarly American shoot grafted on. The German universities in the third decade of the nineteenth century developed the model of the university dedicated almost solely to research. Founders and reformers of

American universities in the latter part of the century combined this with undergraduate collegiate teaching modeled on the universities of Oxford and Cambridge, which had already taken root in American soil. The peculiarly American shoot was first exemplified after the Civil War in the land-grant universities, foreshadowed by Franklin and Jefferson, who asserted the practical importance of knowledge "in the nation's service." This hybrid model is still recognizable in our contemporary universities.[3]

Let me broach a core definition based upon this hybrid model. The modern research university is a company of scholars who are engaged in discovering and sharing knowledge, with a responsibility to see that the knowledge is used to improve the human condition.

I have chosen the terms "discovering" rather than "acquiring" and "sharing" rather than "transmitting" because these metaphors capture more aptly the life of the scholar engaged in research and teaching. The notion of "acquisition" suggests proprietorship, warehousing, and compiling, rather than the searching, journeying, and trial and error that lead finally, when we are successful, to the "Eureka!" experience. "Transmission" implies that the teacher is solely in charge of the object of knowledge, handing it on unchanged to the receptive pupil; whereas teaching, at its best, is a shared experience in which teacher and student strive together towards a clearer explication.

It is important to this definition that the university is a *company* of scholars, a fellowship that provides richly for mutual nourishing in ideas. A university is a community engaged in perpetual self-criticism and self-renewal through conversation and dialogue, an intergenerational partnership in discovery and exploration.[4] Much of what is most distinctive about universities derives from this feature of our lives and work.

We can arrive at such an initial statement of the mission of the university from several different directions, and thus provide a check on our perspective. If we are empirically minded, we can observe what institutions like ours actually do, and attempt to describe it as carefully as we can. If we prefer an etiological or historical approach, we can survey (as Perkins did) the development of our universities and identify the several layers that compose them.

Or we can proceed by an Aristotelian method of comparative categorizing, looking around at other human associations that share some but not all features with universities, and see what it is about the university that is distinctive.[5]

If we adopt the last of these perspectives, we might conceptualize the research university along a continuum that includes, at one extreme, the solitary hermit-scholar, engaged in wrestling out the meaning of the world or answering one single knotty question. Closer to us would be the research institutes, composed of a number of such scholars engaged in parallel pursuits. Some institutes engage only in "pure" or basic research, others in applied research devoted to improving the condition of the world, often according to the conception of improvement held by some friendly funding source.

Universities include scholars of both basic and applied research. We also have the opportunity and obligation to teach, to replicate ourselves by producing new scholars, and to improve the human condition not only through applied research but by training the new generation of citizens and leaders of society.

Next to us on the other side would be the selective liberal arts colleges, which share our interest in research but have an even greater emphasis on teaching. Then would come institutions devoted solely to teaching, including community colleges, vocational schools, high schools, and seminaries. Anchoring the other end of the continuum would be the private tutor, engaged to teach some skill such as music or Italian to a single pupil.

Somewhere within this set we would need to place more specialized and homogeneous institutions such as monasteries, which are dedicated to conserving a certain kind of knowledge for future generations and to improving the world according to their own conception of improvement. We would need room for philanthropic organizations that are established first of all to improve the human condition, but that engage in teaching or research as an ancillary tactic. And we would have to account for a comparatively new phenomenon: corporate educational centers, which convey not only the arcana of their professions but also basic skills of many kinds to their employees.

The concept of a cluster of cognate institutions, each of which shares some, but not all, of our basic purposes, helps to demonstrate what is distinctive about the research university. Most of our concerns about our mission have to do with how these three purposes—research, teaching, and service—are connected, and whether all are still valid for us today. The tensions between teaching and research are the most commonplace of these concerns. It is to these that I will now turn.

RESEARCH AND TEACHING

The functions of discovering and sharing knowledge are intimately related. We obscure this relationship by emphasizing the tensions between research and teaching. Of course, at the pragmatic level of the disposition of professorial time and the deployment of resources, research and teaching often do conflict. Time spent in the laboratory or the library grappling with a research problem competes with time spent elsewhere, including the classroom. Time spent preparing to convey knowledge to undergraduates in terms that will be sensible to them is time not spent describing the results of one's research to informed colleagues. Following up on a graduate seminar over coffee in the common room takes time that might have been better spent at the computer writing the next grant proposal.

Yet it is clear that these activities are not simply opposed to one another. Classroom presentations are enriched by work in the library or the laboratory, which keeps knowledge fresh and pertinent and protects the undergraduates from hearing brilliant but oft-repeated lectures increasingly out of touch with developments in the field. The next grant proposal will be stronger if it follows upon a discussion with graduate students about an especially complex area of current intellectual concern in the discipline.

At an even more fundamental level, the activities of "discovering" and "sharing" knowledge are two ways of defining the same experience. It is true that some kinds of thinking are best done in isolation, and some scholars temperamentally work best alone. But even solitary scholars depend on experiences of sharing. They must have been taught the rudiments of an exploratory discipline, given a sense of what counts as interesting discoveries and where they are most likely to occur. The solitary scholar is an unusual scholar nowadays. More commonly, scholars are incessantly communicative, through conferences, co-authored journal articles, electronic mail, and joint research projects. Such activities are forms of sharing in discovery.

The discovery or acquisition of knowledge is generally enhanced when it is participatory. This participation can take the form of collaboration, in which the partners bring different strengths and knowledge bases to the enterprise and thus extend each other's reach. Or it can mean competition, in which the work of discovery is spurred by the awareness that others are on the track of the same kind of knowledge. In either case, the presence of others engaged in the same enterprise leads to a dialectic in which the final result is fuller and more complete than anything a single person could have arrived at all alone.[6]

This is all very well, one might reply, but why does sharing in discovery require *teaching*, as opposed to the presence of active and interesting colleagues? How realistic is it to suppose that undergraduates, especially, can be meaningful partners in discovery, that sharing knowledge with them can be anything more than the transmission of what is already known?

According to one fairly common conception of the university, teaching is a distraction from our central mission. It should be minimized, if not eliminated altogether. Derek Bok reports that as he was preparing to become president of Harvard University, a colleague in charge of another prestigious institution suggested that his first bold step might be to eliminate Harvard College. His advisor asserted that "teaching introductory economics to freshmen or European history to sophomores is a waste of talented scholars who should have no responsibilities that divert them from what they do uniquely well," which was, in his view, doing research and training graduate students to do the same.[7]

The higher prestige accorded to research, the availability of more trustworthy interinstitutional metrics for judging whether it is well or poorly done, the comparative rarity of the skills required to do it well, and the undeniable fact that it is often more pleasurable to pursue one's own work at one's own pace rather than to translate it for the uninitiated, combine to give research an undisputed primacy in the self-definition of the university. The oft-noted fact that we think in terms of "teaching *loads*" and "research *opportunities*" is faithfully reflected in the academic reward system, by which professors are lured to new institutions with promises of decreased exposure to undergraduates.

These are formidable supports for the primacy of research. Let us ponder, however, what our institutions would be like if we stopped teaching. Many of us have spent joyful and productive periods on sabbatical at institutes of pure research, and sometimes, we think nostalgically, that is the way one ought to live throughout one's life. For some scholars this is no doubt true, and for those professionals, the institute devoted solely to research is a proper home. Most of us, however, would eventually miss the robust variety, the give and take, the intellectual ferment that comes from the coexistence of people of different ages, at different points along the route to intellectual sophistication, tucked into the same small space and required to interact with one another in sustained and ordered ways.

Almost all of us would accept the importance of graduate teaching to our conception of our mission, productivity, and self-definition in our profession. The threats to even the best research centers are intellectual sterility, a sameness of experience and focus, and the nagging questions about who is listening, who really cares, and how much what one does matters to the world. With bright and eager graduate students, there is a regular influx of new ideas and new approaches; the evidence that what one is engaged in does make a difference mounts steadily as one's intellectual progeny move forward in the profession. Graduate students are clearly partners in discovery, and sometimes the most effective partners of all.

Why not, then, adopt the model of the German university and separate the professoriate and their apprentice scholars from the novices, letting those who happen to enjoy teaching undergraduates find jobs in colleges instead?

There are several answers to this question, both principled and pragmatic. Liberal arts colleges, and other institutions in our cognate cluster, also educate undergraduates, but universities take a slightly different approach. Colleges offer small classes, more exposure to regular faculty, more faculty time spent in informal interactions with undergraduates, and different residential, extracurricular, and counseling facilities. Undergraduates who choose a university, however, can expect a more complex curriculum in many fields, as well as the opportunity to take advanced work in graduate seminars or professional fields. They may also benefit from the presence of graduate students and adjunct professors, and from more extensive library and laboratory facilities. Within our system as a whole, it is educationally and intellectually beneficial to have such options available to undergraduates.

Furthermore, undergraduate teaching can sometimes bring significant rewards. This can be true in any discipline—even the most rigorous—when it is taught so as to enhance the sense of wonder and stimulate curiosity, rather than only to instill accepted methodologies. A fresh perspective can jolt one's stagnant preconceptions and suggest whole new ways of looking at the world. More often than not, graduate students are already too fully initiated into our mysteries, too ready to adopt the latest jargon, too anxious to be accepted as members of the guild to ask eccentric, provocative questions. For many of us, therefore, the absence of undergraduates would be a serious loss, however much we might sometimes wish that they would behave less like undergraduates.

For others, the difficulty of preparing oneself to enter the mind of the uninitiated outweighs whatever promise there may be of intellectual surprise. As more and more of our undergraduates come to us deficient in some of the basic skills provided in the past by secondary education, teaching introductory material can be onerous. This can make the responsibility seem only a burden, a pure distraction from one's proper business of research and training graduate students.

Here a more pragmatic answer becomes pertinent: graduate students, however valuable they may be, generally do not come fully funded. Direct support for research is difficult to count on for many scholars; seeking it takes a good deal of time and energy. It sometimes comes with strings attached that deflect us from promising avenues that we might otherwise wish to pursue. Undergraduates, and their parents, support our enterprise with their tuition and fees in the belief that research and graduate training redounds to the better teaching of undergraduates. By accepting the support they give to us, we enter into a bargain with those students and their families. We have an obligation to uphold our end of that bargain.

This rather crass way of putting the matter fails to acknowledge that no student pays the full costs of a university education; endowment income, gifts from alumni, and corporate, foundation, and government support make up the difference in all cases, even for those who pay the full "ticket price." While this support is most obvious in the lower tuition charged at state-supported institutions, which enjoy substantial subsidies from the taxpayers, it is also reflected in the generous amounts of financial aid made available by many private universities. Those who enroll in state universities or attend private universities on financial aid have a larger discount, but in every case we are supplementing what a student or family actually pays with services that are provided without cost to them.

We need to recognize that our responsibility to educate undergraduates does not rest solely on the intellectual enrichment that they bring to other members of the university, or on the tuition and fees that some of them pay. Educating undergraduates is part of our distinctive contribution to improving the human condition, one of the ways we carry out our responsibility to serve society. The most distinctive and effective way we do this is by sharing knowledge with new generations of students, both graduate and undergraduate.

THE OBLIGATIONS OF UNDERGRADUATE EDUCATION

To accept the sharing of knowledge as an element of our mission assumes the conviction that society and the human condition are improved by more knowledge rather than less. One of the most distinctive things about the modern university is our sturdy assurance that we (not only our universities, but also our societies) are better off with free trade in what we sometimes call "the marketplace of ideas." This belief may sound innocuous, but there have been human communities deeply suspicious of such a commitment. Even in our post-Enlightenment world there are those who would argue that certain kinds of knowledge are better not communicated, or not pursued at all.

This should lead us to a more direct consideration of what is at stake in educating people, what we take for granted in doing so. Such discussions are of particular importance as we try to explain how we fulfill our obligations to society. Many of the difficulties we face come from dissonant conceptions of what knowledge is all about—what it is supposed to do for its beneficiaries, on campus and outside our walls. Quite a few observers of higher education in America today refer to our "loss of nerve." Part of what they mean is that we fail to justify what we do in terms that are most consonant with our own vision of our purposes.

Undergraduates and their families expect us to provide an education that advances their productive usefulness as members of society. How can we most faithfully keep our side of the bargain with those families and those students? It is, after all, up to us to decide what we will teach. One of the services that we might most usefully perform is altering their conception of what they need to know and what counts as an appropriate set of goals for the lives ahead of them.

Our society marks value primarily by monetary benchmarks, judging the worth of a person or enterprise by how much it earns or will produce. Unlike traditional societies where not only wealth but also family, status, or religious purity mattered to everyone, ours has no other measures of worth that are generally accepted, even though some institutions or enterprises may have their own criteria. As institutions of higher learning in America have increasingly been called upon to defend the worth of what they do, we have described their value in financial terms. We have adduced evidence that a baccalaureate degree is highly correlated with earning power across one's lifetime, to persuade our consumers that what we provide is worth the increasingly high prices that we charge.

We should hardly be surprised, therefore, when students major in economics or business not because they are all intellectually intrigued by the fields but because they (or their parents) believe that these majors will be more likely to guarantee a high-paying job upon graduation, or press for higher grades because they worry about being accepted at a graduate school that will ensure their professional success. We are sometimes taken aback by such narrow utilitarianism, but if we tell students that we keep our part of the educational bargain by increasing their chances to make a lot of money, they are smart enough to figure out what paths within our institutions are most likely to ensure that goal.

Most of us are idealistic enough to think that the undergraduate years should be years of exploration, risk taking, and intellectual development, before one settles down to serious professional preparation. We believe that education has multiple purposes, and that students who focus too early and too single-mindedly on their career goals are cheating themselves of many of the most distinctive benefits of the collegiate experience. We must do a better job of explaining our advantages and goals to our consumers. This will mean sharing fuller information about how little stress is placed by graduate and professional schools (apart from medical schools) on specific preprofessional education; highlighting the successful career paths of alumni with apparently unpragmatic majors such as classics or art history; and reminding students regularly and imaginatively of the importance of service to others and the balance of work, love, and leisure in a good human life.

Such arguments can be persuasive so long as the aura of the university is still powerful enough to give legitimacy to what we say. But the more we accede to or even encourage the prevailing standards of measuring value, the harder it will be for us to stand up to them effectively to protect other values that we believe are important for society to embrace.

We have been hampered in our ability to defend a robust conception of our purposes in undergraduate education by an absence of consensus in the university itself. It is of critical importance that we undertake a thoughtful dialogue about what counts as a strong education in the liberal arts (as well as in other baccalaureate fields such as engineering). Within the past few decades, the burgeoning of knowledge in many fields, the challenges to orthodoxy in the canonical disciplines of western culture, and the acerbic battles around multiculturalism have caused most faculties to shy away from serious discussion of what one needs to teach or learn. This laissez-faire attitude has allowed us to avoid some internecine conflicts, but it has not served our undergraduates well, and has made it increasingly hard to justify what we are doing in our colleges and universities.

There are elements in a sound undergraduate education that do not change greatly over time—familiarity with excellent work in several fields of human endeavor, with basic historical facts, and with the approaches and accomplishments of science. We need to be explicit about this in describing what we are doing. Furthermore, we need to take steps to ensure that *all* our students are receiving an education that fits this model. Students who take their undergraduate degrees in engineering or other more pragmatic disciplines need some significant exposure to other disciplines; students who choose liberal arts degrees ought also to become familiar with at least the rudiments of technological thinking, in order to understand some of the most essential components of the modern world in which they will live and work.

Many of our students lack analytical and critical tools, and historical and philosophical depth. It is essential that we teach them how to arrive at critically informed judgments about truth statements in a variety of disciplines, and to be suspicious of claims that there is only one single truth, or one viable approach to it. Students are especially vulnerable to shoddy scholarship and to ideological appeals. Shoddy scholarship describes both the approach of the western culture ideologue—who believes that only the traditional Greco-Judeo-Christian canon is worth teaching, even though it limits our perspective on the world to that of upper-class males, mostly white and European—and the feminist theorist or Afrocentric scholar who teaches that everything in the western tradition is irretrievably phallocentric or derivative from Egyptian roots.[8]

We need to educate students to participate in a larger human culture, not just confirm their prejudices, whatever those prejudices may be. The essential contributions of pluralism to a good education are made not only through a variety of disciplines, teachers, and methodologies, but also through working with a variety of colleagues and peers. Anyone learns better in an environment that includes other students who bring a different background and perspective to the same experience or material. Our obligation to educate undergraduates includes assembling a diverse and heterogeneous student body. This will provide the ferment and creative excitement that is itself part of a good education and will prepare undergraduates to participate in a world which promises to be very different from that which any of us have experienced.

EDUCATION BEYOND THE UNDERGRADUATE YEARS

One of the most distinctive facets of the university from the early centuries of its development has been the juxtaposition of baccalaureate education with advanced professional training. This double layer of training has become the definitive characteristic of the university in America, and to a large degree throughout the world. Over time, new professional schools in fields such as business, education, and public policy were developed, and graduate studies in the arts and sciences became the basis for a separate school, alongside the other ancient faculties.

Just as the content of education in the liberal arts has evolved significantly over time, so has the concept of professional training along with the professions themselves. The greater coherence of professional school faculties, and pressures from associations of practitioners to keep the work relevant and useful, have meant that professional training has been rethought and reorganized much more regularly and systematically than training in the humanities and sciences. The mission of a professional school is easier to define than the mission of an entire university, and the curriculum appropriate to that mission is easier to construe and modify than training in the liberal arts.

We have a good example of such renovative activity in the response by several universities to the ethical problems in business and the professions that have become increasingly apparent in contemporary American society. Our reaction has been to introduce the explicit discussion of ethical dilemmas into our professional schools. We hope that as a result, more professionals in law, business, and medicine will be sensitive to ethical dilemmas in their work and better equipped to deal with them.

Graduate education in the humanities and sciences is less easily susceptible to broad changes, since the direction of the program lies almost entirely with each discipline. The primary purpose of graduate education is to replicate scholarship in that discipline. The strength of disciplinary loyalties and the marks of a successful academic guild—conferences, journals, consistent standards for peer review, a core literature, and agreement on an agenda of the most important research problems next to be solved—make clear that this purpose has been served with great effectiveness across the years.

Graduate education derives its quality and resilience from the close symbiosis between master and journeyman scholar. The graduate student comes to be initiated into the profession, to receive the higher mysteries, and to be accorded the insignia, so that he or she can move through the ranks of professional success. Only the acknowledged masters of the discipline are able to provide these benefits. In return, the novice scholars support and participate in the work of the masters, as research assistants and co-authors, extending the reach of their research capabilities and bringing prestige both as students and as intellectual heirs. This symbiosis works so well, and is so fully self-perpetuating, that it is hard to bring about significant changes in the format of graduate education. The content of the material changes, sometimes dramatically, as the discipline evolves, but if people elsewhere in the university or in society as a whole believe that other purposes need to be served in graduate education, it is not easy to accomplish them.

A familiar example of this problem is the recurrent sense that graduate students should be more systematically prepared for teaching. Since many newly minted Ph.D.'s are plunged immediately into a full schedule of teaching undergraduates, both they and their students would be better served if they had more direct preparation for the job. The tasks of a graduate teaching assistant are seldom designed for such a purpose. More often than not, their assignments place them as functionaries in large lecture courses, where their duties are to grade papers, lead discussion sections, and answer questions about the material. The governing motivation of this system is to relieve the professor of much of the detailed work of teaching; the arrangement serves this purpose very nicely. Concerns about the interests of undergraduates and about whether the graduate students themselves derive any useful training from this system have too seldom been seriously addressed.

Conscientious professors sometimes arrange seminars for their teaching assistants, so that they can reflect on their experiences and derive insights about teaching. However, most graduate students have only a vague notion of what is involved in drawing up a set of lectures, devising a syllabus, or taking responsibility for the whole intellectual direction of a course. As a result, the first few years of teaching are very difficult for many novice professors, even though some fairly simple changes in graduate education could provide obvious relief for at least some of these difficulties.

The first steps in reform along these lines are already being taken in several universities, thanks to the recent establishment of centers for teaching and learning. These centers are designed to provide mentoring for those who want to improve their skills, sources of information about new technologies and methods, and opportunities for experiences such as having a class videotaped or analyzed. This system relieves the average professor of graduate students from having to worry directly about training students to be teachers, and provides a cost-effective and centralized location where models of good teaching and training in the skills of undergraduate education can easily be found.

It is easy to forget that apprentice teachers who are also scholars need training in the ethics of our craft as well. We are more alert to the temptations that will beset the graduates of medical or business schools than those that will beset the members of the professoriate. Understanding the meaning of plagiarism, the importance of scrupulous honesty in reporting the results of one's research, and the relevance of concerns about sexual harassment in the scholarly community take specific thought and preparation; we cannot take for granted that such ethical issues are clearly understood by our graduate students.

An opening up of graduate education may also be needed in a parallel direction: in loosening the monopolistic grasp of the disciplines themselves on the training of scholars, and the provision of academic certification and pedigrees. Despite the clear advantages of this system, there are also pitfalls: intellectual arrogance, disputes over turf, and a certain artificiality about the construction of a world that comes in neatly packaged disciplinary boxes. Increasingly, much of the most interesting work done in the university extends across the boundaries of the traditional disciplines, in fields such as political economy, biological chemistry, comparative literature, ecology, and public policy, as well as in areas such as medicine and the law, or the environmental impact of business practices.

If graduate training remains too narrowly focused in the traditional disciplines, it will be harder for graduates to take full advantage of such cross-currents in their own work. Successful scholars need grounding in some systematic approach to the discovery of knowledge, and the disciplines provide this very well. They also need flexibility to work effectively with scholars trained in other fields, to tackle problems that do not lend themselves easily to solution with the tools of any single discipline, and some awareness of where the most valuable cognate fields might lie. Our graduate students will be better served if their training includes exposure to such alternative approaches through interdisciplinary seminars and bibliographies.

As we rethink the organization of graduate and professional training to take into account the growing interdisciplinarity of the discovery and sharing of knowledge, we ought also to consider more broadly our responsibilities to the members of a society increasingly dependent upon knowledge and sophisticated technologies in daily work. Here it may well be time for a bold redefinition of our mission: not just to provide a traditional baccalaureate education followed by graduate and professional training culminating in an advanced degree, but also to serve as resource centers for people at various stages of their lives.

Several elements of such a redefinition are already in place. Many of our candidates for a baccalaureate degree today are not of traditional undergraduate age. They return to us to complete a degree, or begin study for the first time, in the middle decades of their lives. Other middle-aged and older people are satisfying their curiosity, improving their skills, or increasing their earning power by taking courses for pleasure or for specialized professional certification programs of various kinds. Executives and government officials are taking advantage of mid-career programs to retool or refresh their approaches to their jobs.

It is reasonable to expect that nontraditional educational patterns will continue to develop rapidly in a society that puts such a premium on access to information and communication. The universities need to think carefully about how to participate in these developments, so that our faculties and facilities will be put to most effective use, rather than ignore the importance of this phenomenon or allow our core mission of discovering and sharing knowledge to be overshadowed by the provision of specific services and techniques that bring short-term economic gains to institutions hard pressed for resources.

One promising avenue is programs for alumni, who often express the wish for more effective methods of keeping themselves intellectually alive through the "lifelong learning" for which their alma maters supposedly prepared them. Almost every university sponsors alumni seminars or study trips. With the advent of new teaching technologies and more effective organizations for contact with alumni, there are many ways we can satisfy such desires more fully. With the clear trends towards earlier retirement and healthier old age, there are many people who have the time and money to travel and want to develop new skills and keep their minds and bodies vigorous in the last decades of their lives. The company of scholars knows no age limits; the intergenerational partnerships that have always characterized the university are susceptible to newly fruitful variations as career and retirement patterns in our society are changing.

THE UNIVERSITY AND THE IMPROVEMENT
OF THE HUMAN CONDITION

Our responsibility to our students, of whatever age or level of experience, is clear: they come to us to be educated, and we accept them with the implicit understanding that we will serve that need as best we can. The funds to support this activity come in part from the students and their families, but also more generally from taxpayers, as well as from corporations, foundations, and our alumni. This brings us to the more general question of our responsibility for the improvement of society.

General support for universities, both those that derive almost all their money from public coffers and those that rely more heavily on private funds, is provided diffusely in our society because it is understood that we are performing at least two important functions: providing a sound education for the next generation of citizens, and training skilled professionals to perform the tasks that must be done if our society is to flourish. Since we accept the support and enjoy its fruits, we are obliged to carry out our part of the bargain by educating those citizens and professionals to the best of our ability.

Providing such an education is the most obvious way that we improve the human condition, but there are others. The research done by our faculties adds to our knowledge in every field. In many instances, the research contributes to human welfare in directly utilitarian ways: advances in medical science and in more effective legal systems; in agriculture, architecture, engineering, and ecology; and in enhancing communication, transportation, and urban planning.[9] In other areas, such as art, literature, or history, the benefits of scholarly research are less tangible, but no less important, in expanding our knowledge of the intricate dimensions and potentialities in human life.

We know that research can sometimes lead to results that undermine rather than enhance human welfare; progress, even in scientific research, is never without its costs and detours. But on balance, the research done in our universities makes major contributions to human well-being.

We need to be more confident and bolder in reminding governments and taxpayers about this at a time when the whole purpose and character of universities are being questioned. We need to make more explicit the connections between specific beneficial outcomes and the more general situation of our universities. It should be made more clearly evident that the so-called indirect costs of libraries and laboratory equipment, and other administrative costs (so long as they are carefully and conscientiously derived), are genuine expenses of research. Thus, they are costs that should be borne in part by the society that benefits from the fruits of research, and not just by the universities themselves through tuition and fees or endowment income.

However, the use of the general term "society" in describing the beneficiary of activities by the university masks an increasingly serious issue: How do we define the society to which we are responsible? In the past, pressures to answer the question in one way or another have arisen from various interests: local governments and citizens, state legislatures, and alumni. Today they have taken on a new dimension.

One of the favorite buzzwords on many campuses these days is "internationalization." Universities have always been inveterately international in many ways: since medieval times, scholars have stubbornly refused to be constrained by national boundaries in sharing and discovering knowledge and have been among the most effective forces in breaking down parochialism and xenophobia. As our world has become increasingly interconnected, however, we have become more self-conscious about this dimension of our institutions. The new internationalization is still a vague concept in most instances, intended to emphasize the importance of educating our students to function more effectively as participants and leaders in a multinational world, by providing them with classmates and curricula that give them a sense of countries and cultures other than their own. Admitting more foreign students, strengthening programs for international travel or campuses abroad, encouraging faculty members to develop their ties to colleagues in other countries, increasing support for language and area studies— all these are facets of internationalization as it is usually understood.

In several respects, however, the increasingly international face of the university has created new tensions. The admission of foreign students, whether at the undergraduate or graduate level, raises significant financial issues. Do we see these students as a pure source of funding, or do we apply some of the same standards of equity and socioeconomic diversity that we follow in admitting domestic students? If the latter, where does the money come from, and what happens when there is direct competition between domestic and foreign students for financial aid?

Establishing programs in Japanese, Latin American, or Southeast Asian studies might seem pure beneficial instances of internationalism, expanding the horizons of our students in an increasingly multinational world. But funding issues are once again important. Who pays for the new programs? The governments or corporations of the countries in question are one obvious possible source: they have a clear interest in having American leaders better educated in the customs and history of their countries. But receiving funds from them can create pressures on the faculty hired with the funds to do research and teach in ways that present primarily positive versions of those countries and their cultures, and discourage critical analysis of their problems. There is then a tension with the basic commitment of the university to the pursuit of truth.

Another kind of tension arises because at the same time that we have become increasingly conscious of and explicit about the international dimensions of our mission, we are also defending our public utility in quite specifically and narrowly nationalistic terms. We stress our obligation to train effective citizens and leaders for our own country, not just because it is good to have educated people in the world, but because we want the United States to be healthy and strong. In seeking support from the government and the corporate sector, we emphasize the importance of education in building a strong American economy and allowing us to compete effectively with other nations.[10]

This tension between our developing internationalism and our obligations to our own society has become especially problematic in the admission and training of foreign graduate students, in research funding provided by foreign corporations, and in the sharing of potentially crucial research results with scholars in other countries. It would be nice to be able to treat these issues as transitional phenomena, inevitable byproducts of lingering parochialism as we develop closer cross-national linkages and break down historic borders. In the meantime, while we are in the midst of the transition, these issues pose genuine dilemmas for our universities and our polity.

Can we speak of our obligation to improve the human condition without reference to national identity? Or does doing so mean reneging on our fundamental responsibility to our own country and citizenry? American universities are world-renowned, and the provision of undergraduate and graduate education is one of the areas where our country has a clear competitive edge today. Should we pursue this market superiority by aggressively recruiting students and faculty members from around the world, even though this may sometimes mean excluding citizens of our own country from graduate fellowships or desirable posts? Or should we give priority to the education of our own citizens and the improvement of our own polity, economy, and society? These are thorny questions with no easy answers. They must be discussed openly and explicitly on our campuses and in our governments.

Our national government has become increasingly concerned about the outflow of research ideas and trained personnel from our universities into the economies of competitor countries. There is also concern about the potential military implications of some kinds of knowledge. In the post–cold war world, this has generated anxiety about the diffusion of technologies for sophisticated weaponry to more and more countries—protecting sensitive information has become more difficult than when it meant primarily excluding Soviet nationals from access to our universities. In this situation, there is a developing sentiment to set limits on the communication of ideas and research findings, and upon the ability of American scholars to seek and accept funding from abroad. Do universities have an obligation to be sure that the results of our research in sensitive fields are available first and foremost to corporate developers and government officials in our own country, so as to enhance American economic strength and protect American military power?

It would be unrealistic for us to ignore the potentially dangerous consequences of a purely open system of information. Too much control would be self-defeating, if it meant denying access for our faculty and graduate students to vigorous open interchange with their colleagues in other countries. The ideal of vigorous open interchange, however, implies that other countries play by the same rules and allow access for our researchers to the same kinds of knowledge. Where knowledge is differentially developed, this may be a requisite with little practical effect. Where cultural attitudes towards sharing knowledge are different from ours, it may be hard to achieve the reciprocal openness that we seek.

Such issues assume particular urgency today, for several reasons. In the past, it did not much matter what kind of knowledge was communicated, or to whom, so long as specific military or state secrets were not breached. The level of sophistication of scientific and technological knowledge created by university researchers and the implications of such knowledge for military and industrial power have become significantly greater within the past few decades. These developments are contemporaneous with increasing American concern about international economic competitiveness, at a time when we are no longer a hegemonic power and world creditor. This creates strong pressures to hoard useful knowledge for the benefit of our own society.

Furthermore, our ability to communicate quickly and easily to many different transnational audiences has increased dramatically with the advent of computer networks and the new scholarly habits of electronic communication that have grown up around them. Especially in quantitative and scientific fields, national borders have already become virtually irrelevant to communication.

These developments coincide with a period in which the power of governments to control results has become increasingly significant, because so much of the support for expensive scientific research comes directly from government itself. Withholding funds or placing specific conditions on how research can be carried on if it is to be funded are effective constraints in an era when support costs for the research of a single physical scientist in some fields can be as large as the costs of a small department in the humanities or social sciences, and some of the most sophisticated work in several sciences depends upon funding that is available only from government resources.

The alternative of corporate-university partnerships in research funding is becoming increasingly attractive, as the examples of Silicon Valley in California and Research Triangle Park in North Carolina clearly attest. Corporations direct their support to certain kinds of research rather than to others, but in those areas, enlightened partnerships with business are a strong alternative to government support for university research.

Corporate-sponsored research arrangements for development, marketing, and patenting can create their own complex dilemmas for university researchers and bureaucracies, whether the corporations are foreign or domestic. Proprietary knowledge is sometimes important for corporate success, but it is in principle antithetical to the openness in sharing knowledge that is at the heart of the university's mission. Successful research scientists who develop close relationships with particular corporate funders may become increasingly independent from the university and cease to function effectively as colleagues.

Some of the most successful corporate-university partnerships have occurred when several corporations and universities in a geographic area have pooled their resources and ideas. This strategy alleviates the disadvantages of special partnerships, and allows both businesses and universities to show leadership in regional economic development as well as to be very productive in applied research. Such developments, comparatively recent and quite promising, demonstrate the advantages of novel resourcefulness in thinking about the best ways to support those aspects of our mission that have to do with the general improvement of the human condition.

The modern research university occupies a distinctive niche in both space and time, compounded of equal parts of intense nostalgic localism and a generous sense that members of a university are citizens of the world.

The campus, quadrangles, cloisters, common rooms, and libraries are closely linked with the experiences of discovering and sharing knowledge. They evoke intense memories for members of the university in diaspora, and despite their similarities of form and function from one campus to another, they set each university apart as unique in its own fashion. Despite our increasing sense of global connectedness, much of what is most distinctive to the university is clearly localized in specific spaces for inquiry, research, and conversation.

Nonetheless, the university has throughout history been stubbornly cosmopolitan. Scholars are inveterate travelers to conferences, research sites, libraries, and museums. Knowledge in most disciplines is little constrained by language or geography; it is enriched by sharing and by a universalistic perspective. The novel possibilities of electronic communication allow members of universities to do much more easily, cheaply, and effectively what they have always done: exchange ideas along lines of disciplinary interest with almost total disregard for national or institutional affiliation.

Universities also have a distinctive timelessness that provides a generous horizon for our work. We are conscious of our participation in a long heritage of institutions demonstrably similar to ours, reaching back even beyond the medieval European university to the schools and academies of classical times. This sense of history is made palpable in our traditions and ceremonies, our academic processions, colorful regalia, and distinctive feast days—commencements, convocations, and inaugurations. There is a variant of apostolic succession here that gives an assurance of rootedness and continuity even in troubled times.

Yet universities are also forward-looking, restless, pioneering, attempting to discern and even to control the future. Much of our research is concerned with identifying likely outcomes, adapting the lessons of the past to probable future situations, and equipping people to act more effectively on the basis of well-founded hypotheses about what future options will be like.

The love of learning for its own sake, the fascination with exploration and discovery, is a powerful human impulse, needing no further justification for those who are absorbed in it. Many faculty and students would continue their work virtually unaltered even if they knew that the world would come to a cataclysmic end in the near future. But the basic enterprise of the university as an institution rests also on the faith that there will be time for our efforts to make a difference for good. Education makes little sense unless one believes that there will be a future, and that it is likely to be a better one if people are educated rather than ignorant.

These tensions between parochial and cosmopolitan affiliations, between rootedness in the past and restlessness about the future, and between the love of learning for its own sake and an investment in making the world a better place are close to the heart of the university. However we define our mission, the tensions must be acknowledged if we are to have any hope of presenting our strengths and our character faithfully to the world.

Pro Bono Publico

INSTITUTIONAL LEADERSHIP

AND THE PUBLIC GOOD

Tate Lecture, Southern Methodist University, October 1995

Last August my family spent a few weeks on Nantucket Island, off Cape Cod. One day we biked up to the lighthouse at Sankaty Head, an island landmark. Like many historic lighthouses, including Cape Hatteras on North Carolina's Outer Banks, Sankaty Head is threatened by the elements it has warned against for so many decades. The ocean encroaches relentlessly year by year, and the very foundations of the lighthouse are in danger, along with all the houses on the bluff nearby.

On this particular visit, we overheard two Nantucketers discussing a campaign to save the lighthouse and the bluff, by pumping out water from the sand below. One of the men related a snippet of conversation with a neighbor who lived across the road that leads to the lighthouse. Asked to support the campaign to save Sankaty Light, his neighbor said: "Why should I help you? If your house goes into the ocean, I'll be waterfront."

Such selfish sentiments are hardly novel in our society today; but they seemed especially jarring on Nantucket. The early settlers devised a way of life that fit the island, windswept and barren, with a protected harbor and a straight shot at the open Atlantic Ocean. Many of the men were whalers, as you may recall from *Moby Dick*. They ventured into the furthest reaches of the Pacific as well as the Atlantic, following the whales. Such conditions bred sturdy self-reliance, but also made essential those cooperative habits that built a strong community, on the whaling ship, in the meeting house, in the economy of the town, to sustain the thin margin between prosperity and adversity.

Building a lighthouse was an excellent example of the pooling of resources for the common good. Everyone knew that their own lives or the lives of those they loved might someday be saved by that tall, flashing light. It would have been wasteful and foolish for every house on the coast to hang out its own lantern every night; such small lights would have saved few lives off such a treacherous coast. It was much more efficient for the islanders to pool their resources of energy and money to build a single tall lighthouse on the bluff.

This blend of sturdy independence and commitment to cooperation was one of the most distinctive things about our country in its early days. But this fruitful combination of attitudes is rapidly eroding in America today, as surely as the sand on our barrier beaches, so that both our literal and our metaphorical lighthouses are threatened.

THE LESSONS OF THE AMERICAN FRONTIER

Frederick Jackson Turner was right. America is a frontier society; and as the frontier advanced from the coastal enclaves of Jamestown and Boston to the Connecticut Valley and the Appalachians, on to Texas and the plains states, and finally to Oregon and California, frontier conditions led a small brave band of independent-minded folks to create a community on territory that combined threat and promise in equal and uncertain measure. Americans struck out for the frontier because of restless independence; but when they got there, they found that they could rarely go it entirely alone. So they invented new forms of collaboration for survival and companionship.

In the plains states, families who lived miles apart came together for a day of hard work and celebration to raise a new barn for their neighbors. Most things a family did for itself; but no family could raise a barn in a day. This was a clear instance where everyone had an interest in helping build a neighbor's barn, knowing that one could count on similar help if disaster struck one's own.

There was a large measure of trust in this belief in reciprocity. It was always theoretically possible—and you'll have to forgive a bit of parochialism here—that if the Houston family helped the Austins build a barn one fine September day, and Sam and his clan asked Stephen F. for help in turn next spring, the Austins would plead a previous engagement, since, after all, they had already "got theirs." But that was not the way it worked, because people could see quite clearly the linkages between helping others and being helped in turn, and the long-term advantages of reciprocity. And if anyone were tempted just to sit back and enjoy the fruits of his neighbors' work, the social pressures of a small community would be ruthlessly brought to bear to urge compliance or enforce isolation.

This communal spirit became the basis of familiar institutions, drawing upon those informal collaborative activities. Religion was a common bond among the frontier communities. The rough-hewn church or chapel, and before long the synagogue as well, brought people together in worship and provided the basis for shared activities—making music, sharing food, succoring the sick and dying—within the liturgical or congregational traditions of each faith.

The one-room schoolhouse was another familiar frontier institution. Children could, of course, be schooled at home. But few people had the knowledge and even fewer had the time; frontier families lived very close to the margin of survival. Yet they wanted their children to be educated, at least in the rudiments of language, history, arithmetic. And thus one of the earliest professionals on the frontier, after the circuit-riding preacher and the hanging judge, was the schoolmarm.

The simple churches and schoolhouses were followed by the county governments, and gradually by colleges to educate teachers and ministers, as things became more settled and people lived in towns. All these early institutions of government, religion, and education were built upon the frontier habits of collaborating, trusting one another, of friendship extended to civic accomplishment and helping others.

Americans are not innately a more moral people than others. There were violence and deadly selfishness on the frontier, as there are wherever unpredictable humans congregate. We are all familiar with this from the classic westerns of our youth. Why else would we have needed a sheriff or a Texas ranger, except that there were outlaws, not nearly as personally appealing as Robert Redford or Paul Newman? And on the spectacular but very dangerous coast of North Carolina, the name Nags Head on Cape Hatteras takes its name from a perverse inversion of a lighthouse.

The people of Nags Head paraded their horses on the beach at night, with lanterns on their forelocks, so that the nags walking back and forth looked, to sailors off the coast, like boats moving in smooth water. Thus they were lured to the rocks and shoals and drowned, and their treasures made easy pickings for the locals.

We can hardly pride ourselves, as a people, on our record of unstained goodness. Still, that shrewd and distinctive combination of fierce independence and willingness to cooperate flowered as successfully in early America as it ever has in the world.

THE LOOSENING OF SOCIAL BONDS

We have moved very far from that limpid conception of a cooperative public good encompassing our private goods. Our complex civilization puts up multiple roadblocks to simple human feeling, much less durable ties of reciprocity. Newspapers and television describe crimes committed while others serve only as bystanders, afraid to get involved. The uncertain fate of a Good Samaritan these days helps to explain that impulse—the media tell with almost equal frequency of someone who stopped to help a stranger, and someone who was attacked or robbed or killed while trying to do so.

Last summer bystanders watched Deletha Word being harshly beaten for her part in a traffic accident, and then jump to her death in the Detroit River. Many in the crowd saw this as spectacle; one person said they were "standing around like people taking an interest in sports." Some cheered to egg the attackers on. Others, not so callous, were no doubt afraid to get involved for fear of being beaten up or killed, a sentiment we can all understand even if it is hardly admirable. A few people in the crowd around Deletha Word used cellular phones to call 911. Two young men jumped into the river trying to save her. When they emerged cold and exhausted, one of them was arrested and handcuffed by the Detroit police for jumping into the river.

Scenes of impersonal refusal to get involved, or of involvement repaid with cynicism or violence, are so frequent that they seem hardly worth remarking today, no longer as shocking as they were in 1964 with the famous Kitty Genovese case in New York City—except for the agony of those directly involved, which does not diminish, even though it is not shared. But society is diminished, and something that protects us and makes us more human is ominously gone.

The norms of reciprocity are dangerously loosened; we are a long way from the barn raising and the quilting bees. This loss is noted by historians and sociologists as a clear sign of decline and decay, the using up of social capital which is not being replenished.

TOCQUEVILLE'S ANALYSIS OF AMERICAN SOCIETY

To understand America's history of social capital, and why we ought to deplore its erosion, we should go back to the early 1830s, when a young French magistrate named Alexis de Tocqueville traveled to our country, which held for him great fascination. He was a liberal aristocrat who wanted to understand how democracy could be constructed in the modern world, to figure out how the new American republic actually worked, to provide lessons for his own beloved France.

Tocqueville was an amazingly perceptive observer, motivated to study the habits and institutions of America very closely. He was fortunate enough to travel with a cousin of Lafayette, a legendary hero in the new republic, so the two young men had entry everywhere. When he returned to France, Tocqueville published *De la démocratie en Amérique,* an instant success on both sides of the Atlantic and a handbook for understanding American political culture ever since.

In the second volume of *Democracy in America* Tocqueville identifies as one of the most marked characteristics of the citizens of the United States what he calls "individualisme." This sentiment "disposes each member of the community to sever himself from the mass of his fellows and to draw apart with his family and his friends, so that after he has thus formed a little circle of his own, he willingly leaves society at large to itself."[1]

Tocqueville worried about this individualistic tendency, which he identified as the characteristic deformation of a democratic people, free and equal, without the traditional bonds of hierarchy and privilege that hold an aristocracy together. He thought that one of the secrets of America's success as a republic on a continental scale, the first such in human history, is that our free institutions are designed to draw people out of our individualistic cocoons into public actions in which our own private interests are clearly implicated: actions such as building a road or a school.

Beyond these local government institutions, there are other keys to our success—the free press, the powerful sentiments of religion—but the one that especially fascinated Tocqueville was the distinctive tendency of Americans to form associations to accomplish any goal that might occur to us: "Americans of all ages, all conditions, and all dispositions constantly form associations," notes Tocqueville. "Religious, moral, serious, futile, general or restricted, enormous or diminutive. The Americans make associations to give entertainments, to found seminaries, to build inns, to construct churches, to diffuse books, to send missionaries to the antipodes; in this manner they found hospitals, prisons and schools. . . . Whenever at the head of some new undertaking you see the government in France, or a man of rank in England, in the United States you will be sure to find an association."[2]

Associations of this sort, like free political institutions at the local level, bring people outside of themselves, combat the deleterious effects of individualism, and form the bonds that provide the basis of our everyday morality. Tocqueville connects this insight specifically with the Enlightenment "principle of self-interest rightly understood," and credited ordinary Americans with a shrewd understanding of how this doctrine actually works.

"Enlightened self-interest" is part of a moral philosophy advanced by learned Europeans during the same period that saw the opening of the American continent, 1650 to 1750. These philosophers noted that society could no longer count on fear of damnation, or hope for heavenly reward, to hold together a society grown increasingly secular. Nor could one expect unquestioning awe of any earthly monarch to bring about rigorous obedience to earthly laws. But when people understand their situations correctly, it was argued, we will see that we benefit from cooperation, even if cooperation requires sacrifice of the pursuit of one's own interest, narrowly construed.

These philosophers noted the tendency of these valuable impulses to decay with the advance of "civilization," and its corruptions and discontents. In frontier America, where civilization was much simpler and the pressures of daily survival much more keenly felt, there was little time for theorizing; but the attitudes celebrated by these European philosophers were in full flourishing.

In America, the distinctive morality was invented from the necessities of experience, among a far-flung people who needed each other, even if they were determined not to need each other too much. The embodiment of the "public good" in situations like theirs is not a pale abstract conception, but a set of specific practices that improve life and keep it from being, in Thomas Hobbes's trenchant phrase, "nasty, brutish and short"—not a distant prospect on the American frontier.

As Tocqueville looked to the future, the thing he most feared for democratic countries was a new kind of despotism that would be made possible by advanced "individualism," in which individuals draw entirely into their private worlds. Thus the bonds of association are loosened, all public action is left to a distant government, and eventually people become servile to an "immense and tutelary power," paternalistic and providential, which controls all their lives.[3]

Tocqueville did not think such a fate inevitable; but he did believe that we cannot take for granted being protected indefinitely by our free institutions and habits of association against the deformations endemic to democracies.

THE CONTEMPORARY RELEVANCE OF INSTITUTIONS

American society across the generations has encouraged associations to serve the common good, building on the collaborative habits that Tocqueville so clearly noted. Through enlightened tax laws, our government provides support for nonprofit organizations ranging widely from the formal to the casual—churches, museums, boys' and girls' clubs, soup kitchens, public television, charitable foundations. All these enterprises are made possible by tax laws that make it easier for people of good will to contribute to bettering their fellow human beings through giving to organizations established to serve the public welfare. Indeed, the government is now asking institutions of this kind to assume even more of the work that holds society together, as federal, state, and local governments pull back from many programs intended to improve life for the least fortunate. And ironically, at this same time, the very concept of tax exemption for nonprofit organizations itself is under fire as Congress tackles the deficit and reinvents our government.

As President George H. W. Bush made clear in his evocative image of a "thousand points of light," many of these voluntary associations bring together only a few people of good will, dedicated to making their own corner of the world a bit more livable, like small but precious lighthouses on a rocky shore. Others are major institutions that serve millions of people every year. Our country is unique in the opportunities it provides, and in the hundreds of thousands of organizations that we have created for volunteer service.

However, in the face of the bewildering complexity of our society today, many Americans, as Tocqueville would have predicted, have lost faith and interest in these associations. They have withdrawn into their individualistic worlds of family and a few friends, or into a solipsistic stupor with no company save that which can be brought in by TV. Many have lost their ethical bearings altogether, or follow moral road maps that divide them from other human beings in suspicion and distrust. Others have found refuge in novel or reawakened absolute truths, particularly in the bonds of religious communities. These communities may bring solace and benefits; but if they separate their members from the larger society, they undermine any sense of overarching common purpose, of a durable society composed of diverse people who share certain basic obligations to each other.

In such a world, our colleges and universities have an especially important role to play. From the time of the ancient Greeks through that of Tocqueville and into the present century, it was assumed that one of the purposes of education was to train citizens, to teach individual men and women to look beyond our horizons of narrow selfishness, to see our interest in attending to the needs of others, in the reciprocity of the golden rule and the common good.

We fallible human beings will not always discover these truths instinctively, given the powerful impulses of individualistic self-absorption. Nothing is more egotistical than a small human being of the age of two or three. It takes all the power of education—or else of bitter experience—to teach the lessons of delayed gratification, sharing, and cooperative activity. Ethical traditions do not endure unless they are deliberately taught, explained, and understood, within families and religious institutions, and by those in our society charged with educating our children.

Universities, like all institutions, are complex forms of association. Universities are not just bureaucratic structures: they consist of individual human beings of different generations, gathered to accomplish common goals. Our primary goals are to discover and communicate knowledge, to learn more about the world and to pass on what we learn to the next generation. Sometimes we do this well, sometimes not so well; but our basic purpose is clear and ardently pursued.

However, people on campus today, faculty members and students alike, are not residents of another planet. We are part of American society, a society that has become increasingly unsure about moral values, skeptical of absolute truths, daunted by the incredible complexity of the world in which we live. We reflect as well as help to shape the world around us.

Thus, in the past few decades there has been a failure of nerve on the part of higher education, like many institutions in American society. Just as it has become unfashionable to teach civics courses in high school, so the faculties and leaders of colleges and universities have been largely silent about our obligations to the common good. We have been oddly reluctant to recognize the power of what we do, or perhaps more precisely, we have been aware of that power and reluctant to use it. We have shied away from saying straightforwardly that we have an obligation to society to train the next generation of citizens and leaders, and that this entails teaching some of the traditional sources of public good as antidotes to destructive selfishness.

In these circumstances, universities must renew their commitment to civic education, sustaining the traditions that have provided a durable basis for human interaction and collaboration for the common good. Fortunately, universities are particularly well placed to help renew civic purpose in American society today. The elements for doing so are all in place, if we will but acknowledge and build upon them.

UNIVERSITIES AS SCHOOLS FOR ETHICAL UNDERSTANDING

Universities are especially well equipped to teach ethical understanding in the most straightforward fashion. Faculty members in several disciplines are specialists in the core materials of ethics, primarily in philosophy and religion, but also in psychology, classics, history, literature. These professors are knowledgeable about the rich corpus from which ethical truths are distilled and shared— great plays or novels or scriptural texts or works of moral philosophy, crucial heroic or shameful moments in the lives of nations or individuals.

We should encourage professors who are experts in all these areas to discuss moral issues straightforwardly in their classes, not to persuade their students to adopt a particular brand of ethical philosophy or convert them to a particular religion, but to train students to think carefully about ethics, just as we train them to appreciate music or art or to excel in quantitative reasoning.

The emphasis on objective knowledge, and making sure that all truths are carefully considered, are core values in the academy, and we must nurture them. But in doing so, we should not lose sight of the importance of reflection upon good and evil, of the occasions for understanding human ethical dilemmas provided by numerous disciplines on campus.

Beyond the classroom, residential colleges and universities are concentrated human communities, in which students live closely together, sharing all aspects of their lives in an intimacy that they will not elsewhere experience outside the family. These communities give practical experience in the consequences of ethical and unethical behavior.

It is easy to understand the advantages of reciprocity in a dormitory setting. If I refrain from playing my stereo at top volume at 3 a.m. when my roommate has an exam the next day, I can reasonably expect that she will do the same in turn. No weighty tome on the truths of enlightened self-interest is needed to convince me of the benefits of this. Honor codes, athletic teams, student judicial councils charged with enforcing the rules that students have helped to devise—these are excellent places to learn the habits of trust and collaboration that provide the basis of ethical behavior in complex society. We should reflect more specifically upon these lessons, and connect them with life in the outside world.

James A. Joseph, president of the Council on Foundations, has recently published a book called *Remaking America: How the Benevolent Traditions of Many Cultures Are Transforming our National Life.*[4] It's an impressive compendium of the varieties of voluntary activity which are part of the traditions of several different peoples— African Americans, Asian Americans, Latinos, and Native Americans. Each has distinctive lessons to teach about ethical behavior and time-tested practices of mutual support.

In universities, peoples of all these backgrounds are brought together to teach and learn. The diversity is deliberate, not for any "political correctness" reasons, but because we believe, on good evidence, that people learn best when they are not wholly surrounded by people just like themselves. This diversity sometimes creates tensions, as it does in other settings; but it also provides a microcosm of the complex world that these young people will someday lead. Universities are among the few places in America where people have easy opportunities to reach out across the barriers that frequently divide our society, and to learn both the ethical practices of different cultures and the imperative importance of living more humanely together and caring for one another.

Universities are also places where rich and productive research is being done on human beings and society, in the social sciences as well as the humanities and pure sciences. Social scientists add daily to our stock of knowledge about patterns of human life. This knowledge is painfully complex. As Francis Bacon said, "Civil knowledge is conversant about a subject which of all others is most immersed in matter and hardliest reduced to axiom." But some of the insights produced by economists, political scientists, sociologists, or anthropologists—alongside those treasured by students of literature, history, and art—advance our understanding of the world, and suggest improvements in our governments, our economies, our laws.

Universities provide multiple opportunities for deliberately reaching out past one's own selfish horizons to help those in need. Community service projects are a major feature of life on many campuses these days; at Duke, I am told, as many as three-quarters of our undergraduates are regularly involved in such projects, through their fraternities or sororities, church groups, or residence halls. Students may be cynical or apathetic about the political system; but they are quick to respond to the needs of children whose lives and futures are at risk, to the direct impoverishment of people in soup kitchens. The traditional idealism of young people is alive and well on campus, and finds its best contemporary expression in robust community service programs. These lived experiences in ethical practice touch the lives of many students, and transform the lives of some of them profoundly, in addition to enriching greatly the lives of those they help.

Finally, colleges and universities provide a basis for lifelong associational ties, through the friendships formed on campus. Alumni groups have always been a rich source of personal connection. More and more, members of these groups are providing not only the networking that helps young graduates to get jobs, or nostalgic parties that recall the good old days, but also the structure for service projects to improve life around the country.

Duke alumni in Washington, for instance, have adopted public schools, and support the work of students and teachers through tutoring and mentoring programs. Continuing the habits of service that were reinforced during student days, graduates held together by the old school tie are using their alumni organizations to make their present communities better places to live and work.

In 1985 Robert Bellah and four other sociologists published a book that uses Tocqueville's major insights as a prism for understanding

America today. The book, *Habits of the Heart: Individualism and Commitment in American Life*, is a powerful analysis of the "culture of separation" that distinguishes modernity, the "sense of fragmentariness" that plagues our lives.[5]

Bellah argues that in the past the teachings of two powerful traditions helped sustain the livable communities that gave moral meaning to life: the biblical and the republican. These traditions, he asserts, are being eroded today both by what he calls "high intellectual culture" and "popular culture." By "high intellectual culture," he means primarily what happens on the campus.

According to Bellah, "much of the thinking about the self of educated Americans . . . is based on inadequate social science, impoverished philosophy, and vacuous theology. There are truths we do not see when we adopt the language of radical individualism. We find ourselves not independently of other people and institutions but through them. . . . We discover who we are face to face and side by side with others in work, love and learning. . . . We are parts of a larger whole that we can neither forget nor imagine in our own image with paying a high price."[6]

The solution for these ills, I would assert, lies not in retreat from work, love, or learning, but in a more informed understanding of ourselves and the ethical parameters that make life with others possible and enrich our own. For those who believe that social science, philosophy, and theology have got the wrong answers to some basic human questions, the cure is not to become know-nothings or anti-academics, but to learn enough, and help our kids learn enough, to develop better social science, philosophy, and theology.

Institutions are under fire in this society, incomprehensible to people whose worlds are fragmented and narrowly circumscribed. But our only hope for regeneration as a robust society lies in the renewal of our basic institutions, a reaffirmation of our collaborative habits for the common good. Colleges and universities, both public and private, are particularly well placed to lead this renewal and reaffirmation. Indeed, they have a particular obligation to do so. We increasingly recognize this obligation, and take it to heart. We ask for your help and trust in doing so.

Together, we can reawaken those impulses of enlightened self-interest for which Americans have been famous since the days of the Nantucket whalers and the ranchers of the plains. We may lose some historic lighthouses on our stormy coasts, from New England to the Gulf of Mexico. But together, we can shore up those moral lighthouses that will bring our children and grandchildren safely into harbor in the century to come.

Moral Education in the Modern University

Address to the Annual Meeting of the American Philosophical Society,
Philadelphia, 8 November 1996

Colleges and universities assert that we are engaged in educating leaders for our nation and the world. We send our graduates forth with stirring rhetoric about how their education has prepared them to repair all the messes of the past. We argue that a good education requires learning from people with many kinds of backgrounds, and that our responsibilities include training people from all walks of life. Thus we seek students and faculty members of different races, religions, geographies, and economic and ethnic groups, and confidently proclaim the advantages of diversity.

On both these fronts, our rhetoric is better than our performance. The educational experience of many students gives little evidence of preparation for leadership in a democracy. And critics point out that patterns of self-segregation are common in our diverse student bodies, so that the putative advantages of learning from those unlike oneself remain largely theoretical. Nonetheless, I shall argue, our campuses are well placed to take advantage of the educational benefits of diversity, bridge the cultural divides that undermine our political system, and prepare leaders from all parts of society, if we have the will to let them do so.

Colleges and universities have a major influence on developing the character of our students through the varied activities of their college years. The large majority of undergraduate students in many institutions are between late adolescence and early adulthood. Experiences on campus for these students are often exceptionally intense and formative. These experiences shape the character of students every day in minute ways, with too little attention, on the part of the students themselves, or their teachers and counselors, to exactly what sort of character is being formed. Educational leaders—faculty as well as administrators—should give more thought to how we might contribute to the development of graduates prepared to grapple with the daunting problems of the societies of the future.

UNIVERSITIES AS SCHOOLS FOR ETHICAL UNDERSTANDING

During the first years of the Republic's history, colleges and universities accepted as one of their base responsibilities the education of citizens and leaders in a democracy, as they trained teachers for the schoolrooms and ministers for the church. This responsibility was clearly understood: "to train the Christian citizen," through study in the classics, mathematics, rhetoric, and ethics.[1]

By the end of the nineteenth century, this definition ceased to be pertinent for many of our colleges and universities; it came to be seen both as too narrow and as too particular. The definition was questioned long before the 1960s, despite the claims of critics who trace all our educational ills to that tumultuous decade. One of the most significant texts in that redefinition was the report of the Harvard Committee on the Objectives of a General Education in a Free Society, charged by President James Bryant Conant—usually known simply as the "Red Book." The second chapter of that report sketched out a new definition of general education appropriate to the contemporary world, one that would balance the "necessity for common belief with the equally obvious necessity for new and independent insights leading to change."[2]

In addition to seeking a balance between tradition and innovation, the Harvard report also sought to define an education that would work for both the "good man" and the "good citizen," balancing free enquiry and critical individualism with the necessity for individuals to "subordinate their individual good to the common good."[3]

In recent years, a great deal of attention has been paid in this country to resolving the first dilemma posed by the Red Book: combining due attention to the historic canon, the "classics," with appropriate opportunity for learning about burgeoning new fields of knowledge across the curriculum. This tension is memorialized in the "canon wars" and the endless debates over "political correctness."

I would argue, however, that the second dilemma identified by the Harvard Committee—to educate free-thinking individuals who will also be good citizens, contributing members, and leaders of society—is an even more significant challenge for educational leaders today. Just as it has become unfashionable to teach civics courses in high school, so the faculties and leaders of higher education have been largely silent about any obligations to mold citizens. There are many reasons for this reticence, but it is increasingly unfortunate and even dangerous, in light of the pressing need for education in civic virtue in a society that is increasingly, and dangerously, fragmented.

Political philosophers, past and present, have identified a number of aspects of civic virtue. For our purposes, I shall define this term as including several components: an understanding of the interconnectedness of human beings, our dependence on others to provide many of the goods and services, both tangible and intangible, that make life worth living; an appreciation of the need to subordinate some of our selfish impulses to the needs and aspirations of others in order to create a more secure and fruitful society in which to live; a measure of tolerance for those whose ways of doing things are different from one's own; and a readiness to collaborate with others to achieve desirable goals that no single individual can successfully pursue alone.

These are simple principles, but they have substantial implications for ethical behavior. They are more procedural than substantive. They do not require specific agreement on the goods to be sought through collaboration, nor even a prior commitment to values such as liberty or equal opportunity that may in other contexts be thought essential to civic virtue. The principles are primarily prudential, but they spring from an enlightened prudence that recognizes the likelihood of satisfying individual needs and desires through some measure of reciprocity.[4]

Such rudiments of civic virtue are most easily learned in the family and extended to the larger world. In a family, a small town, or other comparatively homogeneous setting, human interactions are not complicated by profound differences in perspective about which collaborative goods are worth pursuing, or by cultural differences so great as to make communication about shared purposes a daunting task. Even in families, there are differences and tensions that make tolerance and collaboration difficult. These differences are multiplied many-fold in the larger society where civic virtue could provide an ordering framework for our lives.

We can no longer assume that citizens grow up in settings where the principles of civic virtue are routinely taught or practiced. Nor can we assume that all citizens will be exposed to such basic principles of morality through religious training, or in their early schooling. As a result, many people in contemporary society are ill prepared to function as productive members of a complex community, much less to take advantage of community to achieve any larger purposes.

Among contemporary institutions, colleges and universities are uniquely positioned to train young people in the rudiments of civic virtue, as I have just defined it.[5] Campuses are concentrated human communities, small enough to be encompassed through a single organization, large enough to present many of the challenges and opportunities that arise in the larger world. Students live closely together, sharing aspects of their lives in an intimacy they will not elsewhere experience outside the family. These communities offer daily practical experience in the consequences of ethical and unethical behavior.

It is easy to grasp the principle of self-interest rightly understood in a dormitory setting. Accommodation to different sleeping habits between those who are accustomed to being in bed by 11 o'clock and roommates who like to study to the accompaniment of loud stereo music requires learning how to compromise, working through differences, perhaps with the aid of an older student who serves as a resident advisor.

Universities also provide multiple opportunities for deliberately reaching out past one's own selfish horizons to help those in need. Community service projects are a major feature of life on many campuses these days, through fraternities or sororities, church groups, special interest clubs, or residence halls. Students may be cynical or apathetic about the political system, but they are quick to respond to the needs of children whose lives and futures are at risk, to the impoverishment of people in soup kitchens. The traditional idealism of young people finds its most common contemporary expression in community service programs.

Too seldom, however, do we provide opportunities for students to reflect carefully on any of these experiences. We cannot just take for granted that students will draw the morals from these actions on their own. We should, more often than we do, focus their deliberate attention on the lessons to be learned.[6]

OBSTACLES TO MORAL EDUCATION

The most significant obstacles to civic education on campus today are in our own practices and expectations. Faculty and staff members, to whom students look as sources of authority and also as role models, are for a variety of reasons hesitant to confront moral dilemmas head-on, or to engage in what might seem to be a form of preaching or social engineering.

Faculty members in every discipline are trained to impart the knowledge particular to their discipline. Staff members in student affairs offices are trained to be sensitive to different situations and to provide supportive, nurturing counseling to each student. Neither faculty nor staff members generally think of themselves as, nor do they wish to become, personal sources of moral authority or insight. Like many parents today, they are hesitant to see or present themselves as models of behavior, and are suspicious of any terrain where they might be expected to offer insights into moral dilemmas. At a time when even parents are reluctant to stand in loco parentis, it is hardly surprising that faculty and staff should hesitate to do so.

It is true that genuine engagement with teaching on the part of faculty members tends to lead to engagement with students as well, to an interest in how they are doing individually, to concern about what they are learning and what sorts of persons they are becoming. Even if faculty members do not think of themselves as "moral educators," those who take their teaching seriously are likely to pose questions and encourage reflection about the larger implications of whatever it is they are teaching.

Professors nowadays, however, face multiple demands and pressures on their time. Many are strongly motivated by disciplinary loyalties and professional relationships with colleagues around the world. Sustained, direct engagement with individual students is not at the heart of our current system of academic incentives and rewards. Addressing this complex matter of incentives in the university is not easy; yet doing so promises multiple rewards, including a greater likelihood of thoughtful attention to the developing character of one's students.[7] Fortunately, on many campuses the place of teaching in the incentive structure for professors is being reexamined. This trend, in itself, is likely to lead to more consideration of the opportunities that faculty members have to help students develop their character during their college years, rather than simply master a prescribed body of material.

Faculty members are also trained to understand the importance of objectivity, of presenting a broad range of views on any subject, so that students can form their own opinions on the basis of all the relevant information. This principle of objectivity is crucial in education as we define it on our campuses, even though most professors recognize that they can never be entirely neutral or Olympian. The most thoughtful explicate their own biases or perspectives when these are relevant—not so that students will feel obligated to adopt these perspectives, but so that they will think about the implications of these perspectives as they make their own judgments about what they are being taught.

It is important that professors not abuse the authority of the classroom by trying to instill or enforce a particular narrow view on any subject. It does not follow, however, that all subjects involving subjective judgment or opinion are off limits for the classroom. The principle of objectivity is sometimes invoked to avoid moral topics and arguments entirely, on the grounds that it is impossible to be objective about such things, that breaching David Hume's impenetrable barrier between fact and value inevitably involves some form of intellectual intimidation. In fact, there are well-understood ways of approaching difficult moral dilemmas, and intellectually honorable ways of exploring them together.

The explorations may involve deliberate attention to the dynamics of the classroom, conceiving it as a kind of public space where students should think about difficult issues of communication and listening, being sensitive to the points of view expressed by others. Or they may involve prefacing abstract discussions in the biology classroom with attention to some major contemporary debate about the allocation of scarce medical resources. An anthropologist or psychologist might reflect on the tensions occasionally encountered in studying fellow human beings, including the potential effects of one's study on one's subjects and their lives.

Similarly, staff members in student affairs offices are trained to recognize and combat unhealthy behavior. They follow certain basic principles in offering advice or support to every student, even as they tailor their advice to individual situations. These counselors should be encouraged to be more explicit about the principles they are following, and about the importance of behaviors that conduce to a more civil community on campus.

These are not easy conversations, but they are important in the formation of character. If colleges and universities do not provide occasions for the conversations, many young people will never engage in them at all.

THE USES OF DIVERSITY

One of the major contemporary challenges to civic virtue is society's great complexity—not just its formidable size and scale, but the large number of cultures, languages, religions, and racial and ethnic groups that compose the United States of America. Members of these different groupings may provide traditional support for one another by forming small subcommunities. But it is rare for citizens to develop a common ethical identification by reaching across the barriers that separate these subcommunities.

The campus is one of the few places in America today where people have easy opportunities to learn from one another both the ethical practices of different cultures and the imperative importance of living more humanely together. Colleges and universities are among the most diverse institutions in our society, in which people of many cultures and backgrounds come together for four years of intense and concentrated experience.

The difficulty, of course, is that rich opportunities for education from diversity remain unexploited. Too many students spend their years on diverse campuses ensconced in homogeneous subcultures, making only the most superficial contacts with peers who are unlike themselves. Furthermore, the fact of diversity in the classroom and elsewhere on campus can become an obstacle to the use of it, if faculty and staff members are overly timid about exploring diversity, or take it as an excuse to avoid unpleasant topics.

At the same time that our institutions of higher education have become more diverse, the willingness to tackle issues raised by diversity appears to have eroded among faculty, students, and staff members. We are often reluctant to pose questions about diversity for fear of offending a member of another subculture. The pride in cultural identity engendered by a critical mass of students from any one subculture can itself become an obstacle to cross-cultural understanding. These difficulties are not unique to our campuses; they are endemic in the world outside our borders. Here again, I would argue, colleges and universities have a particular obligation, and opportunity, to try to transcend the barriers.

In contemporary American society, and surely on our campuses, the most visible and apparently stubborn barriers are those of race. Beliefs about how people of different races should interact, on campus as elsewhere, range across a broad spectrum. Professor Randall Kennedy of Harvard Law School describes four kinds of "racial integration," ranging from "amalgamation" to what he called "pluralist integration." Amalgamation is integration by "the literal blending of races" through intermarriage, to create "a new, distinctly American multiracial hybrid." Next along this spectrum he places "the brand of integration associated with Martin Luther King, Jr.," which neither explicitly promotes nor discourages physical union but "champions the creation of new communal affiliations in which interracial affections are a positive good." Then comes "diversity integration," which Kennedy calls "the most widely practiced and consequential form of racial integration" today. This form concentrates less on interracial attachments and more on power, on the "strategic placement of blacks" in influential forums, in a wide range of institutions from workplaces to boards of directors. Finally, there is pluralist integration, which resists racial blending or mixing "as diversions from the more urgent project of inculcating a strong sense of racial kinship among colored people."[8]

In the pluralist model (to which some might deny the label "integration"), the assumption is that group competition is a fact of American life, that racial inequality will be a permanent feature of our landscape, and that the only workable and desirable form of "integration" is a better power balance among groups, so that previously disadvantaged groups can engage in more effective bargaining. Proponents of this view want to "participate in, contribute to, and benefit from the American polity," rather than withdraw entirely into a separate state or economy, but they do not wish to lose their traits of group identity or solidarity in doing so. Pluralistic integration aims for the effective integration of groups rather than of individuals.

On our campuses these days, all four of these types of integration find adherents. In practice, the leaders of higher education generally strive for a combination of the second and the third—increasing power for members of minority groups, yet also fostering interracial and interethnic friendships and communal affiliations. On campus as in the larger society, however, some of the most effective leaders of minority groups are proponents of "pluralistic integration." They press for separate housing, clubs, and cultural centers. They encourage students to devote their time and energies to understanding and working for their own people, joining social organizations, and taking courses on African American (or Asian American or Hispanic American) history and culture, so that the university years can be used to prepare graduates for leadership in a world where pluralistic integration is either the best that can be hoped for, or the preferred good for which one should strive.

It is important to understand the paths of logic and emotion that lead some students and faculty members to think along these lines. Colleges and universities must be spaces where minority students can support one another and develop a better understanding of, and pride in, the heritage of African American or other cultures. However, just as the unexamined assumptions brought by white students from suburbia to the university must be unsettled, it is important to unsettle the assumption that pluralistic integration is the only way to go.

We should endeavor to construct a community on campus in which all participants experience others in a more than superficial fashion. Constructing such a community involves deliberately fostering learning experiences that lead to a greater understanding of diversity—through the curriculum, the provision of extracurricular programs and symposia, the design of structures and patterns of residential life, and support for student groups that aim for this result, as well as admissions and faculty recruitment practices. An education worthy of the name involves overturning established expectations and opening doors to different worlds. This sort of approach also is most likely to produce graduates who are well prepared to lead in a multifaceted society, empowered by a truer understanding of the potential opportunities of such a society.

As human beings, we are universally in need of the support and comfort of others in times of adversity. There are many ways of providing that support, and in learning about those ways we come to understand more about how other people live. We also have the opportunity to adapt "our own" culture by acquiring new ways of meeting fundamental needs, developed by other cultures.

Our diversity should become a point of healthful tension rather than hostile suspicion or simplistic celebration. In classical dialectical fashion, the thesis of "one's own" societal culture should be set against the antithesis of the beliefs and practices of other people. The resulting synthesis for which moral education should aim is not an undifferentiated homogeneous mass, but a refined, informed, and tempered dedication to "one's own" principles— refined by a clearer understanding of the sources and implications of those principles, informed by an awareness of alternatives, and tempered by some degree of humility in the face of the large number of ways that human beings have of moving through the world.[9]

Such a state of mind is well suited to the practice of civic virtue as I defined it earlier. Civic virtue in this modest sense provides a minimal foundation for acquiring other virtues, for the fuller development of character that we hope will be part of the lives of all our students. It does not determine the course of that moral development, and it allows for numerous conceptions of and paths to the good life. But it does provide a sturdy and supple framework for living in, and leading, a pluralist democracy.

PRINCIPLED INTOLERANCE

Another of the challenges we face in designing effective civic education is the stubborn denial by some subgroups in our society of full humanity to members of other groups, whether along racial, religious, or gender lines. These intolerant groups profess principles at odds with the basic elements of civic virtue, even in the comparatively "thin" procedural definition used in this discussion. They disallow tolerance for other approaches to the good life and forbid open communication with members of other subgroups.

Criteria for admission to our colleges and universities, which emphasize traits such as curiosity and breadth of experience, as well as the self-selection of those who choose to study on our campuses, exclude the most obdurate members of closed societies. Most campuses are, and are known to be, places where open discussion of all kinds of ideas is encouraged, where principles are challenged and rational examination even of deeply held beliefs is fostered. Members of subcultures who are intent on perpetuating their beliefs in the next generation are unlikely to send their children to our institutions.

However, intolerance and the denial of reciprocity are not confined to hard-core members of closed subcultures. Some students profess a strictly defined conception of the good life and are intent either on compelling others to share it, or on protecting it against compromise or dilution in any form. Campuses provide particularly powerful sites for challenging this sort of obduracy, for eroding the sense of closed certainty by exposure to different ways of configuring the world. Equally important, campuses provide excellent opportunities for other students to learn how to recognize and deal with the kind of closed-mindedness that makes deliberation and compromise impossible.

During the past academic year, for example, the legislature of the Duke Student Government was asked to extend recognition,

108

in the form of financial support and legitimacy, to a militantly Christian organization. The leaders of the group—not themselves members of the student body—made quite clear their intentions to convert as many students as possible to their particular brand of Christianity. The student government leaders declined to provide support until they could explore allegations that the group was engaging in unacceptable practices. Their findings led them to deny recognition, on the grounds that the record demonstrated psychological harassment and the isolation of students. The DSG leaders were criticized by other students, including the editors of the student newspaper, for discriminating against the group because of its religion. The discussion of this issue on campus provided an excellent opportunity for thoughtful students to reflect on the purposes and limitations of tolerance in an open society.

In the second volume of *Democracy in America*, Tocqueville ascribed the success of the United States largely to our free institutions, designed to draw people into public activities in which private interests are clearly implicated and actions are undertaken by local government and voluntary associations, such as building roads and schools.[10]

Such institutions (along with the free press and the powerful sentiments of religion) form the bonds that are the basis of everyday morality. Tocqueville describes this common-sense morality in the language of the Enlightenment principle of "self-interest rightly understood." This principle, he notes, is "not a lofty one, but it is clear and sure."[11] It does not aim at brilliant acts of heroism, but it accomplishes its goals, is within the reach of everyone, and works surely and habitually to draw people out of selfish isolation into behavior that benefits others as well as themselves.

How prescient Tocqueville was in many things, including foreseeing the gradual decay of civic virtue in America. In our large, increasingly complex, and multifaceted society, more and more Americans have indeed lost touch with any general associations that bring people together across class and cultural divides. Many have withdrawn to particularistic islands, whether behind the gated walls of a homogeneous housing complex or into the stratified neighborhoods of our cities. Such particular communities, class-based or religious or ethnic, may bring solace and companionship, as compared with the loneliness of the truly isolated individual. But they also tend to separate their members from the larger society, and in doing so undermine any sense of overarching common purpose, of a durable society composed of diverse people who share basic obligations to each other.[12]

Few parts of American society were ever as tightly knit or virtuous as some of Tocqueville's more idealistic passages would lead us to believe. But he was surely right in his diagnosis of those attitudes and deeds that bring human beings together in community, and his prognosis about the centrifugal factors that pull us apart in an increasingly complex society. As many thoughtful observers of these tendencies have noted, there is a great need for social regeneration in contemporary American society, the creation or renewal of ties that bind citizens across boundaries of class, race, and region. Without these ties, we are in danger of a fragmentation rendering us incapable of responding effectively to challenges that threaten us internally or externally—in the economy, the environment, the international arena—and a fragmentation engendering the sort of hostile suspicion or ignorance of others that is a fertile breeding ground for inhumane behavior.

Tocqueville was surely also prescient in warning against taking for granted that Americans always or instinctively will understand the principle of "self-interest rightly understood." He therefore put considerable emphasis on education as a crucial element in preserving American civic virtue. "I do not think," he wrote, "that the system of self-interest as it is professed in America is in all parts self-evident, but it contains a great number of truths so evident that men, if they are only educated, cannot fail to see them. Educate, then, at any rate, for the age of implicit self-sacrifice and instinctive virtues is already flitting far away from us, and the time is fast approaching when freedom, public peace and social order itself will not be able to exist without education."[13]

No one claims that an education designed to mold thoughtful citizens is easy to provide, but there are models for success in doing parts of it on campuses around the country. We need to share information about these successes, and encourage faculty and staff members to take moral education seriously.

We should not underestimate the obstacles to this kind of education, nor overstate our ability to deliver it to all our students. Nor should we assume that our campuses are the only sites for such endeavors. The contributions of schools, churches, civic associations, local governments, and many other institutions will be crucial. But it is no excuse for indifference that others share this responsibility, or that colleges and universities have many other missions besides moral education. At this point in the history of this society, that mission is among the most imperative ones we have.

More Power to the President?

Amid the sometimes heated discussions about the state of contemporary higher education, one theme is beginning to be heard with increasing frequency. Many critics assert that our root problem is one of governance. Our antiquated systems require seemingly interminable consultations with every interested group, provide virtual vetoes for those affected by any significant change, and fail to lodge authoritative power in any office. As a result, they say, it is impossible to address the formidable challenges that colleges and universities now face. Academic institutions have accreted multiple layers of governance over many decades. The views of self-governing bands of clerics who joined forces to attract students in the medieval university live on in the modern view that faculty authority must be at the core of the university, determining who and what shall be taught. The lay governing boards established by colonial colleges in North America to ensure institutional fidelity to fundamental purposes have evolved into contemporary boards of regents and trustees chartered to exercise ultimate oversight and authority on campus. Alongside the faculty and boards, complex bureaucracies grew up to deal with multiple external demands, support the faculty, and respond to the changing needs and preferences of students. Student demands for the power to decide what they should be taught and to control their own living conditions have ebbed and flowed over the centuries. Today they flow moderately, riding on some residual energy from student unrest in the 1960s and 1970s, reinforced by the sturdy consumerist mentality of today's academic customers.

And where, among all these players, is the president?

The American college presidency is a distinctive institution, invented in the early days of our republic to compensate for the lack of a guild of respected scholars accustomed to self-governance. Presidents flourished in the late nineteenth century and the early twentieth. With a few exceptions, they have been less visible, and less obviously authoritative, in recent decades. At a time when captains of industry are once again dominating our world with daunting feats of economic power—as they did during those earlier heydays of academic presidential power—the comparison with anemic college presidents is especially compelling. Through mergers and layoffs and strategic planning, the broad power of the corporate CEO stands in marked contrast to the starkly limited powers of the head of a modern campus. Caught between the "upper and nether millstones"[1] of trustee authority and faculty prerogatives, a president can sometimes feel more like the rope in a game of tug-of-war than a chief executive officer.

Thus, it is to be expected that many of those who trace our problems to defects in our governance systems have hit upon an obvious solution: strengthen the presidency. If only the head of Stanford or Michigan would act more like the head of IBM or General Electric, striking off the fetters of entitlements and veto powers, we would be well on the way to reforming higher education.

In certain moods, all university presidents must thrill at such suggestions. I know I have. Why, indeed, are we such wimps? Would it not be refreshing to decide single-handedly to shut down a program or department to cut costs and reallocate resources? Or to have the deans function more like line managers and less like feudal barons?

But life is not that simple. There are definite pitfalls to believing that our governance problems can be solved simply by increasing the power of the president. To provide a context, consider the modern campus as a political system.

Like the government supported by the U.S. Constitution, our higher education system is characterized by extensive checks and balances, rather than by a clear hierarchy or single locus of power. One of the major elements of our federal political system is the belief that different interest groups will effectively compete with one another to prevent the dominance of any single one. As developed in James Madison's classic essays in the *Federalist Papers* (especially the famous no. 10), such a system is designed primarily to avoid the abuse of power.

As with the U.S. government, the political system on campus

works better at preventing unwise change than at making desirable change easy or even possible. But our version is even more blocked by checks and counterchecks than the federal government's, including not only all the campus forces described above but others who have a significant stake in our work: employees, legislators, alumni, parents, neighbors. In combination with the cautious "political culture" of academia, this makes it very difficult to provide inspiration or incentives for acting boldly or expeditiously.

The view that our problems of governance should be solved by strengthening the presidency can be called Hamiltonian. During the debates on our nascent political system, Alexander Hamilton was prominent among those who argued against the Madisonian position and for a stronger, quasi-monarchical presidency. Adapting this prescription to today's campus, if weak leadership is the core of the problem, the solution is for the president to be given, or to seize, greater power. Some contemporary presidents have acted aggressively on this front, most visibly John Silber when he served as president of Boston University. In a less public fashion, other presidents are taking advantage of readily available instruments of power and creating new infrastructures to accomplish their goals of flexibility and innovation. New schools and programs that break through the traditional constraints of tenure and disciplinary structures, and distance learning through courses provided by nonconventional faculty, are examples of this trend.

Before we explore the Hamiltonian alternative, we should examine other trends and tendencies in campus governance. To continue the analogy with ideas that were current in the days of the founding of our republic, one can imagine a system that could be called Jeffersonian, with power rooted in the people and delegated only with skeptical caution. In the late 1960s and early 1970s on campus, a "more democratic system" meant power for students and sympathetic faculty, often allied with organized employees. It is unlikely that the mood of the sixties will be recaptured anytime soon. But the consumerist mentality to which I referred earlier—on the part of students who are paying generous sums for their education (or whose families or corporations are paying)—is a significant force on campus, especially in conjunction with the current social mood of entitlement to all things. It is difficult to imagine a political system for the modern university modeled wholly on these sentiments; nonetheless, it would be unwise to ignore their potential importance.

Another possibility is an entrepreneurial model in which faculty members would form groups of quasi-independent contractors, much like their clerical forebears in the medieval university, or their colleagues in the private practice clinics in our academic medical centers. They would offer their services not only directly, but also in cyberspace, through videotaped lectures and courses posted on the web. This model would require the creation of an administrative system to organize and market their services, a system quite different from today's campus bureaucracies. In serving business-oriented customers, there is nothing implausible about the entrepreneurial model of governance; indeed, elements of this model are present in today's for-profit universities. Other consortia of this sort may well be devised in the years ahead to market intellectual property, in a more or less uneasy relationship with traditional academic institutions. However, as with the Jeffersonian model, I think it unlikely that such consortia could entirely supplant more familiar institutional models in the foreseeable future.

Still another possible approach would be to adapt the early colonial structure and grant primary authority to the governing board in both the direct and the more formal sense. The renewed activism of a number of boards of regents, especially in public institutions, has moved several contemporary campuses in this direction. The grumbling heard on some boards about the problems that arise because "the inmates are in charge of the asylum" has led some to decide that it's time for saner, wiser heads to assert their authority over the bickering, stalemated folks on campus.

The thoughtful attention by boards of trustees or regents to the governance of campuses is to be applauded as long as the attention is focused on areas in which members have expertise and boards have appropriate authority. But if boards overstep the line between formulating policy and daily management of the institutions, a number of troubling outcomes can be predicted. Few board members have the knowledge or time to devote to management activities, and direct involvement by the board nullifies one of the major purposes of the boards: to provide the strategic, critical, supportive stewardship of informed outsiders who are deeply dedicated to the success of an institution, but *not* immersed in its management.

Boards that recognize the pitfalls in having trustees move in on daily operations, but are increasingly frustrated by what they perceive as inaction or timidity on campus, may decide to react by giving more authority to the president, at the expense of other constituencies. How might this Hamiltonian approach work in practice?

According to the bylaws of most higher education institutions, the board of trustees already delegates to the president a great deal of formal authority for the general management and governing of the institution. To expand the scope of this power, the most significant step would be to weaken or remove the powers granted to other constituencies, especially the faculty. Since boards hold ultimate authority for ordering the institution, a board could rewrite the bylaws to stipulate that the president has the prerogative to create or dissolve academic programs, and to hire and terminate faculty members, without the approval of faculty councils. This would effectively remove the legal basis for the checks and balances in the current system.

Such a bold move would immediately raise serious issues of prior contractual obligations to faculty members and to donors of endowments for existing academic programs. It would have nightmarish implications for a president who tried to run a traditional educational institution (as distinct from a new, for-profit organization) without the collaboration of committed and involved members of the faculty. More fundamentally, some positive defining elements about an institution of higher education would be lost.

Our present system has evolved because each of the major players brings something important to the table. The trustees as stewards, presidents as institutional leaders and managers, and faculty members, including deans and department chairs, as those most knowledgeable about what education and research offer and require—each of these elements in our governance structure is crucial to the successful functioning of the institution. Only a system that gives appropriate voice and authority to each of the major constituencies offers us a chance to maintain what James A. Perkins of Cornell called "the internal coherence" of higher education.[2]

Madison trusted that the conflict among many factions with different interests over a large territory would prevent majority coalitions based on "any other principles than those of justice and the general good."[3] He did not, however, have a robust theory of how a salutary coalition could emerge. Hamilton insisted that "energy in the executive is a leading character in the definition of good government."[4] But he was too enamored of the exercise of authority along Roman lines to explore how the energy might be focused on the common good and made compatible with the due rights and interests of other citizens.

To make our campus governance system work effectively, we need both Madison and Hamilton. Presidents must be willing and able to lead, to inspire, to make tough choices, to bring others onto common ground, to envision. Given the challenges we face, the tendency on many campuses is to choose experienced managers to solve corporate problems. But if presidents lack qualities of courageous leadership and a deep understanding of the academy, the system is tilted out of balance.

Faculty members must be willing to learn enough about complex challenges to provide informed perspectives and help make hard choices. As Don Kennedy has recently reminded us, responsibility is the counterpart of academic freedom—the two are opposite sides of the same coin.[5] To make our system work, faculty members must take their duties in governance seriously, serving not only as suspicious watchdogs on the folks in the administration building, but as effective participants in key academic decision making. Faculty members also need to acknowledge that in today's highly complex, rapidly changing world of higher education, strong leadership from presidents, provosts, and deans makes it more likely that institutions will flourish and provide a setting where all the players can carry out their work.

Boards have a crucial role in reviewing governance practices, clearly defining their own areas of responsibility, and ensuring that the president can exercise effective power as the leader of the institution while respecting the essential authority of other constituencies, including (especially!) the faculty and academic leaders.

Boards and presidents need to recognize the fundamental contributions that faculty members make to the essential work of the university, rather than lament faculty power as a regrettable drag on the system. Yet all of us need to acknowledge that the tendency towards lengthy consultations and mulching new ideas that comes so easily in an academic setting—where careful deliberation and extensive testing of evidence bring rewards in the core enterprises of teaching and research—can easily be overdone in the governance of the institution. As one of our trustees says, if he learns that the end of the world is at hand, he will immediately come to Duke, because everything takes a year longer here. At some point—usually sooner than we on campus get there—it's time to stop talking and take action.

In a recent newspaper article about my first five years at Duke, a faculty member was quoted as saying, disapprovingly, that according to my view of faculty governance the president sets the agenda. My reaction was, yes, this is one of the main reasons presidents are needed. In the life of an institution, *somebody* has to set the agenda, make sure the deliberations are thoughtful and productive, and implement the decisions made. Some of those decisions need to be made by the president or other senior administrators, some by the faculty, and some by the board. But the president is responsible to the board, and to all those who care about the institution, for keeping the whole business on track and pointed roughly in the right direction. An eloquent essay by Frank Rhodes offers an excellent overview of the way presidential power works in practice.[6] Presidents need to be open about how they define their office relative to the success of the enterprise, and trustees and faculty members need to back them up when they do so.

Our goal should be to use the powers of our office in serious—not cosmetic—collaboration with others who have responsibilities and interests in our institutions and to bring partial views together in a vision of the common good. This may sound like a ludicrously lofty goal, given the way all of us actually spend our days. But unless this goal stands behind and inspires our work, we will be deficient in our vision and unable to serve our institutions well.

As Hamilton wrote in the opening paragraphs of the *Federalist Papers*, "Happy will it be if our choice should be directed by a judicious estimate of our true interests, unperplexed and unbiased by considerations not connected with the public good." He noted immediately that "this is a thing more ardently to be wished than seriously to be expected."[7] But he and his colleagues nonetheless had enough faith in the possibility of such an outcome to devote their lives to achieving it. We should do no less today.

The American Campus

FROM COLONIAL SEMINARY TO

GLOBAL MULTIVERSITY

The first stirrings of higher learning in the colony of Massachusetts occurred in 1636. And from that date, through the announcement of the Western Governors' "virtual" University three and a half centuries later, Americans have been staunchly dedicated to higher education as a major force in our society (by "Americans" I mean mostly citizens of the United States, although there are many similarities between the system in our country and that just north of us in Canada).

In the United States, across all those years, a college degree has been the sine qua non for the maturation of young members of élite families and the most significant path to upward mobility for everyone else. The campuses of American colleges and universities have shaped culture and art and entertainment in many American cities, and yet provided semi-cloistered environments for the passage to adulthood for generations of young men and young women.

There are today more than 3,700 institutions of higher learning in the United States, and more than 60 percent of our high school graduates take advantage of some form of further education.[1] The institutions that provide all this training include major research universities, large state-sponsored comprehensive universities, highly selective liberal arts colleges, community colleges, church-related institutions, technical colleges, arts colleges, and proprietary institutions. The bewildering variety of institutions makes it impossible to generalize with any degree of certainty on many points, but it certainly demonstrates American entrepreneurial ingenuity, experimental zeal, and commercial savvy, and also a true commitment to providing access for everyone who

120

wants to learn. This chapter will provide a very rapid overview of the development of our system and then hazard some guesses about what the next generation of institutions will be like. Four themes will be touched upon. First, the theme of access: Who should be educated? Next, the related theme of purpose: For what do we educate? Third: Educated by whom? And finally: Where does this education take place?

The story will begin in the early part of the seventeenth century, when refugees from the British Isles founded institutions of higher learning patterned closely on those that they had left behind.

THE EARLY AMERICAN COLLEGE SYSTEM

In those first decades of the North American colonies, amidst the muddy commons and frame buildings that defined civilization on the edge of a vast new continent, schools and colleges were regarded, according to the historian Martin Trow, as "forces for survival in a hostile environment, instruments for staving off . . . the threatened decline into the savagery of the surrounding forest and its Indian inhabitants."[2] That sense of what American colleges and universities and their surrounding environment were like is one that probably remained stereotypical in Britain and Europe for a long time. But very quickly, American colleges and universities began to evolve from that rather primitive state into institutions that would have been much more recognizable to their progenitors.

Colleges were founded primarily to educate leaders for the colonies—preachers, teachers, and lawyers, needed badly in a new society. The colonial authorities granted power to these new colleges to award the degrees within their own colonial territories, of which there were thirteen. Like their British counterparts, these governments attempted to prevent the establishment of any rival institutions in their own colonies so as to guarantee doctrinal orthodoxy and service to established society. The earliest were Harvard College in Massachusetts and William and Mary in Virginia, founded with deliberate reference to the models of Oxford and Cambridge.

Higher education from the beginning in America was provided in a residential campus setting where groups of scholars gathered to teach and to learn. The curriculum focused on liberal learning for undergraduates, including the classics, philosophy, mathematics, history, natural history, and theology. All of this was seen as the best preparation for any useful professional life.

Libraries were a very important part of the new foundation, in a part of the world where there was little other access to sources of learning or repositories of culture. There was a very strong sense of faculty responsibility for disciplining students, which extended to many aspects of life outside the classroom. As in Britain and in contrast, for example, with some medieval Italian universities, students had relatively little power to determine what they were taught or by whom.[3]

The presence of these several prominent institutions in the various colonies—there were nine colleges in all at the time of the Revolution—created a sense of ownership in each different territory. The strength of colonial feeling also militated against founding a single national university, which America has never had. There were many attempts to found one, particularly during the eighteenth century, but like parallel attempts to found a central national bank, these efforts foundered on the strong sense of identification with Virginia, or with Pennsylvania, or with Massachusetts.

As in Britain at the time, it was taken for granted that these foundations would provide higher learning for white males of the propertied classes, especially those who adhered to the Protestant faith. Dartmouth College in New Hampshire was established just before the Revolution to educate Indians along with "English youth." Higher education for young women, slaves, and indentured servants was virtually unknown, except as provided in rare, individual cases by individual families. The few American Jews could be educated only by assimilating into the surrounding society.

Yet even in these early years, some aspects of the colonial system diverged fairly significantly from the British model. Responsibility for governance of the colleges was placed in a president and a governing board composed of local citizens, usually including both clerical and lay members. Such a board of trustees, of regents, of overseers was a distinctive innovation in colonial colleges, designed to assure that the graduates of these new institutions would be trained in godliness, morality, and devotion to public good.

These overseers were given community responsibility for assuring, in other words, that the institutions accomplished their social purposes. That innovation took root. Today more than forty thousand citizens serve in a purely voluntary capacity as members of governing boards of all sorts and conditions, in virtually every institution of higher learning in America.[4]

The role of the president in colonial times was especially unlike anything that had evolved in Britain or on the continent of Europe. The president was responsible for all aspects of the administration of the college. He was the senior and sometimes only member of the faculty, the college chaplain, the disciplinarian, the advocate for his institution with the local community.[5] This prominent role for the president stood in marked contrast with the more familiar system in which teaching fellows elected the master and were responsible as a body for governing the institution. At first, of course, the new system arose because there was no indigenous scholarly guild in the colonies to elect the master and run the institutions. But even as scholarly communities were created along these lines, the American system continued to lodge considerable power in the president. The president's power, combined with but also limited by the powers of the governing boards, created an opportunity here for innovation and visionary leadership, which may help to explain why American institutions took some fascinating experimental directions. In the late eighteenth century and the early nineteenth, more and more universities were founded—such as the first state university, in my own state of North Carolina, just before the turn of the century, and many others. During this period, the influence of the nine original colleges remained strong, but very quickly new patterns began to be developed.

THE DEVELOPMENT OF HIGHER EDUCATION
IN THE NINETEENTH CENTURY

The number of institutions of higher education in America grew exponentially between the Revolution and the middle of the nineteenth century, just before the Civil War. The citizens of the United States moved westward restlessly, in search of open land and new opportunities, and they carried with them a great faith in the power of education as a civilizing force and as a prerequisite for republican government. Alexis de Tocqueville regarded the education of the people as one of the most prominent causal factors in the success of these democratic institutions growing up on American soil. He vividly described frontier families carrying with them their bibles and a few precious books, hungry for news and conversation in their rude huts carved out of the vast wilderness.[6]

Many of the institutions established in these new regions of our country in the first part of the nineteenth century were founded by religious groups—particularly Methodists, Quakers, Baptists, and Presbyterians. It was easy for these institutions to receive charters from the governments of the new states and territories, since they were eager to provide the structures for a newly civilized life. Some of the many colleges founded in those days took root and have survived, but hundreds of others fell by the wayside across the decades, lacking the essential support of their communities or a long-term appeal to any student constituency.

Not only were new institutions founded in the western territories, but establishments were also founded to serve new constituencies such as Catholics, Jews, urban workers, and former slaves. Beginning just after the Civil War, there was a particularly strong movement to provide higher education for women. Even for an innovative society, this was a revolutionary step.

When the first colleges for women were founded in the mid-nineteenth century in the United States, they were designed with great care, both in the curriculum and in their physical attributes. The course of study was established with the particular needs and desires of women in mind, as these needs and desires were then understood. So were the layout of the buildings, the graceful landscaping, the height of the stairs, even the pattern of china in the dining room. But one of the most important serious results of this development was a cadre of women scholars who were prepared to teach and administer institutions.

At Bryn Mawr College in Pennsylvania in the 1880s, women were for the first time trained exactly like young men and for the same reasons: to become educated persons, professionally active in law or medicine or scholarship, advancing the boundaries of learning. Over time coeducation, described as the idea that men and women should be educated in the same way, by the same faculty, in the same classrooms, became more and more the accepted pattern in the United States. Newly founded institutions such as Stanford University in California, or the University of Chicago toward the end of the century, adopted this practice before this ideal took root anywhere else in the world. Trinity College, the precursor of Duke University, was instructed by its major benefactor in 1896, as a condition of his gift, to offer education to young women on the same terms as young men.

Colleges were also founded for free Negroes and former slaves. Like the women's colleges, many of these institutions disappeared when integration, like coeducation, began to provide new opportunities for Americans of African descent. However, also like women's colleges, a robust set of historically black colleges and universities continues to thrive even today in America, and provides an attractive alternative to historically white coeducational institutions. This is one of the many dimensions along which our system flourishes because of our diversity.

Along with education for women and for blacks, there were three other very significant steps which shaped American higher education in the final part of the nineteenth century. The first was the Morrill Act of 1862, through which Congress created a new category of land-grant universities. The second was the establishment in 1876 of the Johns Hopkins University in Baltimore on the model of the German university. And the third was the considerable infusion of public and private wealth into colleges and universities during those decades.

The Morrill Act provided funding in the form of grants to the states of large areas of federal land, equivalent in area to the whole of Switzerland or the Netherlands, to support colleges and universities.[7] Colleges either created or strengthened by these grants had to include instruction in practical subjects such as engineering or agriculture or mechanical arts along with more traditional subjects. In some states, existing institutions benefited from this largesse, but in others new institutions were created especially as land-grant universities and installed on campuses that closely copied the traditional features developed in New England.

The emphasis on practicality in these land-grant universities provided a stimulus for research and development in areas which had not hitherto been regarded as fit subjects for scholarly study or deliberation: engineering, agriculture, mechanics. This gave a new dimension to the purposes of education in our country, and proved very influential in the development of public attitudes towards higher education. There was a growing sense that universities ought to serve useful purposes by training leaders in very pragmatic ways rather than being isolated ivory towers.

This attitude extended as well to the belief that universities should provide education very widely for all interested citizens, not just those destined to pursue traditional professions. The aspiration of Ezra Cornell's land-grant institution in Ithaca, New York, as it was expressed in the university register of 1869–70, was to be "an institution where any person can find instruction in any study."[8]

At the same time that the provisions of the Morrill Act were pushing institutions of higher education in America in a more practical, service-oriented direction, the influential model developed by Johns Hopkins provided an impetus for development in the opposite direction, towards the German model of the university as a home of "pure science," the locus of lofty and abstruse research and specialized graduate training. This ideal had an immense influence in America in a very short time. It seemed as though a university could not be a serious place of learning unless it provided graduate training and encouraged specialized research by faculty members.

Established universities such as Harvard and Yale, and new institutions such as Stanford or Chicago, adapted the Germanic Johns Hopkins model by grafting it onto the traditional undergraduate liberal arts training provided by the collegiate structure, within the larger research university context. Thus was born that distinctly American hybrid: the research university, dedicated to excellence both in undergraduate education and in graduate training.

Many of the institutions described above became strong through generous support from private fortunes. That is why so many of our great universities bear family names. Families such as the Stanfords, the Rockefellers, the Hopkins, the Dukes, and many others were persuaded to invest substantial amounts of their new wealth in higher education. This created a very strong foundation of private financial support for higher education which has continued unabated to the present day.

Certain states such as Michigan, North Carolina, and Wisconsin also invested significantly in their state universities during this period. Citizens of these states took enormous pride in the prominence of these institutions and supported them through taxation so that they were easily accessible to all citizens. Thus there was also established a tradition of strong public support for education in several key states, which set educational standards for, and raised the aspirations of, universities elsewhere.

At this point also, many universities both public and private began to reach out deliberately beyond the borders of the United States to attract students from abroad, especially from the Asian countries to which American denominations had sent Christian missionaries. For the first time, in the last decades of the nineteenth century American higher education became a net importer of students, since the growing strength of our institutions meant that fewer and fewer students went to Britain or Europe for professional training or polish, and more and more students from other parts of the world came to the United States to study all kinds of subjects.

The last third of the nineteenth century was a very rich period for the development of higher education in the United States. It provided considerable scope for strong leadership by vigorous presidents such as Andrew Dickson White at Cornell, Charles W. Eliot at Harvard, Daniel White Gilman at Hopkins, and M. Carey Thomas at Bryn Mawr.[9] But at the same time, the growing size and complexity of these institutions meant that the presidents could no longer exercise the kind of individual dominance in the daily operations of the university that they had previously had. New administrative structures grew up to take care of day-to-day operational needs.

This same period also saw the beginnings of a much stronger sense of professional orientation by faculty members, with the emergence of disciplinary consciousness and disciplinary organizations in the social sciences at the turn of the century. Thus there was both a new administrative infrastructure and a growing sense of faculty responsibility and faculty pride in what one might call a guild solidarity. These two factors together clearly limited the power of the president, but they also led to experimentation with new ideas and created a formidable alternative source of institutional authority.

And so in a whirlwind fashion, we come to the twentieth century. In the first decades of this new century, educational opportunities were once more offered to new populations. The City College of New York, which had been founded in the nineteenth century to "educate the whole people," became very prominent in the 1930s as a beacon for waves of immigrants to the United States. Poor young men flocked to CCNY for an excellent education at a very low cost without the traditional amenities of a campus, but with the extraordinary advantage of a superb faculty, drawn largely from the swelling ranks of European refugees. Commuter campuses were established in other cities, appealing to the upwardly mobile working classes. However, even in these novel institutions, almost all the undergraduate students were of the traditional age, between eighteen and twenty-two years.

This traditional ordering by age changed rapidly after the Second World War. Among the most important stimuli for this development was the G.I. Bill, the Serviceman's Readjustment Act of 1944. This bill was designed to make a college education affordable for the generation who had fought the war. Veterans could use their federally provided tuition stipend at any college or university that would accept them. There were no governmental stipulations about how training would be provided, nor were there efforts to establish standards or monitor performance.

The G.I. Bill changed both the sense of who would go to college and at what age a college education might be sought in the United States. It is now common for both men and women well past their mid-twenties to seek a college education or to return to complete one interrupted by military service or for family or financial reasons. Many American institutions have undergraduate degree candidates as old as sixty-five or seventy.

The 1950s and 1960s were a period of significant expansion for higher education around the world, and the United States was no exception. Many new four-year colleges and universities were established. Community colleges—two-year colleges granting the associate degree, rooted in particular cities or counties—were established to provide practical education in vocational skills with components of the liberal arts as well. Over time this system of community colleges has become a very successful part of our educational establishment, providing adult education, non-degree programs, and retooling and retraining for hundreds of thousands of Americans.

Another postwar development of great significance was the entry of the federal government in a major way into sponsorship of scientific research on university campuses. The U.S. Office of Scientific Research and Development under the leadership of Vannevar Bush during the war laid the foundations for a significant collaboration in advancing basic scientific discoveries in American higher education between the government and the research universities and, increasingly, industry and business. The National Science Foundation, the National Institutes of Health, and several departments of the government including defense, energy, and agriculture have since that date provided billions of dollars of research funding for campuses around the country.

The third major step taken by the U.S. government during this period was the passage of the Education Act in 1972, which codified the promise of government aid to all kinds of needy students in the United States, especially those at the baccalaureate level. Once again, it was significant that the grants and loans provided by the government were made available directly to the students, not as block grants to the institutions, although the funds were administered by the colleges. And again the federal government followed a path of self-denial. Instead of using major funding for student aid or research as a lever to influence the policies or behavior of college and universities, the money came with no strings attached.

With the growth of federal funding, the line between public and private institutions in the United States has become considerably blurred. Private institutions depend more and more these days on support from federal and state governments for both research and student aid, as well as for tax-exempt loans for major building projects. At the same time, public institutions have sought to become much more flexible and savvy in their financial bases, and have reached out very effectively to private donors. Some state universities, including especially Michigan, Virginia, and Texas, have very substantial endowments.

American higher education has always been highly competitive —in the quest for students, for faculty members, and for funding sources—and market-driven rather than ordered by political fiat. In many ways this has been healthy, but it has created some significant contemporary challenges. As traditional sources of funding have come under pressure, many institutions have begun to diversify and search for new markets. Distinctions among different types of institutions appealing to baccalaureate students, such as those for specialized research and those for technical training, have become increasingly blurred. More and more institutions are becoming full-service organizations, so that many American universities today provide education across a very broad range, from remedial education for admitted baccalaureate students whose standards for preparation have not been high, through a full range of graduate and professional training, to extension programs for senior citizens and executive education programs for corporations and newly chosen government officials. All these diverse programs may well be offered by the same institution. As a result, our universities and even our four-year colleges are becoming less clear in their sense of mission, less differentiated from one another and from the community colleges and technical institutes.

At the same time, the burgeoning of knowledge in every field, the increasing specialization of faculty members in various disciplines, has meant a blurring of the earlier clarity of what should be taught in any course of study, especially for the baccalaureate degree.

These developments mean that the answer to my question "What is being taught in American higher education?" is increasingly complex and even opaque. This lack of clarity, along with the dramatically increased costs of higher education over the past decades, paid as tuition by students and their families, has led to a new level of public scrutiny directed at American colleges and universities.

This scrutiny comes in two related forms. First, a growing number of anxious parents are concerned about whether they will be able to afford a college education for their children as tuition costs climb higher. They are convinced that education is the necessary ticket to a good life in America and want to make sure that the education is worth the money they expend. The mentality of the American public has shifted from a historically somewhat awed pride in our colleges and universities to a consumerist mentality. We are being asked to justify the market value of what we do, and there is increasing interest in for-profit, money-making institutions, such as the University of Phoenix, which provides an education targeted specifically to the career development needs of adult students.

In such a context, the traditional liberal arts education is often regarded as unworldly and unlikely to prepare anyone for anything that earns a salary. This view is exacerbated in the public mind by the perception that scholars in history or literature or the arts have become dabblers in arcane, politically radical nihilism. This perception is exaggerated and unfair, but in a world of deconstruction and post-everything, it is hard to explain to ordinary folks what the intellectual excitement is all about. Professional education fares better, but here we face increasing competition from educational programs designed by corporations to accomplish their own specific goals, such as Motorola University.

Political leaders in both state and federal government reflect these public concerns, of course, and thus, for the first time in American history, a trend that I have been describing is reversed: over the past two decades, governments have developed a taste for monitoring, and to some extent controlling, activities on campus. Governments are requiring evidence of acceptable outcomes in education; they are imposing complex regulations concerning the use of funds for certain purposes; and they are using the power of the purse to influence or require institutions to pay more attention to gender equity, access for the disabled, particular research activities, and other social goals.

In some states, there are movements to decide who can be admitted to institutions of higher education, particularly in Texas, California, and Maryland. This tendency neutralizes university efforts developed over decades to diversify the student body by giving some degree of preference to black or Hispanic students. And thus for the first time, the steady tide of openness and accessibility that I have been describing for students from all kinds of backgrounds, a tide that has marked American higher education for almost two centuries, is threatened with reversal by government actions.

In other states, there are discussions of limiting or abolishing tenure for faculty members or setting rules about how much time faculty members must spend in the classroom. People apparently have a hard time grasping that a faculty member is doing useful work even when he or she is not standing at a podium. Getting across the message of how faculty members actually spend their time and the very deep involvement of most professors is hard to do when the public assumes professors do nothing else but teach.

At the federal level, the current suspicion of the humanities and the arts has led to dramatic reductions in funding of university activities in these areas. Oversight is hardly unfamiliar in Europe, but the traditional independence of American colleges and universities, governed by presidents and faculties and lay boards able to stand or fall on their own, has been one of the hallmarks of our system throughout the past. This is now being challenged in novel ways by state and federal governments, by the courts, and by the students and families who pay our bills. At the same time, the most dramatic development of all, the introduction of information technology into the classroom, is changing the landscape of higher education more rapidly than any factor in the past has ever done.

WHAT LIES AHEAD?

Futurists delight in propounding radically new scenarios for higher education in the twenty-first century, based in large part on the wonderful capacity of information technology—computers, multimedia—to provide education to anyone, anywhere, at any time. Some people are convinced that most traditional institutions of higher learning, in America and elsewhere, will cease to exist within a few decades, swallowed up by more efficient competitors, rendered obsolete by the World Wide Web.

132

Let me venture my own prediction under the headings of the four themes that I have pursued throughout: Who will be educated in America in the year 2020? What will they be learning, and from whom? And where will the learning take place?

It seems likely that in the twenty-first century higher education will, for more and more Americans, become a continuum across the life span rather than a punctuation point that marks the rite of passage to adulthood. With the broad access to many kinds of educational programs made possible by computers, education will also become much less expensive for the consumer, although the start-up costs for the providers of the education will continue to be significant. This technology will sustain the trend towards more and more accessibility in a new way.

Higher education will also become more practical, more focused on providing the training that people need to get the job, to pass the Bar, to become a chartered accountant, to qualify for medical residency. The concept of general education will surely suffer, especially as part of the background preparation for a successful career in any field. This will come both because of the growing pressures for practicality in education, and the increasing difficulty in deciding what exactly a well-educated Bachelor of Arts should learn. But the gifted amateur will not become extinct. Adults may expect to explore geography or geology, music or art appreciation, ethics or Shakespeare or Italian through technology and continuing education. The quality of the education, the motivations that might impel one to take advantage of it, and what kind of staying power these newly gifted amateurs will have are open questions; but I am confident that education will be provided through extension programs, arts councils, and museums. In these ways, more and more people will be educated in the decades ahead, and they will be learning a great variety of materials and subjects.

What about the other two questions? Who will do the educating and where will the education be provided? American higher education today is populated by a bewildering variety of what might be called ungraciously "knowledge providers." The tenure-track faculty still decide what should be taught and do most of the teaching in research universities and in the selective liberal arts colleges. But in many other types of institutions, these faculty members are outnumbered by a varied and growing core of part-time faculty members hired to teach a particular course, who are sometimes called "gypsy scholars," as well as graduate teaching assistants, adjunct faculty members, contract workers, even software specialists.

Such developments might seem to place increased power in the hands of administrators who can hire these folks to do these jobs and set the conditions of performance. However, faculty members, especially those in high-profile institutions who are renowned for their skills as teachers and specialists, hold some trump cards that may shift the balance back in the direction of faculty power.[10] The central administration can only facilitate or impede: it cannot control the imaginative exploration of new forms of teaching. As sophisticated instructional technology makes it easier for good teachers to put lectures on video and design courseware for the computer, the skills of good teaching and imaginative new forms of mass presentation become more and more marketable, far beyond one's particular campus. Potential providers of mass education through licensing software sense a very lucrative new opportunity here.

One can envision a situation in which faculty members join, as medieval companies of scholars did, to offer their services to students, but this time through proprietary courses packaged as videos, as CD-ROMs, or over the World Wide Web or its successors. There will be no need for student services administrators, admissions officers, presidents, deans, or boards of trustees to make this kind of education possible. Such a prospect, of course, raises some very thorny issues about accreditation, marketing, and quality control, but it also offers more and more opportunities for increasing numbers of people to learn from skilled teachers and accomplished scholars.

So where will all this education take place? I have stressed deliberately that institutions of higher learning in our country have been closely tied to campuses, to particular spaces, and this tie has led to the identification of members of the faculty, the student body, and the alumni with particular communities of scholars and learners. The identification can sometimes become very fierce, as in the incredibly fanatical loyalty that members of my own university community feel for the Duke basketball team, or the sense of great beauty that some of these campuses evoke nostalgically in the minds of their graduates. What happens when education is provided by these new information technologies over long distances or in unconventional commercial settings? Isn't it inevitable that the campus will disappear?

It seems very likely that many traditional campuses will disappear. Others, I believe, will find that the decades ahead offer some attractive new ways of building on their traditional advantages. To do so we have to be quite clear about the mission and the advantages that we offer and prove very nimble and appropriately visionary in responding to these new opportunities.

THE FUTURE OF ÉLITE HIGHER EDUCATION

A typology has recently been offered by two students of higher education, Bob Zemsky and William Massy, to distinguish three broad types of institutions in higher education in America today: brand-name, mass-provider, and convenience institutions.[11] In the future it seems clear that what are called "mass-provider institutions," which include many of our state universities, land-grant institutions, and four-year colleges, will be severely pressed by the new low-cost "convenience institutions" if they attempt to offer, as the mass providers traditionally have done, a traditional education on traditional campuses in a traditional way. The new, low-cost convenience institutions are appealing mostly to adult learners. They are very flexible in their offerings, focused on providing outcomes that can be demonstrated to employers and heavily reliant on the Internet and multimedia communications. British observers are already familiar with examples of such institutions, including the very successful Open University. In order to survive, mass-provider institutions will have to adopt some of these same techniques.

It is less clear that the brand-name or élite institutions in America will be deeply threatened by the new convenience institutions. The distinctiveness of universities such as Stanford, Yale, Harvard,

Princeton, or Duke lies not only in prestigious names, long track records, or comparative financial stability, but also, and most importantly, in their goals.

Martin Trow offered a definition of these goals twenty years ago that remains helpful today. What do our finest colleges and universities attempt to do which sets them apart from mass-provider or convenience institutions?

First of all, says Trow, élite higher education seeks to socialize students, not merely to train or inform them; that is, to shape qualities of mind, feeling, and character. In the second place, this kind of education is carried on through a relatively close and prolonged relationship between teacher and student. It depends on the creation and survival of the social and physical settings within which that kind of relationship can exist. And finally, although the specific content of the curriculum in these institutions may vary widely, this type of education tries to convey to students that they can accomplish large things in the world, that they can make important discoveries, lead great institutions, influence laws and government.[12]

In this sense, brand-name or élite education is clearly distinguished from the transmission of skills or knowledge through a fleeting, impersonal relationship between teacher and student, or across the distant learning of the Web. It is also distinguished by a commitment to adding value and satisfying several specific goals. These features run directly athwart the mass-market, consumer-oriented, low-cost distance learning trends that I have described above. And yet, the elements in "élite education" retain an immense appeal to potential students and their families: not just the brand name, but the provision of an experience that can never be fully replicated through a virtual substitute. On this basis, I am confident that for the foreseeable future there will be a steady market for the richly varied and intensive undergraduate education that a small number of places provide, as a rite of passage for young American adults.

Our problem will not be filling our classrooms and our residence halls, but making sure that we can include within those classes young men and women of all kinds of backgrounds, including those who cannot afford to pay the costs of this expensive and intensive training. A baccalaureate degree at Duke University, which usually takes four years, now costs $30,000 a year. There are very few families who can afford to pay that without some help. For such students and their families the appeal of a much less expensive, much more convenient baccalaureate degree will surely be great even if they wish they could take advantage of a Duke or a Stanford. It is here that we are most vulnerable, and here that we need to redouble our commitments to retaining our accessibility by making best use of our resources, so that we do not become havens for the élite, defined by wealth rather than intellectual capacity.

In the training of Ph.D.'s, it can be assumed that the brand-name universities will have a very large head start, most of all in the pooling of academic talent that a place like Oxford, Duke, or Harvard will provide. It gives us a significant advantage, because even if fewer and fewer students will seek Ph.D.'s to teach in conventional universities, the need to prepare teacher-scholars to work in many new fields of interdisciplinary research and many new forms of outreach and teaching will not evaporate. We will need to adapt and think about our graduate training to make sure that we do not just replicate traditional tenure-track faculty members from the past, but also young people trained imaginatively to teach and do research in a variety of settings. Nonetheless, the major research universities will continue to attract many students who wish to be trained as teachers and scholars.

The competition will become most intense in professional training, in the production of lawyers, doctors, or MBAs. Here the advantages of campus-based education seem much less obvious, and the advantages of distance learning very clear. However, opportunities for close relationships between faculty and students, and among students themselves, retain an immense advantage for professionally educated graduates of universities such as Duke. There is no way in which these close personal relationships can be replicated over the Web.

Our model for the future will need to be similar to the one we have begun to establish at Duke in a program called GEMBA (the Global Executive MBA). The candidates for GEMBA come from all over the world, and there are forty-five of them in each class. They do not have to give up their jobs or leave their homes for extended periods. They spend several brief but intensive sessions together with classmates and faculty members, first on our campus and then, punctuated by several ten-week stints of learning through distance mechanisms, in locations deliberately chosen around the world to maximize the global virtues of what they are doing: Salzburg, Shanghai, São Paulo. Thus they come together periodically for two intensive weeks and then study apart for ten weeks, being kept together through an enormous investment of their time and energy over the Internet. Most of their education is provided through distance learning, but the time they spend together in these four two-week periods over eighteen months is absolutely essential to the success of the program. Having significant "face time" together makes it much easier to bond in cyberspace, to enter into virtual discussions that have the flavor of the real thing. Instead of communicating with disembodied, impersonal e-mail addresses, the students and faculty members in this GEMBA program know each other well and communicate as friends and colleagues. The distance learning that they enjoy is carefully crafted by faculty members who have spent a great deal of time developing these programs, adapting their traditional means of transmitting information through software to create a true virtual classroom, a faculty lounge, a student lounge where only the students can talk, chat rooms, and formal seminar periods which are described by time rather than by space. "We will have a discussion of this particular topic for the next two days. Log on and enter it. It is, for this period of time, an open session; we'll then move on to our next topic."

Using this kind of model, along with or in collaboration with other institutions, I believe that élite educational institutions in the United States will not only survive but flourish in the years ahead. The evocative and intensive importance of the campus may be diminished but need not be abandoned. Campuses bring benefits and attributes that virtual universities attempt to create through cyberspace; but cyberspace will never match the advantages of the real thing.

In conclusion, let me briefly address the place of American universities in the global framework of higher education.

American higher education today attracts students from around the world. There are more than 450,000 students from other countries on our campuses.[13] Many of our students and faculty members also study and do research abroad. But just as citizens of the United States have a recurrent tendency to isolationism and xenophobia, American higher education today is in some ways quite parochial. Our students and family members are too often ignorant of what is happening in other countries, compared with our counterparts in other systems. Since English is the dominant language of international scholarship, a dominance reinforced by its use as the lingua franca for the Internet, there is little incentive for American scholars to learn other languages. Because American scholarship is recognized as preeminent in many fields, there is little incentive for it to keep abreast with the work done in other countries.

Thus we have the paradox that our system is highly international in some ways, particularly in the number of students who come from abroad to our shores, and highly insular in others, especially in the awareness of scholarly activities elsewhere.

One of the greatest unanswered questions about the future of American institutions is how much we will become involved in genuine collaboration with institutions in the rest of the world. A considerable amount of energy is being devoted by our institutions to cultivating markets abroad, but that is not the same thing as entering into genuine intellectual partnerships with universities in the rest of the world. The potential advantages of collaborating are great, and the ease of doing so with the kinds of technologies that I have been describing is striking. Therefore we may hope that our tendencies towards insularity will be overcome. The future of higher education will surely become more global, with or without conscious direction, and with or without thoughtful American participation. But we shall surely all be better off if we in the United States think about what we are doing and join forces to accomplish visionary goals rather than risk the consequences of global drift.

ACE Address

Chicago, 19 March 2000

I am honored to give this lecture in Bob Atwell's name. Bob has been a leader in higher education for decades; both policy makers and educators have benefited from his wise counsel. More important, generations of students will flourish because of his commitment to access to higher education.

I was tempted to use this occasion to give advice, in their absence, to this year's brace of presidential candidates. But although I believe that academic leaders should speak truth to power, a more pressing task is to speak truth to ourselves. If we think more clearly together about what higher education needs to do to face the challenges ahead for our profession, that will surely involve thinking more clearly about the challenges ahead for our world.

Since there are so many fascinating paths one might explore in keynoting a conference on higher education in the twenty-first century, let me begin by noting that there are two important speeches on this topic that I am *not* going to give. One is about the international dimensions of our topic; the other is about information technology. I will make several references to the latter topic—indeed, it would be weird to ignore it; but that is not my major theme.

I am aware, as we all must be, that new information technologies are having, and will continue to have, profound consequences for the way we educate. Powerful forces, both economic and intellectual, are moving us in the direction of greater reliance on these technologies. They offer much that is good, as well as substantial pitfalls. It is in any case abundantly clear that a large proportion of higher education in the coming decades will be offered through new delivery mechanisms and new consortia of providers. I take that as a given. My goal is to help us step back from these trends, so that we can better choose from the exciting new techniques and partnerships the ones most likely to be fruitful for our students.

I have chosen to talk about *American* higher education, even though I am convinced that one of our most pressing needs is to throw open our windows to the world beyond these shores, build real partnerships with universities in other countries, learn from best practices elsewhere. The most common international reference in speeches about American higher education today is a complacent reassurance that we have the best system of higher education in the world. Perhaps so—but that statement has become a shibboleth, and may soon, in some respects, be out of date. That, however, would be another speech.

As a practicing political theorist, I will use a particular prism to help focus our attention on higher education in the United States: the perspective of one of the most astute of all observers of our society, Alexis de Tocqueville.

To refresh your memory, Tocqueville was a young French aristocrat who visited America in the 1830s, and was fascinated by almost everything he saw. His two-volume *Democracy in America* analyzed our politics, religion, mores, and geography, attempting to place this novel social order within the context of both history—the republics of classical times—and the old states of Europe, with their deeply riven social classes, dominant, decaying aristocracies, and ancient, threatened monarchies. Because he was such a gifted observer, elegant writer, and unusually talented social theorist, what Tocqueville tells us about our society still resonates more than a century and a half later. Some of his predictions seem right on target; others fall wide of the mark. But even when he was wrong, Tocqueville was stimulating, and he usually covered his bases by noting features in our society that stood as exceptions to his generalizations, or as seeds for possible future change.

Tocqueville described the United States of America in the 1830s as a highly *egalitarian*, largely *homogeneous* society, deeply *individualistic*, with a preference for pragmatic approaches to the world tempered by a restless faith in perfectibility and progress. I will use these four categories to frame my analysis of where America stands today, and what our agenda should be in this new era ahead.

In observing American society from a European perspective, Tocqueville was first struck by what he called the "equality of condition"[1]—by which he meant the lack of clearly delineated social classes, relatively even distribution of wealth, and parity of citizenship on this side of the Atlantic. He saw this as the most distinctive hallmark of American society—and also what the rest of the world was likely to become as the old European states crumbled and dissolved.

Tocqueville noted one major and exceedingly disturbing exception to this generalization: the continuing presence of slavery on American soil. But apart from the condition of "the Negro," Americans seemed to Tocqueville largely equal in their situations. He was struck by how much Americans prized equality, setting it even above liberty as a social value to be protected.

Whatever may have been the case in the 1830s (and Tocqueville clearly exaggerated the equality that he saw, by comparison with the societies he knew in Europe), it may seem that on this, his central observation, Tocqueville is obviously outdated. American society is marked by increasing inequality, and the world as a whole exhibits staggering inequalities both within and among societies. In 1998, for instance, seventy-five average wage earners in the world's poorest country (Sierra Leone) did not collectively earn what one average American worker did,[2] while here at home it took more than 420 average workers to equal the income of the average CEO.[3] Furthermore, Americans today rarely express much interest in equality; the word seldom appears in our public discourse. Our people have shown themselves to be far more concerned about threats to our liberties—religious, economic, or arms-toting—than about the diminution of equality.

However, Tocqueville noted that equality of condition is an unusual situation for humankind, and he saw inevitable pressures towards inequality even in the America of his day. In a democracy, he said, "numerous artificial and arbitrary distinctions spring up," as individuals endeavor to distinguish themselves from the mass of their fellows: the personal pride of individuals will always make them seek to rise above the line and form somewhere an inequality to their own advantage.

In this regard, Tocqueville singled out the exceptional importance of money in American society, compared to the old world he knew. With all other distinctions leveled, the focus of Americans was primarily on getting and spending. The most probable source of a new privileged class, in his view, was the power of manufacturing in the American economy. "If ever a permanent inequality of conditions and aristocracy again penetrates into the world," he said, "it may be predicted that this is the gate by which they will enter."[4]

Tocqueville also noted that "when hereditary wealth, the privileges of rank, and the prerogatives of birth have ceased to be and when every man derives his strength from himself alone, it becomes evident that the chief cause of disparity between the fortunes of men is the mind." In fact, he argued that these two sources of inequality are correlated: when "natural inequality" reasserts itself, he claimed, "wealth will spontaneously pass into the hands of the most capable."[5]

So two interconnected factors—differentiation on the basis of wealth and of mental capacity—were the probable sources of future inequality in the egalitarian society that Tocqueville observed on our shores.

His prediction might seem to be good news for educators, since our core business is honing intelligence, sharpening the minds of our students, including those most likely to wind up in positions of leadership and influence. And in many ways, contemporary life does reward intelligence; access to ordered information and sophisticated skills are crucial for success. Tocqueville would not have been surprised by our preoccupation with what we call "the knowledge society," although I suspect he would have found the grammatical construction barbarous.

But in drawing this connection between amassing wealth and

natural talent, Tocqueville surely understated the cumulative advantages of wealth, and the obstacles confronting bright children of underprivileged backgrounds who want to improve their fortunes. Both factors underscore the importance of accessibility, so that all our citizens who possess qualities of mind that lend themselves to the force of education will have the opportunity to flourish.

Yet we know that thousands of students who could benefit from a college education don't even consider it, based on their misconceptions about what it will cost them to attend and the amount of aid available. Even more important, our long-standing commitment to access to higher education—which is one of the most admirable and durable manifestations of the belief in equality that Tocqueville identified in us—is now significantly eroded. Funds for aid for children of the poorest families are becoming scarcer. Support for students by the federal government has shifted away from the needs of the nation's poorest to respond to middle-class fears about the price of college. More of the funds available for aid on many campuses are being channeled to attract talented students to a particular college, rather than to make it possible for underprivileged kids to attend any college at all.

This tendency is not the result of any single fiat or decision; all the actors in this scenario are behaving rationally, given the pressures they face. But the result is disturbing—a reinforcement of what Duke's Phil Cook and his co-author Bob Frank called "the winner-take-all society," in which the good things of life are cumulative for some people and continually elude others.[6] To reinforce existing inequalities in our society by restricting access to higher education means cutting off the avenue by which generations of Americans have successfully achieved much greater opportunities, and by which our society has avoided some of the most glaring inequalities that have brought division and conflict to societies throughout history.

At this point we may feel like the rabbit in Aesop's tale, who after delivering an impassioned and eloquent plea for all the animals to have a fair and equal share overhears the lion's wry aside: "Nice speech, but it lacks teeth."

144

This is precisely where I believe leaders of colleges and universities should shape the terms of our discourse. We need to speak truth to *economic* power, which we have been less willing to do than speaking truth to the folks in government. Admittedly, such truths may bite much closer to home. All of us are dependent on generous support from individual donors, wealthy community leaders, foundations, or corporations. All of us benefit from the richly productive economy of our country these days, and the market forces on which it rests. But this makes it all the more imperative that all of us—not just the radical sociologists or the ethicists or theologians, but college and university administrators too—speak out frankly about the long-term threats to a society where wealth occupies too large a space on the social landscape. Some measure of the hunger for getting and spending is no doubt good for a society. But one of history's clearest lessons is that dramatically increasing inequality based on unbridled greed is corrosive and dangerous, especially in a democracy.

In a recent issue of the *New York Times*, there were two articles on stress.[7] The first, on a sadly familiar theme, described a recent survey of working mothers, who spoke of the great difficulties of managing lives in which many of them work long hours, some of them at more than one job, continually seeking decent child care, attempting to find time for their families, and barely making ends meet. The other article was front-page news: the stresses felt by children of tremendously wealthy families in Silicon Valley these days. Their concerns were of a very different sort: Will my friends like me for myself, or only because Daddy lets me invite them on vacation for two weeks in Switzerland? How can I hold up my head at school if we have only two houses and three BMWs, and not a single private plane?

The comparison between these worlds would give a Tocqueville rich material for reanalyzing American society in 2000, and it ought to sober us all today. Universities should be places where the culture of inequality based on wealth is regularly and eloquently called into question, where the radical inequalities exemplified by those two articles are cause for deep concern. We should reinforce impulses towards philanthropy and humanitarianism that benefit our whole society, not just our own institutions. We should also speak up for enlightened social policies, to improve the lot of our poorest hard-working fellow citizens and their families.

To those who would say that this is none of our business, we have a ready answer. Those children who languish today in substandard day care, who learn violence from drug-addicted and despairing parents, who watch mindless programs on TV for countless hours each week rather than have anyone stimulate their innate curiosity about the world—these children are our future students. Thus we have a strong interest in making sure that they come to us prepared to learn, prepared to take advantage of what we have to offer. This is our business, after all.

As presidents, we still command the respect of many people in our society. Our voices will be heard, even by those who may not like what we say; if we wish to be heard, we must use those voices. And if we wish to be respected, we must look to our own house as well, and resist the alarming tendency for inflated corporate compensation to spill over into higher education. Our students pay tuition, and generous donors support us, so that we can provide a better education, support path-breaking research, and serve our communities, not to bolster our own compensation to emulate our counterparts in the for-profit world. That is *not* our business, after all.

AMERICAN HOMOGENEITY

Another of Tocqueville's bold predictions was that the Anglo-Americans would eventually control all the vast continent which lay before them as they pressed towards the Mississippi and beyond. "This gradual and continuous progress of the European race towards the Rocky Mountains has the solemnity of a providential event; it is a deluge of men rising unabatedly, and daily driven onwards by the hand of God." As a result, eventually "the Anglo-Americans alone will cover the immense space contained between the polar regions and the tropics, extending from the coasts of the Atlantic to those of the Pacific Ocean."[8]

The geography we take for granted as we jet between our coasts was by no means a foregone conclusion in 1832. However, Tocqueville spoke only of the European settlers. He was persuaded that the Anglo-Americans would preserve a definite homogeneity of customs and cultures as they overspread the continent; he failed to foresee waves of immigrants who have transformed and enriched our population.

Our homogeneous society has become more and more pluralistic, multifaceted, and diverse. There is every reason to believe that this tendency will continue and even accelerate in the decades ahead. Census predictions regularly project majorities of non-Anglo citizens in many parts of our country, and increasing numbers of such citizens in every region, within a very few years.

In the middle of the twentieth century, as some of Tocqueville's intellectual heirs among social scientists strove to come to terms with America's increasing pluralism, they hit upon concepts such as "cross-cutting" and "reinforcing" cleavages to describe what they saw, hoped for, or feared. As they observed increasing diversity, they hoped that this very pluralism might become a source of strength, if citizens of different backgrounds learned to identify with others who shared some, but not all, of their conspicuous characteristics.

Thus, for example, if Americans of different races share multiple religious affiliations, Hispanic evangelicals might feel kinship with co-religionists as well as predominantly Catholic members of their cultural and linguistic group. The same could hold for socioeconomic class, or any other major cleavage—at least in theory. These would be "cross-cutting" cleavages, which sociologists uniformly regard as a "good thing" in holding our country together rather than having it become deeply divided along major reinforcing lines of class, race, or religion.

In practice, however, our citizens have shown a disturbing tendency to align themselves with "none of the above." Hispanic evangelicals may feel a major kinship only with other Hispanic evangelicals, or even with just the Hispanic evangelicals from a particular home country or subculture. Dominican immigrants in the Northeast, Cuban-Americans in Florida, and Chicanos in Texas may feel little linkage with each other despite Spanish-speaking backgrounds, much less a linkage with, say, Anglo Catholics; the same may be true of Asian-Americans with roots in different countries and languages. The result is increasing fragmentation: nobody feels any great kinship with anyone but that small group of others who share every salient trait—some combination of gender, class, religion, race, and ethnicity.

The accompanying advice for higher education is both simple and hard: our institutions must take responsibility for educating a diverse citizenry, preparing people for a pluralist society, by bringing to the fore those common principles of political and moral understanding that hold us together in one polity. Our principles must be made and kept explicit.

Universities and colleges are among the most diverse institutions in our society; people of many different cultures and backgrounds come together for an intense and concentrated experience. We must take advantage of this diversity. Institutions of higher education are among the few venues where people can easily reach across the barriers that divide us. Indeed, our institutions consciously bring diverse groups of students together because we believe that this diversity of experience prepares them for life in a multicultural world. Majority students, as much as minority students, benefit from being educated in a diverse environment. Thus, despite the many advantages of distance education, there is good reason to protect campus-based learning as well, so that real encounters among diverse people can enrich the education of each one of them. That kind of learning is hard to do in cyberspace.

Bok and Bowen are right.[9] We know it from our own campuses and the students we teach. However, we have relied too long on our intuition and personal experience on campus, without pausing to be sure that the public and politicians are still with us. One of the great virtues of *The Shape of the River* is the degree to which the authors have carefully documented the outcomes of our efforts to diversify. It is imperative that we educate the public better on these matters; to do so effectively, we need more such studies.

It is against this backdrop that issues of affirmative action and need-blind admissions play out. Tocqueville noted even in the 1830s that in certain areas of the country, "slavery recedes, but the prejudice to which it has given birth is immovable."[10] In his view, the presence of an enslaved black population was "the most formidable of all the ills that threaten the future of the Union." Foreseeing that the bitter fruits of slavery would be with us long after the peculiar institution itself was abolished, Tocqueville would not have been surprised that our nation continues to wrestle with the long-term effects of racial oppression.

Those of our contemporaries who exhort us to do away with any consideration of race in our policies would do well to ponder Tocqueville's insights. Racial prejudice rooted in slavery has a long life, and its effects continue to tarnish and threaten our national character and prospects.

AMERICAN INDIVIDUALISM

Another of Tocqueville's broad generalizations was his claim that our citizens were stubbornly individualistic. Tocqueville warned that unless equally strong forces counter this tendency it will dissolve ties among citizens and threaten the future of democratic government. "Private selfishness," as he put it, is the "rust of society."

Fortunately, Tocqueville believed, American society contained effective antidotes to this radical individualism, most notably the amazing propensity of our citizens to associate.[11]

Tocqueville's contemporary intellectual heirs have been disturbed by the increasing power of individualism and withdrawal from the civic realm in our society. The best-known of these observers, the political scientist Robert Putnam, asserts in his essay "Bowling Alone" that the decline of traditional associations, and the failure of Americans to form new ones, is precisely what leads to the domination of unchecked individualism and the erosion of civic virtue in our time. We have used up a large proportion of our "social capital," and with each passing year millions more people withdraw from the affairs of their community.[12]

Tocqueville's understanding of the powerful tendency towards corrosive individualism was right on target; but he probably overestimated the American propensity for association in the longer term. Unless we can find ways to reestablish this propensity, one may easily imagine American society sinking more and more deeply into solipsism, and the springs of civic connection further weakened.

Higher education surely has a significant role to play in this arena. Campuses are natural seedbeds of associations. I sometimes think that even Tocqueville would have been surprised by the incredible number of different forms of association that undergraduates at Duke devise to accomplish their shared purposes, from Students against Sweatshops through the Self-Knowledge Symposium and the Creative Anachronism Society to the Cameron Crazies. Their experiences do much to combat tendencies towards withdrawal and narrow individualism, and may, we hope, instill a taste for similar activities after the degree has been conferred.

Tocqueville put faith in "the customs of the people," our manners and practices, as more potent than legislation and government itself in shaping civic life. In an arresting phrase that has become current among sociologists, he described such patterns of behavior and thought as the "habits of the heart." If we recognize the importance of education in civic virtue for our students, our campuses are well designed to nurture and reinforce healthy habits of the heart.

Students on residential campuses share aspects of their lives in an intimacy they will not elsewhere experience outside the family. These are communities that offer daily practical experiences in the consequences of ethical and unethical behavior. An important part of our responsibility should be to draw attention to these experiences and help students learn their lessons. We build character not by inculcating particular forms of morality or belief, but by teaching students to think carefully about ethical choices, and providing them with the tools to do so—just as we provide them with tools for quantitative reasoning or aesthetic appreciation—and the means to sharpen those tools.

Universities also provide multiple opportunities for deliberately extending one's consciousness beyond the horizon of ego to help those in need. Although many young people may be cynical or apathetic about politics, they are reassuringly idealistic about volunteering and serving their communities. Quick to respond to children whose lives and futures are at risk, to the poverty of those who frequent soup kitchens and the loneliness of the elderly, they reach out to real people whom they can know and touch. These experiences are profound training grounds for the "habits of the heart."

What about the contention that such habits may get overwhelmed by, and totally lost in, cyberspace? The jury is still out on the relation of the Internet to the propensity to form associations. Some observers contend that virtual relationships are our newest form of association, vindicating Tocqueville by the bewildering variety of linkages that are now being formed. Others say that these associations are a poor substitute for the real thing, that virtual relationships are thin and distorted, that the peculiar anonymity of cyberspace skews constructions of the personality and precludes forming real bonds. Such critics would argue that people who spend a great deal of their time glued to their screens are actually withdrawing into solipsism, rather than risking the hurts and claiming the rewards of real, messy human relationships.

We need to know much more than we now do about the special characteristics of virtual relationships, about how they can be used positively and how they supplant or threaten direct, positive, morally challenging relationships among human beings that help to build character. The fascinations of the World Wide Web are sufficiently compelling that students, we may safely assume, will continue to explore it eagerly. We may try to guide them by demonstrating some of the great power and also the problems in this new form of human connection, but they are always likely to be ahead of us. Until the psychology of virtual reality is better understood, our goal should be to encourage these present and future citizens to develop their natural propensity to bond, congregate, and hang out not just over the Internet, but also in synchronous, nonvirtual reality—real time and place. Encouraging people to know other people, in all their complexity, may be one of higher education's greatest gifts to the future.

The fourth characteristic of the new country noted by Tocqueville was our exceptional pragmatism. As he put it, "the spirit of the Americans is averse to general ideas; it does not seek theoretical discoveries." That was a common claim of European observers throughout the nineteenth century; however, given the predominant role of American science in our contemporary world, that perspective appears to have been shortsighted. Tocqueville was closer to the target when he asserted that the citizen of a democracy "cares more to know a great deal quickly than to know anything well; he has no time and but little taste to search things to the bottom."[13] He saw our intellect as broad and shallow, like a soup bowl.

Tocqueville also noted that Americans were marked by an incredible restlessness, demonstrated in their eagerness to pursue gratification, and the assumption that we can always leave our present position and find a better one—whether that means picking up stakes and lighting out for the territories, or changing jobs to maximize our earnings. "To minds thus predisposed," he says, "every new method that leads by a shorter road to wealth, every machine that spares labor, every instrument that diminishes the cost of production, every discovery that facilitates pleasures or augments them, seems to be the grandest effort of the human intellect." (Boy, did he have us pegged!)[14]

Tocqueville also mentioned a touching American faith in progress and perfectibility, though we seem to seek progress almost wholly in material terms. For our countrymen, there is always a better way and a reward for those who seek it. In one vivid passage, he reports: "I accost an American sailor and inquire why the ships of his country are built so as to last for only a short time; he answers without hesitation that the art of navigation is every day making such rapid progress that the finest vessel would become almost useless if it lasted beyond a few years. In these words, which fell accidentally, and on a particular subject, from an uninstructed man, I recognize the general and systematic idea upon which a great people direct all their concerns."[15]

The lessons for higher education here are clear. We need to remember and advocate for the long view, the durable process, the deeper thought, the broader reflectiveness. Our campuses must encourage the cultivation of ideas that go against the grain, celebrate the unconventional, provoke the challenge. We must vigilantly protect basic research, for example, as a core enterprise not merely of our institutions but of our society. The bottom-line regimens of corporate shareholders and governments will inevitably tilt towards funding discoveries that have some probable short-term payoff. Providing federal support to ensure the strength of the basic research enterprise within universities has proven to be sound public policy (as well as sound educational policy): as we continually remind our representatives in Washington, here is the engine that has driven our economy and technology. True enough; but it is important to remember that pure science is also the source of some of humankind's grandest ideas and boldest adventures.

We must stand up for the importance of the odd, oblique, abstract enquiry; of knowing for the sake of knowing; of the truly free exchange of ideas, as one of the most important services we can provide for our society and the world. In Tocqueville's words, "men living in democratic ages cannot fail to improve the industrial part of science"; therefore, all our efforts "ought to be directed to support the highest branches of learning and to foster the nobler passion for science itself."[16]

We must also be mindful of the importance of aesthetics, the lens of history, the perfection of beauty, the smooth, sharp edge of "high culture." We in higher education are more than the curators of civilization's intellectual treasures: we are the interpreters and translators who will keep them alive, the raconteurs who tell their stories, the griots who renew their magic, and the interlocutors without whose sympathy for tradition and love of innovation the culture goes grainy and out of focus. American popular culture overspreads the world like kudzu, and our responsibilities include making sure that it does not choke out all other forms of creating, thinking, and knowing.

Hence the crucial importance in the new world of the liberal arts, despite all the pressures that militate against them in favor of a utilitarian approach. Fortunately, Tocqueville counseled us that in a society where "the chief cause of disparity between the fortunes of men is the mind," knowledge becomes greatly valued as a mark of distinction. In a society where basic physical needs are satisfied, the human mind is freed to explore "the infinite, the spiritual, and the beautiful."[17] "The utility of knowledge becomes singularly conspicuous even to the eyes of the multitude; those who have no taste for its charms set store upon its results and make some efforts to acquire it." As a result, "not only will the number of those who can take an interest in the productions of the mind be greater, but the taste for intellectual enjoyment will descend step by step even to those who in aristocratic societies seem to have neither time or ability to indulge in them."

This observation jibes with our own faith in the importance of education for all kinds of people, of all kinds of interests and backgrounds, at all stages of their lives. No longer simply a rite of passage for the young, or a source of credentialing for the would-be professional, education in the new era will become the staff of life and the stuff of everyman's—and everywoman's—dreams. This is one of the most exciting, and most promising, prospects that lies ahead.

My message today may strike you as deeply conservative. It concentrates on familiar forms of education, campus-based and provided by a community of scholars whose common purpose includes thinking carefully together about the kind of education they are offering. I am convinced that just as radio and movies survived the onslaught of TV, so campus-based education will retain a significant place in our new agenda. There are simply too many advantages of real-life engagement within and outside the classroom; the power of place is too deeply wired into our brains. Many wonderful innovations will be enabled by the Internet and successor technologies we cannot yet imagine. We should embrace them; use them wisely; do with them what was impossible before. But we need also to be cognizant of and precise about the limitations of technology.

Ideally, all forms of education in this new era will be a fertile combination of place and cyberspace. Some types of education—continuing, executive, professional—will and should rely more heavily on distance education. This form of conveying knowledge allows us to reach learners who would otherwise be disenfranchised—thus bringing to many more of our fellow citizens the precious advantages of higher education. Distance education also offers very attractive conveniences to learners who can retain their homes and their jobs, yet still tap into the resources of institutions far from their home towns.

Other kinds of education—for example, the Ph.D.—will surely continue to depend on direct encounters and real relationships. Undergraduate education can no doubt be offered in both dimensions; still, it seems likely that many students will continue to covet the kind of campus-based community that has conventionally led to the bachelor's degree, and many families will want to provide it. The issue will be not whether high-quality, campus-based undergraduate education survives, but how many institutions can afford to offer it, and who gets to take advantage of it. This will boil down to who can afford both the direct cost and opportunity cost of what is, after all, a fairly luxurious and resource-intensive endeavor. The constraint—as Bob Atwell has always understood—will be neither desirability nor feasibility, but accessibility. One of our main responsibilities should be ensuring that the special advantages of campus-based baccalaureate education do not become once more, as they were in Tocqueville's time, the exotic preserve of the children of the wealthy, leavened by a few prospective clerics.

So these aspects of my message are undoubtedly conservative. Yet my speech may also appear radical, in that it calls for a role for higher education that is not neutral, not simply responsive to the market or social trends. I have called upon each of us to show real leadership in using our own bully pulpits—and the power of the education we provide—to speak forcefully on issues that we know a great deal about, so that society as a whole will be the better. My call to arms would not have seemed noteworthy to our nineteenth-century precursors, who took it for granted that higher education has a moral responsibility. But it is incontestably radical today. It's time to return to that root tradition.

We are, to be sure, a diverse group of associations, and diversity has been one of the great advantages of American higher education. I hope and expect that this very diversity will be enhanced in the coming decades as we sort out distance and on-line learning.

There is, after all, a great deal of educating to be done, and we all stand to benefit from the testing of alternatives. But we must not lose sight of the basic purpose for which society supports us: and that is not to make a profit, nor to figure out how to package the most wisdom at least cost, but to provide the very best education we can to all those who come to us in search of it.

The Liberal Arts and

the Role of Élite Higher Education

This is not the first period in history when large-scale technological and social change has transformed higher education. The campus as we know it is the multilayered result of many such changes over the decades—in governance, curriculum, and student access. Yet through all these transformations, some version of the traditional liberal arts preparation for the baccalaureate degree has survived. Today some observers fear, and others hope, that liberal education has finally become obsolete.

We live in what pundits call a "knowledge society," in which mastery of certain kinds of information is essential to success. As a result, nontraditional knowledge purveyors are springing into action everywhere—corporations training workers, for-profit "universities" enrolling career-changing adults, new high-tech companies marketing degrees. In every part of our lives, sophisticated technologies offer exotic new ways of conveying information, and theoretically provide almost unlimited access to it.

In such a world, what is the place of a traditional liberal arts education? At least for the moment, we are helped by evidence that higher education brings quite tangible benefits in earnings over time.[1] The first step in the process is the baccalaureate degree. Prestigious institutions that confer this degree in the humanities and sciences are highly competitive. Students may seek these degrees more for their networking benefits or the power of the "brand name" than for the kind of education offered. But consumer preferences rooted in such factors tend to have a long life.

Thus young people who want to hold power, make money, or make a difference in the world still flock to these colleges and universities. Another way to describe the aspirations of these students is to say that they wish (or their parents wish them) to become, or remain, members of the "élite." An ambiguity in the meaning of this word works to the benefit of selective colleges and universities. We describe these institutions as élite because they choose their students carefully from a much larger pool of applicants and offer an expensive education by the most distinguished faculty members they can attract. Because their graduates, even if not born to wealth and privilege, are disproportionately represented in privileged and powerful positions in society, these institutions are also associated with the concept of the élite in a socioeconomic sense.

This conjunction poses some tricky issues in our society: "élitism" is often regarded as inherently undemocratic, perpetuating historical inequities. But the benefits of spending four years in highly specialized settings at a formative time in life, with talented peers and magnificent resources for learning, are quite significant. Our job is to make sure that these institutions are truly open to bright students of all socioeconomic backgrounds and that we provide them with the very best liberal arts education we can devise for the world that they will go on to lead.

HOW DO WE DEFEND THE LIBERAL ARTS TODAY?

Familiar defenses of liberal education offer a beautiful ideal, playing on the multiple meanings and linguistic roots of the key word "liberal." This form of education was first designed in classical times for free persons, rather than slaves or metics. It frees the mind, offering personal liberation from ignorance and constraint. In a recent essay, William Cronon traces the meaning of *liberal arts* beyond the root Latin *liber*, providing affinities with Old English *leodan*, "to grow," and *leod*, "people," as well as the Greek *eleutheros* and Sanskrit *rodhati*, "one climbs," "one grows." As Cronon summarizes this ideal, "Liberal education is built on these values: It aspires to nurture the growth of human talent in the service of human freedom."[2]

These aspirations of a liberal arts education overlap with some of the goals of contemporary culture. Self-development is an attractive concept for many people. But neither peace of mind nor social success is guaranteed by the baccalaureate degree. Many paths promoted on TV, or in the kinds of seven-step handbooks available in airport bookshops, promise a much more direct way of reaching these goals. It is hard to explain to our contemporaries, raised in a society of sound bites and instant gratification, how the oblique routes taken by the liberal arts through arcane and apparently useless forms of knowledge lead to many worthwhile destinations.[3]

Justifications of the liberal arts usually focus on skills or competencies, the basic habits of mind and spirit instilled by a liberal education. The ability to read, write, and converse with supple ease and interest; a familiarity with human history and diverse cultures; some understanding of the scientific method; an appreciation of art; quantitative reasoning; critical thinking—these are the markers that we use in describing what we aim to do, and they are crucial skills for men and women of any era, in any profession, in any endeavor.

All these claims, I believe, are sound; but how do we accomplish the goals? The next few pages spell out some key assumptions that lie behind justifications of liberal education and its distinctive character.

THE VALUE OF DISCIPLINE

A liberal education achieves its goals first by training the mind in a disciplined way, as one trains the body in physical fitness to improve health and prolong life. Learning Greek verbs is an especially dry example of such exercise, like performing a certain number of push-ups every day. The liberal concept of a discipline is broader and more expansive, more akin to a life regimen.

Undergraduate students are typically exposed to a wide range of subjects in their early college years. This gives them some conception of the foundations and forms of knowledge available to them. Then we require them to choose an area of concentration, a major subject, believing that the organized pursuit of knowledge brings special benefits. This approach differs from that of the dilettante by positing intriguing relationships among the different parts of a particular form of human understanding and demonstrating confidence that pursuing these relationships with sustained persistence bears its own fruit.

For the student who does not intend to pursue the major subject in greater depth through graduate education, this discipline becomes an end in itself. It turns out not to matter a great deal, from the point of view of intellectual growth and later benefits, which discipline is chosen. The acquisition of the habit of mental discipline includes learning how to pursue different parts of a complex subject, how to impose the right kinds of questions on unfamiliar material to find the key to understanding. This is a large part of what we mean when we say that liberal education teaches people how to learn rather than to master a technical skill that may someday become obsolete.

Some of the same benefits in mental acuity can of course be gained by mastering a technical skill. In liberal education, however, the mental discipline itself is the basic point, rather than the content of what is learned. If undergraduates choose to concentrate in an interdisciplinary program, or design their own major, it cannot simply be a potpourri of whatever happens to interest them at the time. We insist on having a clearly structured path through the material that brings the same benefits of mental discipline as traditional majors. Programs that fail to honor this requirement have become something else—a Chatauqua, or an intellectual cruise ship menu, but not a liberal education.

THE DELIGHTS OF EXPLORATION

A second tactic employed in liberal education is wide-ranging intellectual exploration. This open-ended quality might seem to be the opposite of the requirement for mental discipline; but experience has shown that these two characteristics fit together with exceptional facility and reinforce each other.

One of the mechanisms for encouraging exploration is the distribution requirement. Undergraduates in most institutions must become minimally familiar with several types of knowledge. Fascinated (or discomfited) by the large number of courses offered for a baccalaureate degree, students are guided by the requirement not only that they choose a major subject, but also that they obtain some familiarity with each of the basic areas of knowledge. This encourages suppleness of mind and lays the groundwork for future exploration of different aspects of the world.

Furthermore, some of the most formative moments in a liberal education occur outside the classroom. A campus (especially a residential campus) provides multiple encounters with other students and faculty members in extracurricular activities, sports, and volunteer service. Bringing together seekers of knowledge across the generations, the campus is a uniquely powerful setting for such structured yet serendipitous exploration—a "free and ordered space," in Bart Giamatti's felicitous phrase.[4]

This kind of exploration is especially useful in educating citizens.[5] Members of large, complex, modern communities who understand something about science, technology, culture, human nature, and politics will be better prepared to make well-informed decisions about what kinds of policies, or political leaders, deserve support. They will be more cautious about accepting bold claims that turn out to be false, less subject to manipulation by those claiming superior knowledge.

Equally important, a taste for intellectual exploration and the acquisition of skills that enable one to indulge that taste are important keys to personal satisfaction. The person who is encouraged to be curious and knows how to satisfy curiosity is a more interesting friend or colleague and more comfortably at home in solitude. Mental resources that enrich leisure time, direct travel plans, and widen one's personal horizons are of great value throughout life.

THE IDEAL OF A COMMON LANGUAGE

One of the traditional justifications for a liberal education has been that the leaders of a society should have some common reference points. Shared familiarity with certain works of art, literature, and music to which allusions could be made provided a kind of elegant shorthand within which arguments and claims could be couched without having to spell out the layers of meaning and implication in every new idea. Acquisition of this common language was the primary form of upward mobility for members of the lower classes in many stratified societies. By learning the symbols used by the élite, the young person could emulate them and thus, by assimilation, join them.

At a time when knowledge has burgeoned so greatly that various curricula provide quite different approaches to the common goal of a liberal education, it is hard to assume that graduates will all have read even a small number of generally acknowledged classics. Nonetheless, some kind of familiarity with the major cultural accomplishments of the western world (and increasingly of other cultures as well), and the basic frameworks of the natural sciences and mathematics, still provide a rudimentary common language for leaders these days.

This ideal has yielded some interesting permutations in the increasingly pluralistic society of the United States, where people of many different backgrounds, cultures, languages, and beliefs aspire to leadership. Many faculty members today stress multicultural understanding while retaining the ideal of a shared, structured curriculum. Their goal is a curriculum that does justice to the core of the liberal arts developed in the West and also to the contributions of other cultures to human understanding and enrichment.

When such a complex combination is successful, students from many backgrounds can recognize themselves in the curriculum. As a result, they are more motivated to participate in the educational experience. Future leaders learn some valuable lessons about the cultural expectations and accomplishments of the diverse people with whom they will work. This creates considerable pressure on curricular choice and internal coherence; it also provides the stimulus for some very interesting juxtapositions of knowledge. Fortunately, the faculties of many institutions have designed rigorous yet flexible curricular structures that incorporate nontraditional as well as classical kinds of knowledge.

A common language derived from a similar education, even in such an attenuated form, is a valuable asset in an increasingly global world. Corporate, nonprofit, and governmental leaders increasingly have no choice but to engage in multinational cooperative endeavors. They readily appreciate the value of some common reference points. Congruent goals—in business or elsewhere—smooth the way, but things are made much easier where the informal context of conversations includes some shared sign-posts of experience and understanding.

Thus, paradoxically, this third feature of a liberal education has become even more important in a period of growing international contacts and rapid social and technological change. Common reference points make it easier to work past the inevitable mis-understandings that arise from differing cultural expectations, the nuances of different languages, and the implications of different historical experiences.

THE VALUE OF VALUES

One further practice in the traditional liberal arts education that has been regarded with some suspicion over the past few decades is reemerging as a significant asset: training students to think care-fully about values in human life. This goal is rooted in the convic-tion that both the individual and society are better off if people are trained to consider critically the consequences of their behavior for themselves and others.

In the past, a liberal education was openly and specifically value-oriented, proposing to make students more virtuous human beings. Such a claim can seem quaintly irrelevant or even danger-ous today. We are acutely aware of the pitfalls of narrow sectarian-ism, the contradictory teachings of different ethical and religious systems, and the huge divergence in human cultural practices. We may feel that the most prudent course is to avoid any claims about teaching ethics or building character in the classroom.

Thoughtful observers are concerned, however, about several fea-tures of modern society that stem from a breakdown of ethical awareness. The erosion of the standards of civility that ease hu-man interaction, the rising tolerance for cruelty and violence, the increasing incidence of cheating and fraud: these are all dis-turbing aspects of our world today. To reverse these tendencies, there is renewed emphasis on character building or civics educa-tion in primary and secondary schools, and a well-defined move-ment towards teaching ethics in professional-school curricula. Given the ancient connection between a liberal education and developing character, it seems especially shortsighted to ignore education in ethics during the undergraduate years. Thus, many campuses are developing education in ethics as part of the liberal arts experience.[6]

In its modern guise, teaching ethics does not mean imposing particular creeds or theological systems. Instead, students are taught to think clearly about ethical dilemmas just as they learn to reason more carefully in other areas. Students draw upon texts and historical models as well as extracurricular experiences that stimulate and focus their thinking and apply lessons learned in the classroom to their own lives. They are encouraged to think about what they value and admire in others and aspire to become themselves. The goal is to help students of many different religious and moral beliefs live a more ethically informed and sensitive life.

There are interesting links between this form of education and the roots and character of the liberal arts. Moral education stems from the same core axioms as liberal, moral, and social philosophy: the value of the examined life, the basic equality of members of the human species, and the ideals of individual freedom and self-control. Yet the impulse to provide ethical education derives also from themes closely identified with conservatism in our culture: respect for tradition, the concept of honor, and awareness of the fragile complexity of institutions and of the impulses towards destructive cruelty that can mar even the most beautiful human moral and religious systems.

WHAT KIND OF AN ÉLITE?

The four themes sketched out above do not cover the entire range of accomplishments of a liberal education; they do, I think, provide a good sense of the basic assumptions that lie behind this form of education and some idea of the keys to its success.

What about the audience for whom this kind of education has traditionally been intended—the children (most often, in the past, the young men) of the privileged classes, preparing to take their places in the leadership of a society, as clerics, warriors, barons, professors, artists, senators, doctors, lawyers, corporate CEOs? How

164

do we square this aspect of a liberal education with our contemporary beliefs in equality and advancement by personal merit rather than the accidents of birth?

One familiar way of dealing with this quandary is to explore the two different senses of the word *élite* that I referred to earlier. In one sense, *élite* refers to those who are privileged by class or caste. In many societies, these privileged persons are expected and given the opportunity to govern, guide, or manage others. Another meaning of *élite* embraces what Thomas Jefferson called the "aristocracy of talent," the naturally gifted of whatever social background who have the personal qualities to excel in their professions and lead other people. These are the students whom élite institutions have attempted to enroll in recent decades.

American society, like most societies these days, has mingled these two concepts in an uncertain brew. By precept (and sometimes fortunately in practice as well), we provide higher education for all who can benefit from it, without regard for family background or privileged access to resources. Yet a young person from a privileged background is clearly more likely to enroll in a school that offers a liberal education. Others may have formal access to such an education, but the access may be (or seem to be) more difficult. There are many reasons for this: the cost of the education; earnings forgone while getting it; lack of information about available scholarship and admissions opportunities; insufficient appreciation of, and thus support for, this kind of education in the family or social group; and uncertainty about what a liberal education involves and whether the student will fit in.

This gap between our goals and our achievement raises several troubling questions about élitism in our society. We need to face these questions directly and honestly if we are to understand, articulate, and carry forward our educational mission. Our colleges and universities, supported by our federal and state governments, have for many decades attempted to bridge the gap between precept and practice.[7] This was done by providing generous financial aid for talented students of all backgrounds and attempting to share information about these opportunities widely. There are signs that this commitment may be crumbling, both on campus and in government, as financial aid practices, attitudes towards affirmative action, and tax policies are changing. Given the consumerist mentality of parents and students and the benefits that accrue to an institution from recruiting talented students, financial competition among schools for the "best" students has sharpened markedly. A sense of entitlement appears to be growing up among some talented students from well-to-do families: they feel that they should be given "merit" aid to demonstrate that the college or university really values them and wants them to attend. In such a climate, the pressure to use financial aid funds to attract students from more affluent backgrounds has become significant.

Except in a handful of the very wealthiest schools, the result is a reallocation of scarce funds from disadvantaged students to those with more conventionally attractive admissions credentials. In both federal and state government, pressures from vocal middle-class families worried about the price of education, and shifts in ideology that undermine the principle of government support for an education accessible to all, have had a similar effect. The single largest source of federally supported financial aid is no longer allocated to those most in need but rather, through recent changes in tax laws, to those who vote most consistently—the middle and upper-middle classes.

If these problems are not addressed, we will see the reversal of a trend that has lasted for more than a century: the opening of selective colleges and universities to more and more gifted and ambitious students of varied backgrounds. The result will be the recreation of enclaves of the privileged that offer the benefits of a liberal education, while those from less privileged socioeconomic classes obtain their education in less desirable circumstances and with fewer opportunities. This should cause concern to anyone who worries about the increasing tendency towards a winner-take-all society in which those who have inexorably get more and those who don't fall further behind. More fundamentally, this trend should worry everyone who is committed to the ideal of a liberal education for all talented young people prepared to embark upon it and to educate one another in doing so.

Commitment to equality of access for talented students does not mean that everybody ought to be given a liberal arts education. This insight raises another issue that needs to be faced directly in defenses of this kind: Who should get a liberal education?

Statements about the worth of a liberal education make clear that the experience is valuable in fundamental ways. It affects the kind of person one becomes, the richness and satisfaction of life, and the ability to contribute meaningfully to one's community. Of my four key assumptions, only one—the third—has anything to do with a specific group or class of leaders. All the others touch on aspects of a full human life that are relevant for everyone, not just those who will occupy positions of power or special responsibility. If we can make the case for the fundamental value of a liberal education in personal growth and fulfillment, how can we justify giving the benefit of this experience to only a small number of students?

The only way to justify the present situation in our democratic society is to admit that the kind of intellectual talent that enables students to benefit from a liberal arts education, like all other forms of talent, is not evenly distributed across any population. A liberal education works best—in fact, it truly *only* works—for students who have qualities of mental acuity, curiosity, and intellectual stamina that prepare them for such a demanding regime. For those who possess this particular form of talent, a liberal education is, for the reasons I've sketched out, a wonderful preparation for life. For those who do not, other kinds of education, personal experience, and community involvement can lay the groundwork for a satisfying life. Our task as a society should not be to route everyone through the same kind of education. Instead, we should think creatively about different educations and life experiences that lead to fulfillment for people with varied talents and capacities, so that each person can have a shot at living life to the fullest. This means recognizing that a liberal education is one way, but not the only way, to prepare people for a rewarding life.

Intellectual quickness, in the form of the ability to understand complex issues and find solutions, is an essential attribute of leadership in several areas of human life. Thus it should not be surprising that there is a positive correlation between those who benefit from a liberal education and those who tend to wind up in positions of leadership. Our most pressing task is to make sure that all those in our democratic society who possess this quickness, and the aspiration for leadership, are given the best education possible. Family circumstance alone should not determine who gets such opportunities. There are many entrenched barriers to the realization of this goal, including very unequal preparations in primary and secondary school and unequal forms of family and community support and encouragement. But these barriers should not deter us from doing our best to identify talented young people early in their lives and give them the tools and encouragement they need to prepare for a liberal education.

It is important also to be clear that these generalizations hold for people of *all* backgrounds, including members of racial minorities. *The Shape of the River* provides compelling evidence that when measured by their long-term success in life and their ability to provide significant leadership for their communities, students from minority backgrounds, including those from both disadvantaged and more privileged families, benefit greatly from study in selective colleges and universities.[8] We must make sure that we are truly educating leaders for all kinds of professions and all parts of our increasingly pluralistic society.

HOW WELL DO WE LIVE UP TO OUR CLAIMS?

Some contemporary critiques of colleges and universities recognize the value of what we claim to do but fault us for falling down on the job in any one of a number of ways. These critiques take several forms. I have addressed, at least in passing, a couple of them above: that we have diluted the traditional liberal arts curriculum beyond recognition by pandering to new groups and forms of knowledge or that we have deformed our admissions standards to offer a liberal arts education to people with nontraditional preparations and many backgrounds. Although we have not addressed these issues with complete success, I am confident that we are on the right track.

Another concern of the gloomsters comes closer to hitting its target, in my view: that we do not often enough provide our students with the exhilarating educational experience promised by our ideals and our promotional brochures. To live up to what we promise requires paying close attention to the educational needs of all our students—their diverse backgrounds, personal experiences, degrees of preparation and readiness. It also requires that we put undergraduate teaching high on the priority list for support in institutions that increasingly have multiple purposes and opportunities.

Selective liberal arts colleges today, as a group, do an especially good job of emphasizing teaching while not neglecting the importance of faculty research.[9] Research universities provide a stellar alternative model. They offer students access to a broader range of courses and interdisciplinary programs and to potential involvement in truly cutting-edge research in many more fields than smaller institutions can provide—even smaller institutions of very high quality. However, because of the range of other activities and responsibilities in these larger institutions—professional education, graduate training, operating large medical complexes, distance learning, agricultural or technical research, government consulting—it is easy for the devotion to baccalaureate education to be diminished or submerged. Indeed, even liberal arts colleges are not immune to these cross-pressures.

Sustaining our ability to offer an excellent liberal arts education while fulfilling all our multiple missions requires an imaginative, multifaceted strategy and the institutional will to pursue it.[10] We must think in new ways about the activity of teaching, the interconnections between teaching and research, the value of information technology, the role of graduate students, and our expectations of both partners in the close student-faculty engagement that we call a liberal arts education.

WHAT MATTERS TO THE FACULTY?

According to our critics, the key to our problem lies here: most professors at a modern research university teach infrequently and ineffectively, spending their time in esoteric research of dubious social value to impress their professional peers and carve out an easy sinecure for life. What really motivates faculty members? Most young professionals who choose to become faculty members in a school of arts and sciences assume that they will teach undergraduates, and many look forward eagerly to doing so. They have recent experience of great teachers with passion and charisma, teachers who inspired their own vocation. They also recall dull or distant teachers and are convinced that they would never inflict such poor teaching on their own students.

Over time, this fresh eagerness is dissipated by the realities of professional life. Faculty members at a research university are expected to engage in many types of work—teaching undergraduates, supervising graduate students, research, service to the discipline, consulting, service to the university—as well as to juggle family and personal responsibilities. In stark contrast to the stereotype of the "lazy professor," many, perhaps most, faculty members work intensely, for long hours. Overwork is only part of the problem. Teachers are also subject to "burnout" over time, unless they can refresh their skills and reignite their excitement in the classroom. As more undergraduates come to college deficient in basic skills, teaching introductory material can be especially onerous. It is easy to become jaded with entering the mind of the uninitiated, with bringing yet another generation up to speed in the rudiments of the discipline.

For all these reasons, hours spent teaching tend to become fewer, rather than more, as faculty members develop other professional skills and find it rewarding to exercise them. My generalization holds not only for indifferent teachers but even for professors with well-developed skills who enjoy their students. The linguistic conventions that refer to teaching *loads* and research *opportunities*; the effectiveness of promising a very light course load when wooing a faculty superstar to another university; the appeal of time released from teaching as a reward for service on campus— all of these demonstrate this consistent preference.

Yet most scholars continue to prefer the university campus and its multigenerational set of scholars to the rarified atmosphere of a research institute, except for the occasional sabbatical. The urge to share one's knowledge with others, to lead others along the path of discovery in one's discipline, continues to be one of the major motivations for the life of scholarship, for mature as well as younger professors. So why is research, especially, preferred to teaching as an intellectual pursuit?

Part of the answer lies in the incentive structure for faculty members. Research universities—and increasingly, other types of institutions—rely heavily on research productivity in making decisions about which faculty members to employ for the long term. It is easier for administrators to obtain "objective" estimates of successful research than of successful teaching, at least by the metrics that we conventionally employ. Asking other professionals to judge their peers' research provides the most clear-cut way of deciding which professors are likely to continue to be productive, highly regarded members of the faculty.

Successful research is the best single indicator of that elusive trait we call "quality of mind," the intellectual sharpness and vigor that we want to ensure in our faculties. If professional peers find work provocative and relevant, this is our best indication that faculty members will teach their students material that is fresh, challenging, and well grounded, rather than simply read from lecture notes designed to play well to an undergraduate audience. Research success also transfers easily from one institution to another and thus makes a faculty member potentially more marketable. This has obvious implications for differentials in salary and status.

Our conventional assessment structures thus provide powerful incentives for ambitious faculty members to concentrate on research. But it would be wrong to assume that these incentives are the only factor. The joys of pure research are great, and the fruits of successful intellectual endeavors are profoundly rewarding both personally and to one's students and colleagues. For many faculty members, nothing is more exhilarating than a discovery that works out as the researcher passionately believed it would. In many more cases than the public usually recognizes, research results are also important to society as a whole. Even apparent candidates for the infamous Golden Fleece Award can be unexpectedly fruitful in helping us to understand ourselves and the world. The structure of ancient, "dead" languages, for example, can form the basis of our most sophisticated computer languages today.

However, teaching can also be a deeply rewarding activity. A brilliantly successful lecture or seminar can be as exhilarating as any other experience in life. Indeed, unless a faculty member is one of a handful of truly outstanding scholars in his or her field, teaching is often more likely to be rewarding than research, since path-breaking research findings are less likely to be part of one's daily fare. Because our systems for professional assessment and establishing salary and other forms of institutional support as well as our professional status systems are so intricately bound up with research success, however, it is difficult for a professor who cares deeply about teaching to sustain this passion in the face of multiple institutional messages that research is more valued. If research universities are to be successful in sustaining a strong liberal arts education as part of their mission, they will have to change this. Teaching must be deeply valued, and our incentive and reward structures must reflect this valuation.

RETHINKING THE INCENTIVE STRUCTURE

All faculty members at élite research universities and liberal arts colleges should be expected to demonstrate their ability to do research and remain current in their fields. But every faculty member should not be judged simply by the standards of the most productive researchers, as though research were the only thing that mattered in the university. Faculty members and administrators need to work together to find more reliable ways to measure excellence in teaching and then provide significant rewards to professionals who teach well. Both institutional recognition and generous salary increases should be realistic goals for fine teachers, not only for scholars with strong name recognition on other campuses.

One of the most notable features on campus these days is the changing composition of the professoriate. Fewer scholars are hired for conventional tenure-track posts; more are employed in part-time or full-time contract work, with an emphasis on teaching. Research expectations for these faculty members are much less than for tenure-track professors, and it is important that they feel valued by their institutions and be motivated to teach well. This is another reason for making sure that we reward fine teaching and demonstrate our esteem for those who excel in this craft. The issue is one of reallocating limited institutional resources. It would be unrealistic to expect that salary competition and demand for the faculty members most productive in their research will dramatically diminish, but we can bend our efforts towards cutting back on other institutional expenditures to free up money to support good teaching.

A professor invited to join the faculty of arts and sciences in an institution that aspires to offer a fine liberal arts education should expect to engage in undergraduate teaching. The alternative—a two-tiered faculty, with one part concentrating solely on research and graduate education, and the other on undergraduate teaching —may have been successful in certain institutions in the past. But the costs in morale can be significant, with damaging results for the enterprise of undergraduate education. The graduate faculty risk losing as well the intellectual energy and zest that come from involvement with bright undergraduates.

In any case, a significant portion of the budget of the arts and sciences division of any modern college or university is provided by tuition-paying parents of undergraduates or by state funding provided specifically to make such an education possible. This makes it imperative for us to involve some of the energies of virtually all faculty members in the endeavor of providing high-quality teaching as one of the obligations of their employment. To do so successfully, we need to find ways to sustain the love of teaching in young faculty members even as they encounter significant incentives to engage in other activities.

RETHINKING THE TEACHER'S CRAFT

Teaching and research are, ideally, deeply symbiotic. Helping students to understand the process of discovery and engaging them in some form of independent inquiry should be one of the basic goals of a liberal arts education. At the same time, sharing knowledge and learning from the questions and insights of students can jolt a teacher's stagnant preconceptions and suggest whole new ways of looking at the world. This, at least, is the ideal. In reality, of course, neither teaching nor research is always exhilarating. Both pursuits involve repetitive work that is not inherently rewarding. Few teachers look forward to grading, but then neither do we enjoy writing yet another peer review of a badly written research paper for potential publication. Like every profession, scholarship involves both routine work and intellectual excitement. It is important to find ways to keep the routine to a minimum and introduce new sources of intellectual excitement.

Preeminent among these sources should be the new instructional technologies. It is true that cyberspace can never match the unique advantages of the physical place where students live and learn together, with multiple opportunities for education both inside and outside the classroom. And the personal interaction between teacher and student will always remain central to the particular qualities of liberal learning. But the amplification of new, exciting ways of conveying and sharing knowledge can be one of the most important ways of preserving the excitement of teaching for faculty members and of involving students deeply in their own education. Rather than see new technologies as a threat to the liberal arts, we should take full advantage of their radical possibilities.

Well-designed computer programs are effective substitutes for routine drills in language instruction and can provide introductory materials in a variety of disciplines. At the other end of the spectrum of learning, computer assistance in doing independent study can facilitate student and faculty research. Mid- or upper-level courses can be enlivened with clever exercises and simulations, increasingly available in every discipline. In certain fields, programs for grading quizzes on basic material are available and will surely become even more sophisticated. Communication among students and between students and faculty members is enhanced by the use of electronic mail, chat rooms, syllabi and question sets posted on the Web, and numerous other electronic aids. With appropriate incentives and support, faculty members can find exciting new ways of conceptualizing material to be shared in class.

These ways of rethinking the teacher's craft promise also to make better use of faculty time with students. The lecture format works well for faculty members who are gifted in presentation and skilled at involving even large classes in substantive classroom discussion. For many faculty members, however, there are better ways to spend teaching time. As more material is shared through innovative computer programs and less in the conventional lecture format, more time is available for seminars, discussion sections, one-on-one research projects, small group tutorials, and other forms of close interaction that clearly bring benefits to student learning.

Supporting faculty members who want to think freshly about familiar material through team teaching with a colleague from another discipline; rotating courses so that no faculty member is permanently "stuck" with an undesirable assignment; encouraging faculty members who are talented teachers to provide guidance to colleagues in settings where guidance is not directly tied to the assessment process—all these and many other ways of helping teachers to rethink their craft should be developed on every campus, and the best practices should be shared with colleagues elsewhere.

Faculty members should also think in fresh ways about the role of graduate teaching assistants. Too often, TAs are assigned the routine tasks of teaching, those associated with the mundane drudgery of the craft. As a result, they have a hard time getting excited about teaching or learning much about its splendid opportunities. To compound the problem, parents and students regard them as a deficiency in the program of the university. Employing TAs is seen as inserting an intermediate layer between the student and the "real" professor.

In fact, with the right opportunities and support, many graduate teaching assistants are outstanding teachers, having the high degree of excitement and fresh commitment that comes with the first opportunity to engage in their professional craft. Many have an insouciant ability to communicate ideas directly and effectively to undergraduates. Giving TAs the chance to participate in designing their courses, reconceptualize the material, and discuss their experiences with the professor and other graduate students not only trains TAs to teach but also contributes significantly to the richness of the undergraduate experience. By the time they have almost completed their dissertations, many graduate students can do a fine job of teaching a course on their own, especially with appropriate guidance and support from faculty members in their field. Conceived and carried forward in this way, the use of graduate teaching assistants can be a real plus for the university curriculum, a venture in intergenerational scholarly discovery rather than a deficit.

Finally, it is important for faculty members—and indeed for universities and colleges more generally—to clarify the institution's expectations of undergraduate students. One of the primary sources of burnout among teachers is student apathy. If students come to our campuses for an undergraduate degree assuming that the admissions process is the ultimate test, that they can float through four years with a "punched ticket" and work only on things that immediately appeal to them, the implicit bargain that we call liberal education is not possible. We need to be clear from the start about the institutional expectations for what students should contribute to this partnership.

Candidates for a degree in the liberal arts should be aware that they have been chosen for their intellectual promise and apparent aptitude for the demands of a particular form of learning. Students, and their parents, should understand that a high degree of intellectual engagement and a willingness to live through periods of intellectual austerity, difficulty, and challenge are essential to a successful education and its promise for greater personal and professional reward in later life. If students are not willing or able to operate within these constraints, they should be encouraged to find some other form of preparation for the future.

In a speech to the graduating class of Duke University in 1931, President William Preston Few said, "As I look back over the life of man, I think I can trace a long historic conflict that has been waged through all civilization between beauty and fullness of life without a moral meaning, on the one hand, and austerity and barrenness along with religious intensity, on the other." Few went on to speculate on the unresolved conflict in the human spirit, which "has produced that strange ebb and flow so conspicuous in all human history. It has always been difficult for human society to preserve the gains made generation after generation, and any high and enduring civilization still awaits the synthetic power . . . to combine a full and beautiful living with moral energy and enthusiasm for the causes of humanity."[11]

Few's description of this historic struggle reminds us that it has never been easy for societies to combine material success, aesthetic achievement, and technological progress with a true belief in the dignity and value of every person and a moral commitment that all should share in the benefits of a good life. Failure to achieve this synthesis has, as Few notes, contributed to the decline of many civilizations over time.

One of the main purposes of a liberal arts education today should be to prepare tomorrow's leaders to tackle this challenge. Of course a liberal arts education provides no guarantee that leaders will avoid Few's dilemma; some of history's most vivid examples of failures to achieve his ideal had a classical education. Nonetheless, building a "high and enduring civilization" that effectively melds both these impulses is an aspiration worth instilling in our students. And today as in the past, a strong liberal arts education provides our best hope that leaders might understand both the power and the difficulty of this goal and dedicate themselves to achieving it.

"You Say You Want a Revolution?" Well . . .

Let me put my own cards on the table at the beginning: I speak not as a latter-day Luddite, but as someone who finds information technology in higher education intriguing and powerful in many ways.

My own Duke University, like many others, has used distance education to good effect to bring together widely scattered audiences—MBA students on different continents, as well as nurses in rural hospitals in eastern North Carolina.

But my assignment is to put all this into some kind of historic perspective—and to remind us of features of the traditional university that we should try to preserve as we contemplate the coming revolution.

My tag-line quotation, in case you didn't recognize it, is from those forward-looking scholars, the Beatles. John Lennon's words, written in a highly revolutionary year, 1968, were as follows:

> You say you want a revolution,
> Well, you know,
> We all want to change the world.
> But when you talk about destruction,
> Don't you know you can count me out.
> Don't you know it's gonna be all right.
> All right, all right.

In that vein, I will make four points, very concisely, so that we have ample time to discuss this fascinating topic.

First, the doomsayers are wrong. Second, predicting the future is very difficult. Third, quite a few things about the traditional university will endure because they are valued and valuable, whether or not we take any particular steps to preserve them. Fourth, some other features of our institutions are also very much worth preserving, but may well not be sustained unless we take special effort to protect them.

THE DOOMSAYERS ARE WRONG

Everyone's favorite guru, Peter Drucker, made a prediction six or seven years ago. Thirty years from now, he said, the big university campuses will be relics. Already we are beginning to deliver more lectures and classes off campus by satellite or two-way video at a fraction of the cost. The college won't survive as a residential institution.

I am quite confident that he was wrong about that—superficial on one count and premature on the other. Drucker underestimated the cost of high-quality distance learning; as we have learned, these are very expensive things to do well, and we have not yet reaped any benefits from the technological revolution in terms of dramatic cost cutting for an educational product of equal quality— although we will very probably find that we can do so in the future.

And Drucker was far too pessimistic about the demise of universities. These are profoundly resilient institutions.

The advent of the printing press was regarded by some doomsayers as ending university education, since everyone could have easy access to information and would have little reason to undertake the arduous regime of the trivium or quadrivium. As we know, the academy changed in some ways but persisted, grew, and flourished in the new environment.

And I take some comfort from two predictions made about higher education more recently. One was an earlier version of Drucker forty or fifty years ago, in the form of several confident predictions that the invention of television would make schools and colleges obsolete. The other was a proposal in 1899 from the commissioner of the U.S. Patent Office to the administration in Washington suggesting that the office be closed down on the grounds that everything had already been invented.

The new world of instructional technology is highly competitive, as institutions scramble to be the first to offer a particular kind of degree on line or to develop new venues for our educational products. We assume, on shrewd historical evidence, that being first in the field and establishing a reputation as the obvious provider can bring considerable benefit.

But being on the "bleeding edge" carries peculiar risks, as well as the formidable costs of start-ups and initial investments. The barriers to entry are substantial, and requirements include much more than the ability to design a great website.

In a book entitled *The Innovator's Dilemma*, Professor Clayton Christensen of Harvard Business School described how great companies have floundered when they have ignored "disruptive technologies" that drove changes in economies, markets, and products.[1] These technologies are not immediately recognized as threats by mainstream institutions; at first they seem eccentric or peripheral, so they are not taken seriously. In higher education, it is easy to argue that on-line learning is just such a disruptive technology, and in many ways this undoubtedly is true.

However, one of the lessons of Christensen's book is that it is very difficult for mainstream leaders—all of us in this room—to know just what innovative technologies are going to do. If we could know that, we would never be blindsided.

We are early enough in the infotech revolution, I would argue, that the same applies to us. It's clearly big, but big in what ways, and with what effects? Extrapolating from past trends is overly simplistic—and overprediction about the "brave new world," as Prospero warned Miranda in *The Tempest*, is a risky affair. When the euphoria dissipates, the passionate belief in distance learning may encounter the same fate as passionate belief in the "new economy."

The message here is, of course, how difficult it is—as with all revolutions—to predict the course these new technologies will take, and foolhardy to assume that we can today see clearly the details of the path ahead. Nonetheless, we have to be able to plan and navigate, not just drift, and formalizing strategy requires that we make some predictions about the future. So I will do just that.

DURABLE TRADITIONAL FEATURES OF OUR INSTITUTIONS ARE LIKELY TO SURVIVE

While the revolution unfolds, there are some things that are likely to last, without requiring our special efforts to support or sustain them, simply because they are so valuable and valued.

One example is undergraduate residential education, developed in the United Kingdom and widely imitated around the world, especially in the United States. This sort of education provides a distinctive combination of academic experience with other aspects of life that we call "extracurricular"—social life, clubs of every conceivable variety, sports, dormitory living, volunteer service—all of which adds up to an eagerly awaited and nostalgically remembered part of life for many young people in our society.

The experience is valued for several reasons—some not particularly admirable, but no less durable for that: the reputational cachet of the degree, the proven financial benefits that come with it, and even the disinclination of parents to have eighteen-year-olds around the house for four more years earning their degrees on line upstairs.

But some of the reasons why we value the experience are more admirable. It can indeed be an important rite of passage, a way of developing and maturing that depends precisely on the context, the whole environment, the interplay of different activities in a very personal and direct experience. It is not possible to replicate that experience in cyberspace, and it is not likely to disappear in the near future.

A second example is the path to the Ph.D. Some research can be done on line, of course, and many of the powers of new information technologies are enhancing doctoral education every day. But this is in no way a substitute for the mentoring that professors provide to doctoral candidates—a direct and personal experience that is very hard to replicate in all its fullness on line.

These earliest and core scholarly experiences are thus likely to be sustained in something not too far from their traditional forms, I would predict. They will be enhanced and deepened by the powers of information technology, which bring as much to the curious first-year student as to the thesis writer. Information technology will allow for study abroad with connections to home, and for combinations of courses brought together in imaginative new forms. The possibilities are endless.

But the key factor here, and my major point this morning, is that the combination of place and cyberspace is precisely what is so powerful, and this is almost certain to remain a dominant theme.

Cyberspace alone is a pale imitation of real physical contact, but cyberspace brings a whole new dimension to an education that also retains a spatial dimension. Places may change their character, but they will continue in some form to be crucial.

In every aspect of education—traditional, professional, executive, continuing—the ideal goal will be some distinctive combination, a combination different for each type of learning. In some—executive, continuing—cyberspace alone can be a pretty good substitute, even, in some cases, preferable. But the most interesting and durable forms of education, I would predict, will include both types of space.

As I'm sure most of us are aware, MIT recently made a breathtaking announcement: our colleagues there have decided to spend $100 million in the next few years putting instructional materials for all their courses on the Web—lectures, syllabi, attachments, reading lists. The curious, bright high school student in Pakistan or the isolated scholar in Paraguay will be able to tap into the rich materials of MIT's great faculty immediately and at almost no cost beyond that of adequate communications equipment.

This indeed is a brave new world! Early reactions from some people were: "Won't this render an MIT education unnecessary?"

That seems very unlikely. Our colleagues are betting—and I agree—that it will simply enhance the sum of information available to others, provide models and examples, open new doors, increase knowledge powerfully for the whole world, and provide wonderful publicity and name recognition for MIT, making it even more likely that people around the world will want to come to

Cambridge to learn even more from the authors of these syllabi or confer with them at their symposia.

In this connection, I would affirm with conviction, lies the durable appeal of intellectual community as the core of the university.

We keep hearing about the cyberspace "community" and how technology has enabled or will enable us to sustain virtual learning communities free from the tyranny of time and space. But the jury is still out on whether cyberspace connections, as fascinating and powerful and addictive as they apparently have become, create communities in any true sense—or whether the student seated in front of her computer is still, in Robert Putnam's famous phrase, "bowling alone."

There will certainly be new types of institutions to provide new services, and familiar institutions will be changed and modified to perform new functions, but through all this universities will continue to do a pretty good job of organizing the way knowledge is delivered. The resilience that our institutions have shown in the past few decades will continue, I predict, to make these ancient institutions, in some recognizable form, durable and relevant in the years ahead.

Residential communities have challenged every generation of students to learn how to deal with difference—never more so than today. And never has it been more important to do so, given the increasingly close interconnections of our world.

There is also a third aspect of traditional universities that will survive: some loose, perhaps transforming version of our institutional core, our governance, structure, and support—what we call administration.

Networks will grow, yes, but anarchy is very unlikely to prevail—there will be structures for providing knowledge—and they will most likely be recognizable versions of universities.

We should not be too concerned about how closely these new structures will parallel our familiar forms. However, for the user—and increasingly, with certain types of education, for the provider as well—on-line education can be considerably less expensive and far more convenient than place-based learning. This leads me to my fourth and final point.

Some features of the traditional university may indeed become obsolete unless we make deliberate efforts to support them for the
important values that they bring.

Access, especially to undergraduate, campus-based education,
is one such feature. The danger is that as more and more varieties of on-line degrees become available, including baccalaureates
in cyberspace, and as they become less and less expensive as new
technologies and new modes of delivery of knowledge are per-
fected, the baccalaureate residential experience will once again
become the province of the wealthy and privileged—as it was up
through the nineteenth century.

If this happens, both our societies and our universities will be
impoverished. Education does not work nearly as well among ho-
mogenous students; they will have a very distorted view of the
world, will be less well prepared to manage and partner with diverse workforces and colleagues; their prejudices will be reinforced
and their horizons left narrow. And many deserving young people
who could profit greatly from a distinctive residential education
and contribute much to the education of their fellows will never
know this opportunity.

The solution? Renewed commitment to need-based financial
aid and making university, government, and social resources available to support this priority.

Another feature that may need special protection is a sense of
community and belonging among the faculty. We may well find
that we need to provide deliberate incentives to sustain this sense
and to prevent faculty members from becoming independent contractors—deprived of the networks of cross-disciplinary contacts
that a real community provides, immured in their narrow disciplinary networks, and responsive mainly to the financial opportunities of the best deal for going on line.

The durable thread here is the long experience of the benefits of
such community for all concerned, even if individuals sometimes
see their interests elsewhere. But both our society and the univer-

sities—and all of the individuals involved—stand to lose in the longer term if the faculty's sense of belonging together disappears for good.

The solutions lie in finding ways to encourage retention of membership in the academic community through appropriate rewards for on-line exploration and development of new intellectual property on campus rather than forcing those activities outside—and being ready to spend real dollars to recruit and retain committed teacher-scholars as full-time, tenured members of the university community with reasons to care about the place and help steward it, rather than succumb to the temptation of hiring contract employees who have no loyalty to the institution and no reason to feel committed to sustaining it.

A final example of a university feature that may need special protection is the strong and admirable tradition of providing—through research, outreach, and civic participation—service to the community, nation, and world, something that is very difficult to do in cyberspace.

Over time, especially in the United States, through the land-grant universities and the great public universities and community colleges, and more and more through private institutions as well, we have compiled an admirable record of making a difference in our cities, our neighborhoods, our regions—through volunteering, involvement, leadership, example. In a time when other bulwarks of community and pro bono service are under increasing pressure, if we wish to sustain the many benefits of livable communities where people care about their schools and other benefits, it would be foolish indeed to let the historic and crucial participation of faculty and students in these enterprises be gradually dissolved.

Powerful forces—intellectual and financial—are moving higher education in the direction of increasing reliance on information technology. We are in an age of exploration: the landscape is still largely uncharted. We would do well to consider carefully what seeds we plant in this brave new world, so that we can concentrate on cultivating those most likely to bear fruit for our students.

To end on an optimistic note, I quote from the Durban seminar cosponsored by the American Council on Education and CHET in August 2000. The author is not noted but may well be in this room: "If [universities] are not flexible enough, they may become redundant. . . . But if they are too flexible, they may cease to be universities, at any rate in a recognizable form. If they abandon their commitment to liberal learning, to critical knowledge, to disinterested scholarship and science—in other words if they sacrifice their core, their fundamental values on the altar of novelty—universities may not be worth defending. . . . Of all the institutions created by human effort it is difficult to find one more benevolent, more creative, more emancipatory, more dynamic than the University. It is hard to believe that such an institution will not continue to be central to our aspirations, individual and collective."

When Should a College

President Use the Bully Pulpit?

Like many other college presidents, I have often been called on to speak out, or have been criticized for not speaking out, on some issue of public moment. This has led me to wrestle mightily with the question of whether "the university," in some form, should make its voice heard on issues of great public importance or concern.

What does it mean for "the university" to take a stand? As universities become increasingly complex, with multiple purposes and very diverse memberships, how and when can one person claim to speak for the whole institution?

Few would deny that faculty members and students, as individuals, have the right to say whatever they wish—signing petitions, writing op-eds, making speeches. Such statements are inevitably interpreted by some irritated readers as implicating the whole university, but most people readily understand the distinction between the views of an individual faculty member and a formal statement by the institution. The complications arise when those of us who have responsibility for the leadership of the institution as a whole speak out about controversial subjects.

We may claim that we do so only as individuals, that we don't abnegate our individual right to free speech by taking the job of president. Yet such a stance is not easily sustained in practice. Anything a president says about controversial issues while in office can be taken as an official statement. It's very hard for observers to separate the person from the position.

Furthermore, if an officer takes a substantive stand on a thorny topic, those on the campus who hold the opposite point of view may be less likely to speak out—especially if they lack power and job security—even if the senior officer has no intention of silencing anyone. In this way, if a university leader takes a position that he or she believes to be in the public interest, that action unintentionally can create a potential chilling effect on the campus and thwart the robust exchange of ideas.

Must university presidents therefore be silent on all controversial public issues? Many people would defend that position. They would argue that no one can legitimately speak "for the university," and that our best course of action is to focus on ensuring the unabated free play of argument and counterargument among others.

That stance has merit, but it neglects the positive potential of using the "bully pulpit" of a university presidency. It also ignores the fact that some major issues affecting society also have significant implications for universities. When they do, silence may be dangerous, since the field will be left to those who understand little about higher education.

Therefore, I find it useful to distinguish three kinds of issues—although they are often blurred in practice—for a president trying to decide when and how to speak out. They present successive degrees of difficulty.

The easiest cases are those where a topic has clear relevance to the other public purposes of the university. Few would deny that the president ought to make his or her voice heard when the basic goals of the university are at stake: support for research, financial aid that makes education more accessible, academic freedom. People on and off campus may not agree about the specific comments that the president should make, but the connection to the university's well-being is undeniable.

More difficult are cases where the university has an interest but the connection is less clear-cut—for example, drug use, gun control, or health care. We cannot function well if people pack heat in the classrooms or regularly hold up our students. That became very clear to me a few years ago when a disgruntled ex-employee walked into my office and held my secretaries hostage at gunpoint. University medical centers depend heavily on policy decisions about the type of services they should provide, who should receive them, and how they should be paid for. However, people who live and work on our campuses are likely to hold widely differing views as citizens on these matters. As a result, a president should use care in deciding whether and how to speak out on those sorts of issues.

Finally, there are issues like divestment from South Africa, support for the government of Israel or the rights of Palestinians, the war in Iraq, corporate ethics, sweatshops, and boycotts. People seriously disagree about whether the university should become involved in such matters at all. To some, these issues are so tenuously connected with the fortunes of the university, and the range of political disagreement is so broad, that no good case can be made for bringing the university formally into the discussion. For others, the issues have such profound consequences for our society that it seems imperative for a respected institution—and, by implication, its leaders—to try to influence the outcome. It is in those areas that presidents must determine their course of action very deliberately, realizing that a large contingent of those who care about the university will criticize whatever presidents do—including doing nothing.

Especially in those vexed third-order cases, a president might well want to distinguish between speaking out as an individual and speaking for the university. Although I have already noted that it is difficult to sustain the distinction in practice, in certain instances it is worth trying.

For example, I recently addressed a conference on the campus on corporate ethics and took a strong stand that boards of directors should be actively involved in ensuring accountability and trustworthiness in the corporations that they lead. Because of my years as a corporate board member and my training in political and ethical philosophy, I considered myself to be speaking as a corporate director and an ethicist, rather than making an official statement for Duke University—and that is how I believe my audience heard my remarks. Nonetheless, that I am president of Duke was the reason I was asked to speak to the group, and I am sure that this penumbra colored what was heard.

Similarly, I have regularly expressed my general concern about sweatshops. But it could be said that I was speaking "*for* the university" when, only after due procedures and consultation, decisions were made that Duke would join the Fair Labor Association and the Worker Rights Consortium, and I announced those decisions. Thus, I draw a salient distinction between speaking out and making policy, between expressing an opinion and taking steps that commit the university as a whole to particular types of actions. In close cases, I might note this distinction and try to make clear which type of statement is on the table, even as I realize that the distinction is difficult for others to acknowledge.

Whenever I must decide when and how to speak out, I consider a few key questions. They don't yield easy answers, but they represent the kinds of filters that I think presidents should employ:

> How important is the moral principle involved? Are human rights and liberties at stake?
>
> How clear-cut are the moral issues—are there strong moral arguments on both sides of a dilemma, or is the preponderance of moral argument in favor of one side?
>
> How close to the university is the issue at stake, and how much involvement does it have in the question?
>
> Am I called upon by other thoughtful and engaged people in the university to exercise judgment and take a stand on this issue, or rather am I going out looking for dragons to slay?
>
> Do I have any special competence or experience that might give more credibility to the expression of opinion and make it more likely to be sound?

It can sometimes also be relevant for a president to assess how many people on the campus would agree with a stand that he or she might take, and proceed if there is considerable sentiment in favor of that stand. Yet in some situations a president may be bound in conscience to speak out, even if most people on the campus take the opposite view.

In fact, quite a few people these days deplore the idea that university presidents have become a bunch of wimps, concerned only with raising money and keeping the peace—pale shadows of the giants who walked the earth in ages past, whom an entire society revered as moral arbiters. I have no desire to be a wimp, but also no illusions about becoming widely recognized as a moral arbiter even if I wanted to. That's simply not the way things work in our society of sound bites and talk shows, a society that no longer easily accords moral leadership to anybody in whatever post.

However, I find it hard to accept the view that many of my colleagues in university presidencies would affirm: that the only place we can stand comfortably as presidents is on some neutral middle ground, that our only role is to protect unimpaired free speech for others and the right of both sides are heard. Some of my colleagues believe, as an argument for neutrality, that both sides in contentious issues are attempting to capture the "moral authority" of the university. But if that "moral authority" is never used by those who can speak for the university, then in what sense is there any moral authority at all? Moral authority is eroded and devalued if it is used too often; but if it is never used, it becomes moribund.

I do sometimes feel morally bound to speak out as president of Duke. And I am well aware that the authority of my office lends weight to what I say. My responsibility, I would argue, is neither to be silent nor to chime in on every possible occasion, but to think very carefully about how I use that kind of influence, and never to do so lightly.

Are We There Yet?

*Address for the Thirtieth Anniversary Celebration, Institute for
Research on Women and Gender, Stanford University, 3 November 2004*

Good evening to everyone. I'm truly honored to be part of this
celebration, to see good friends and confirm the importance of this
institute to the university and to all of us.

My title is taken from a common experience on family auto-
mobile vacation trips: hardly have you left the city limits of your
home town than one of the children will ask, "Are we there yet?"
The "we" tonight is all of us—women and men, in our country and
around the world. In the aftermath of the election, we are deeply
aware of how our country needs to move forward, we hope together, and the jagged divisions that make it difficult for us to do
so. And the "there" in this journey that I'm especially concerned
about tonight is a world in which gender contributes to human
personhood and creativity without overly constraining individuals
in stereotypical roles.

Are we there yet? The short answer is no; the more helpful answer is that we are in some demonstrable ways further along the
road than we were when we last asked the question here at CROW
and IRWG, in 1974 or 1984 or 1999, and that has to be good news.

This talk is dedicated to two friends who contributed enor-
mously to research on women and gender, and thus to moving us
ahead on this journey together. They were both crucial members of
this community, and both died untimely deaths: Shelly Rosaldo
and Susan Moller Okin. Their contributions are revealed as more
and more important with every passing day; they were uncommon
women, and we miss them greatly.

First, a word about the journey we've taken over the last thirty years, the journey we celebrate tonight, by the Center for Research on Women and the Institute for Research on Women and Gender. These institutions have traveled an impressive road, and have, we believe, an even brighter future.

Those of us who were present at the creation in 1974 and the years immediately following envisioned a truly pioneering venture, radical for the time or indeed for any time in history. The Center for Research on Women brought together a large proportion of the active women scholars at Stanford (of which there were—and are—too few), and also some sympathetic men, to launch research on women at a time when this topic was quite marginal to what serious people did. The scholars engaged in this research—faculty members, affiliated researchers, graduate students—were so excited about the enterprise that they reached out with missionary zeal and brought others into the fold. It was such an exhilarating place to be that even those of us with disciplinary expertise in entirely different fields (and that was true of almost everyone at the time) were caught up in the fervor, and had our lives and work transformed.

We played by feminist rules, which meant that we spent a great deal of time in discussion and consciousness raising; not the most efficient way to get things done, but a great way to form close intellectual bonds. We made a successful bid for the editorship of SIGNS, which provided a wonderful opportunity to work together to shape an emerging field. In 1980 CROW's Task Force on the Study of Women at Stanford recommended the formation of an undergraduate program in feminist studies. The choice of the name was contentious but deliberate, at a time when women's studies programs were being founded around the country; the university administration accepted the proposal nonetheless, as it had supported the founding of CROW. Alumnae returned to celebrate the twentieth anniversary of feminist studies at Stanford in 2001.

As we were reminded in the faculty panel this afternoon, the work done across the years by researchers first at CROW and then at the Institute for Research on Women and Gender has fulfilled the hopes of the early pioneers, making a real difference in the world, exploring many different fields, prompting fruitful intellectual collaborations, opening up new areas of discovery. The institute is now well established, involving many people as engaged scholars, associates, interested students, and staff. It is one of hundreds of centers for research on women and gender around the world, having provided a template and shown the way. But there is more work to be done to establish the institute on a firm financial footing, and the work of scholarship of course is never done.

Londa notes that one of the major areas of research that the institute will be pursuing in the coming year is "how employing gender analytics has contributed to human knowledge."[1] That's a very important, and very exciting, question. Thirty years ago, our goal was to get people in the university to pay significant attention to the lives and work of women; we've made a lot of progress towards that goal, but there is still a pernicious sense abroad that research on women and gender is a specialized niche that can be done well or badly but doesn't make much difference to the "real world" of mainstream scholarship, whatever that mainstream may be in your particular discipline. Those of us here tonight know that isn't true, but we're having a hard time convincing some of our colleagues, and making this case clearly will be a significant contribution.

Thus, as far as IRWG is concerned, we are not "there yet," but we are impressively far along the way. The leaders and supporters across the decades who have made this happen deserve our celebration, and our gratitude. Yet none of us is ready to declare victory and go home, in the sense of believing that all gender problems have been solved, that we know all we need to know about these topics, that there are no special challenges left so we can go on to other things. Far from it: the depth and importance of the work that lies ahead is at least as breathtaking as what we faced in the mid-1970s, and that opportunity and challenge are what we celebrate tonight.

THE JOURNEY IN THE LARGER WORLD

I am well aware that the whole image of a "journey" as a way of discussing gender issues may be problematic. How do we know we are heading anywhere, rather than just going around in circles or wandering aimlessly through the wilderness? And how can we plausibly speak of "we" when there are so many different human beings with lives that overlap only in the most marginal—or the most basic—ways?

I do believe that there are ways in which progress for women in general terms can be measured, and I believe that progress for women wherever it occurs is progress for our entire species. With Charles Fourier, the eccentric but brilliant nineteenth-century utopian socialist, I believe that the progress of women towards full personhood, respect, and a wider range of opportunities in our lives is not only the best measure of human progress, but the most powerful engine of that progress too. (When I went back to check that reference, by the way, I found that I had gotten it years ago from Susan Bell and Karen Offen, *Women, the Family and Freedom*—one of the many products of the last thirty years of research at IRWG!)[2]

Let me suggest several dimensions or areas of human life that one can look to to determine whether progress has occurred. I will point to eight of those, not because I think the list exhaustive but because I believe that all the areas are important and that we have enough knowledge to measure how well we are doing. In no particular order, they are:

- the extent to which women hold authority or positions of leadership in a society;
- the degree of flexibility in household and domestic arrangements;
- good provisions for the care of children;
- control over sexual and reproductive choices;
- a reduction in sexual harassment, or an increase in the sense of safety and security in the workplace and the world;
- access to education;
- chances for meaningful work, getting good jobs, equal pay, and opportunities for promotion;
- the degree to which cultural depictions of women acknowledge our personhood rather than dwelling solely on female sexuality.

Clearly the specific meaning of these indicators will be different in different societies. In some developing countries, where women have been enclosed within domestic walls and denied opportunities for education and economic advancement, access to education may mean learning to read and write, and economic opportunity the chance to secure a small loan in order to sell produce or handicrafts. In western industrial societies, access to education means that all professional schools and fields of study are equally open to women and men through the final degree, and economic opportunity may mean the opportunity to aim realistically to be the CEO of a Fortune 500 company, if that's your goal in life.

If I were grading our progress in the United States today, I'd give us anywhere from an A− to an F on these eight measures, scoring us higher in areas such as education, and lower in areas such as the cultural depictions of women as persons.

I will support my contentions by illustrating what we learned at Duke University two years ago when we undertook a comprehensive women's initiative on campus. Before I turn to that body of evidence, however, I want to say a few more words about how a couple of these areas interact to support or impede human progress.

PUBLIC AND PRIVATE CONUNDRUMS

As a political philosopher, I have always been struck by the degree to which success for women in what we conventionally call the "public realm" depends on progress in the "private realm" as well. These two terms are mightily contentious in feminist theory these days. But whether a woman who chooses to form a family can aim realistically for holding authority or getting promoted in a demanding job depends fundamentally on the state of her household. Does she have sole responsibility for the domestic arrangements and child care? Does her partner support, encourage, and facilitate her ambitions?

This problem is boringly familiar, indeed axiomatic, although that doesn't mean we have made a great deal of progress in addressing it. The lack of flexibility in household arrangements for all but a very few privileged women, the lack of good reliable child care for all but a few very privileged families, is the daily stuff of the women's movement. And it's not as simple as just saying to your partner, "You should do more of the work," or "Let's get more help around here." There are agonizing dilemmas about whether you want your child raised by someone else, whether you can stand the guilt of not being at home with chocolate-chip cookies when the child comes home from school, or contributing your share to the volunteer mommy arrangements in their lives. Those of us in my generation have all seen how these tough choices stress our daughters and daughters-in-law, as well as their husbands. Gaining the formal opportunity to pursue a demanding job or hold public office was a crucial step, no doubt about it. Making this operationally meaningful for most women has been a much more difficult enterprise.

Individuals, families, and institutions are still finding their way through a complex maze of expectations, facing imperatives that are sometimes mutually contradictory. Nor is the change unidirectional. A small but not insignificant number of well-educated young women who might a decade ago have assumed that their lives would include, in equal measure, professional success and nurturing a family are explicitly choosing one or the other. At the same time, a growing number of well-educated young men are committing themselves to substantial involvement with their homes and children against the traditional expectations of their chosen professions.

One interesting question to me is why the dualistic pattern doesn't seem to hold in the opposite direction, or holds much less weakly. What I mean is this: It's obvious that providing more support and flexibility in the private sphere is essential if women are to make more progress in careers and in the public arena. But it's not so obvious that it improves the situation in the private sphere if more women have high-powered careers and hold public office.

On the "public" side, there are a few women in public office, and a few women in high-powered jobs in big companies—and a few men too, God bless them—have made it their business to work towards improving opportunities for other women by instituting better child care arrangements, establishing policies that support flexible work time without damning somebody forever to second-class status by making this choice early in life, and a number of other useful instruments. But there are very few such people, and it's not obvious that they are more likely to be female. In fact, discouragingly enough, it appears that women who hold high-powered jobs may be *less* inclined than some men to acknowledge the challenges facing ambitious women with families, even if they themselves had to overcome the challenges to get where they are.

So it's true that there are undeniably more women judges, governors, mayors, senior vice presidents, and university chancellors than there were when CROW was founded—or even when IRWG celebrated its twenty-fifth anniversary five years ago. We are, in other words, making slow but steady progress on our first metric. But rather surprisingly, that doesn't seem to be helping much with the intractable obstacles that still face women in the other spheres, and for this reason, the progress towards more high-powered jobs and public office will inexorably remain very slow indeed.

This issue cuts close to home for me, based on conversations I have had with many women in high-powered corporate jobs who are very reluctant to rock the boat by expressing any interest in domestic arrangements or demonstrating any sympathy for feminism. Some of them just don't get it; others get it very well, but have made a decision that taking up "women's issues" is a sure-fire way to get branded as not serious about your work, not really "one of the guys" after all.

It cuts even closer to home because I realize that whereas at Stanford and at Wellesley I was free to be as feminist as I jolly well pleased, when I got to Duke, I made a more or less conscious calculation that I wouldn't put issues around women and families high on my priority list in the early years, since that would just confirm the suspicions of those who doubted that a feminist from a woman's college could possibly understand Duke, much less run the place. It's not that we ignored the issues, but we did very little.

During my last three years at Duke, I repaired that omission consciously and on a fairly public scale. I'm glad I did, and we accomplished a lot. But my experience does allow me to understand how difficult it is to put women's issues at the forefront if you want to be taken seriously as a major player. I waited until I was already taken seriously and then used my prestige and clout to turn to women's issues. That may have been the right strategy; but I am still sorry it took me so long.

THE EVIDENCE FROM DUKE

In May 2002 I charged—and chaired—a steering committee of sixteen women and men to launch a women's initiative at Duke. The group presented its final report more than a year later, in September 2003. It's available on the web from Duke, by the way, if you are interested in following up on what I will describe briefly tonight. This initiative had its roots in Duke's history of educating women, which extends back for more than a century, just as Stanford's does. More immediately, it sprang from a set of conversations that I had with many people in 2001–2, spurred by my desire to understand the situation of women on campus better before the end of my time as president.

The dilemmas documented in our report are not unique to Duke, nor unique to women. Mentoring, child care, self-confidence, professional development, equitable promotions, and pay—these are of interest to any community intent on fairness. Some things that we found were specific to Duke, but I am confident that the broad outlines are pertinent to other comparable campuses—and to our larger questions of how well we are faring on our journey towards a brighter future—and that's why I wanted to share some of the results with you tonight.

The steering committee for the initiative was a broadly representative group of people who each had the authority to carry out decisions in their areas of responsibility across Duke, and to bring together subcommittees of students, faculty, and staff members in each major area. We formulated questions, supervised multiple forms of data gathering and analysis, and came up with both policy actions and recommendations for others.

Some of the policy choices were so clear-cut and pertinent that we moved forward on them immediately. Others are still in the process of being implemented, and still others are still being formulated for the future. Taken together, they help chart a path from where Duke is to where we hope to be: a truly coeducational, more egalitarian institution.

Professor Susan Roth, a member of the department of social psychology at Duke and now dean of the social sciences, wrote the report. She's a hard-nosed social scientist who convinced us that the report would be persuasive to the skeptics only if we could back up every single one of our claims with hard data, and so we did. I did, however, introduce the report with a more lyrically feminist essay, just to make sure that we didn't lose sight of our more visionary goals.

Twenty undergraduate focus groups were drawn from a wide range of student organizations; graduate and professional students were studied through additional focus groups and a web survey; we held another six focus groups for alumnae in cities where they were highly concentrated; faculty were studied through a Women's Faculty Development Task Force, which collected both quantitative and qualitative data, and a Medical Center Focus Group Project team; and employees were studied through surveys, forums, focus groups, roundtables, and reports. Even trustees were surveyed by a participating member of the board.

And what did we discover? Using as our benchmark 1973, when Duke's Woman's College merged with its male counterpart, we found a good deal of statistical progress. Conveniently, that was of course exactly the period when CROW was established, as part of the same broad social movement.

In 1973, 28 percent of the students in the Graduate School of Arts and Sciences at Duke were women; in 2003 the corresponding figure is 47 percent. Across all graduate and professional schools, in 1973, 20 percent of the candidates for advanced degrees were female; today, 43 percent, with parity in the social and biological sciences, the medical school and the law school, and progress being made in business, the natural sciences, and engineering. More than half the professional, technical, and managerial staff today at Duke are women, and about a third of the university's senior administrators—vice presidents, vice provosts, deans—are women; this would surely not have been true in 1973. Fourteen of the thirty-six members of our board of trustees are women, compared with five in 1973.

In the faculty, the numbers are not so impressive. In 1973, 8.4 percent of the Duke faculty outside the School of Medicine were women; today, 23 percent of the tenured and tenure-track faculty across the university are women, with somewhat higher percentages among other "regular" faculty ranks and in several of the schools. Progress, but hardly an indication of robust success.

This fact, and the continuing small number of women in the ranks of the very senior leadership, provide the first evidence that the progress towards full inclusion of women in the faculty and administration of Duke University remains slow and uneven across the institution. These data provide a striking contrast with the progress that has been made and is being made in the admission and graduation of students in each of the schools of the university.

Findings like these have often been interpreted as evidence for the "trickle up" or "pipeline" hypothesis, with the connotation of a steady flow—that women are making their way into the professions gradually, achieving equality first in the classroom and then in the ranks of the junior professionals, eventually to be equally represented at all stages. Our analysis does not support this hypothesis, nor the alternative that the pipeline is "leaky" at every stage along the way. It is clear that the flow through the pipeline now moves smoothly until particular specific points are reached. There is a stubbornly durable blockage at the point when a candidate could be moving into the junior faculty, and another blockage at the stage of promotion and tenure, or of movement into the senior administrative leadership. We suggest that the appropriate metaphor is of a pipeline that is obstructed, or blocked, at specific points, rather than with "leakages" all along the way.

Women and men, our data make clear, increasingly follow the same paths through Duke to the point where they take their final professional degrees. But then striking differences begin to emerge, in terms of the numbers of women who choose to commit themselves to the goal of becoming full members of the tenured professoriate or the senior leadership of the university, and are able to sustain these ambitions to the point where the goal is achieved.

To provide the context for these findings, one needs to combine quantitative data analysis with more subtle qualitative observations, gleaned from conversations and focus groups. We were reminded, for example, that most undergraduates come to Duke with a fairly well-developed set of cultural expectations about how women and men should behave, communicated in powerful ways by the messages of contemporary popular culture and formative high school experiences. We have learned that contrary to what one might wish for in a residential educational institution dedicated to personal growth and the exploration of diverse experiences, these cultural expectations are powerfully reinforced for many students at Duke. These norms are clearly not conducive to equal participation as members of a community of scholars; but they are profoundly influential in the lives of our students. They are strongly gender-specific, in terms of everything from what one should eat or how one should dress to romantic and sexual encounters, even reaching into what is regarded as appropriate in terms of intellectual assertiveness or interest in leadership.

The ideal of "effortless perfection" described eloquently by many Duke female undergraduates in our initiative creates a suffocating climate, a climate that too often stifles the kind of vigorous exploration of selfhood and development of enlightened respect for members of the opposite sex that one would hope to see at a place like Duke. It also perpetuates a strongly heterosexual norm, and can make things especially difficult for lesbian, gay, bisexual, and transgendered students.

On the positive side, students, faculty members and employees report very little direct sexual harassment. But there is a disturbing sense that equal respect and perceived equal opportunity for advancement are lacking, surely not across the board, but in many situations. Here, as in a number of other instances, race can be a crucial factor along with gender, and the experiences of African American women, especially, differ in significant ways from those of white Americans.

Finally, graduate and professional students, faculty members, and employees alike report consistently that their lives are very complicated in terms of juggling career and family. The lack of accessible, affordable child care was reported early and often as one of the major obstacles to professional development that women face.

Here, as in other ways, economic class reinforces gender differences. For lower-paid employees, making ends meet and providing opportunities for their children often means that one or both parents work two jobs, and child care arrangements depend on the help of family and neighbors as well as affordable child care providers. More highly compensated employees can pay for arrangements that make parents feel comparatively comfortable working long hours outside the home, although none of this is ever easy. As one medical faculty member put it: "It really does take a village. And I've hired a village."

HOW DOES THIS ALL ADD UP?

If we take these findings and refer back to my list of eight metrics, my grading standards should be clearer. I would give us very high marks in this country for access to education, at least for many women although surely not for all; obstacles of class, race, and ethnicity have by no means disappeared. But as far as our institutions are concerned, the barriers to advancing to a final degree in your chosen field appear to have fallen in most areas, and to be eroding fast in others.

The opportunities for getting a job, getting promoted, and holding authority are clearly much less bright, on the Duke evidence. We still have a long way to go for equity in these areas. And the poignant concerns expressed by Duke people about the need for more and better and more affordable child care, and for more flexible work arrangements to compensate for inflexible requirements in the home, make clear that here too we still have a long way to go.

That so few people in any part of Duke spoke of sexual harassment as a major problem is good news. Yet the vivid descriptions from our undergraduates about the pressures they feel to look beautiful, dress well, and generally knock them dead socially make very clear that cultural depictions of women still emphasize sexuality and stereotypical femininity. On this score, we have a very long way to go indeed.

One disturbing finding relevant to our work as faculty professionals is that the undergraduate women (and quite a few graduate students and junior faculty as well) spoke longingly of having more contact with older women, women who have made it and struggled with these same issues successfully, who can mentor them and support them sympathetically. We thought we had a lot of support structures in place for our students, and indeed we do, but they spend a great deal of their time in peer-specific situations, and the contacts with women professors or successful alumnae are few and far between. We can, and should, give them more.

My hunch is that the findings would not be wildly different if you did a similar study at Stanford. And you would probably find that there are havens of sanity—that things are better for women athletes, for example, who feel less pressure to conform to these stringent norms and have more of a women's community to support them—and examples of good behavior, on geological field trips or in outward-bound experiences for freshmen where nobody can possibly expect you to have your eye makeup perfect every morning. Faculty and administrative support networks are also a positive sign, and there is evidence that they may be increasing on some campuses, after a period when they went into decline.

Tonight, in closing, I want to recall a fascinating circumstance about each of the times I have previously given a speech at CROW or IRWG.

On 13 May 1981 I presented some of my ongoing work in feminist theory to the Wednesday noon discussion series, under the heading "The Nature of Woman and the Liberal Arts." It was, I pointed out, the third time I had had that honor, and I went on to say: "It is an appropriate symbol of the interdisciplinary quality of feminist studies, especially at Stanford, that I, a political theorist and historian of ideas, have each time focused centrally on poetry."

The first time I used as my text Adrienne Rich's "Diving into the Wreck." The next time I interviewed the poet Susan Griffin as part of a series on West Coast Women Poets. And in May 1981 I framed my thoughts with another poem by Adrienne Rich, "Planetarium." I first heard this poem read by Diane Middlebrook at a CROW retreat at a ranch in Woodside, a memorable sunny Saturday which I can still picture after almost thirty years, where we gathered for "a sustained exchange of feminist scholarly ideas" and also good food and wine and even swimming.

Then on 8 February 1988, as a visiting scholar at the institute on leave from Wellesley, I addressed the Associates' Day Program on "Women, Power and Authority." I closed that speech with another favorite poem, by Muriel Rukeyser, called *Myth*. As a tribute to continuity in this anniversary celebration, and because it remains one of my favorite poems, I'd like to end with it today.

Long afterward, Oedipus, old and blinded, walked the roads
He smelled a familiar smell.
It was the Sphinx.
Oedipus said: "I want to ask you one question.
Why didn't I recognize my mother?"
"You gave the wrong answer," said the Sphinx.
"But that was what made everything possible," said Oedipus.
"No," she said.
"When I asked, 'What walks on four legs in the morning, two at noon, and three in the evening,' you answered, Man.
You didn't say anything about woman."
"When you say Man," said Oedipus,
"you include women too. Everyone knows that."
She said: "That's what you think."

PART II   Duke University Addresses

Opening Convocation Address

26 August 1993

Like most of you, I have only recently arrived at Duke, and I've been learning my way around. I've discovered that it's easy to find the Chapel, but not much else; the roads seem to have been laid out specifically to divert you from the shortest way to your destination. But as I'm sure you have already discovered, you and I have come to live in a very beautiful place.

As you begin to find your way around as a novice Dukie, as you sort out your belongings and your classes and your new friends, I encourage you to take time to make this wonderful campus your own. Let us agree to enjoy it together, to explore its treasures and make it our home.

On West Campus, where we are now sitting, everything is splendidly, unrelentingly Gothic, each quadrangle meticulously laid out. At first you may think they all look alike; but look again—there are small, delicious nuances of difference from one quad to another. When you need to catch your breath from the frenetic pace of orientation week, take time to look more closely at those stone decorations. Each one of them was lovingly carved to represent familiar and strange beasts, local flowers and trees, the symbols of the various disciplines, and in a most generous gesture, the seals of several dozen other universities. All of these are close around you— begin to discover your own favorites.

West Campus looks just like Hollywood's idea of a college campus, and indeed you'll find that occasionally your scholarly peregrinations will be interrupted by film crews and bright lights, when yet another film company is immortalizing your alma mater for yet another movie.

Then there is East Campus, the original site of the early core of Duke University, Trinity College, then later for many decades the home of the Woman's College. You will discover soon, I hope, that East Campus has its own character and charm, which some observers have called "Georgian repose," as distinct from West's "Gothic restlessness." But East is also our urban campus, close to the city of Durham, including the trendy shops of Ninth Street and Brightleaf Mall, as well as many of the people who work at Duke and live in the city as our neighbors.

And then there is everywhere else—North Campus, Central Campus, the utilitarian red-brick science and engineering buildings punctuated by high-tech additions in bold new architectural styles. Don't overlook the Sarah P. Duke Gardens, an amazingly large and beautiful garden with many different kinds of areas—the rose garden, the wildflowers, the new Asian garden—people come from far away to see these gardens which are in your own back yard.

Of course you will discover the hustle and bustle of the Bryan Center, the playing fields, the sacred precincts of Cameron Indoor Stadium where you will soon develop into certified Cameron crazies. Then there are the professional schools, law and business, and the enormous Duke University Medical Center, which houses some of the world's most advanced research on diseases like cancer and Alzheimer's and AIDS, and one of the best hospital complexes anywhere.

While you are at Duke, you will have many claims on your time and your attention. That is part of the point of choosing a university setting for your education. You will also find out that a great many things are going on at Duke that are only tangentially related to undergraduate education. That is also part of the point of choosing a university.

In choosing Duke, you have come to a place that offers a splendid array of undergraduate courses in every discipline you have ever heard of, and many that will be entirely new to you. You have also come to a place where undergraduate teaching is only one of the responsibilities of the faculty members who will teach you.

Your education will be enhanced in ways you cannot even predict. The faculty here are seriously committed to undergraduate teaching (which is not true of the faculties of every university) and yet are also engaged in world-class research in their fields. It means that they may have less time than you would like to answer every one of your questions; it also means that you can look forward to learning about things that are at the very forefront of whatever field you study, from someone who is highly respected by other professionals who really know the business.

That so many other things are going on at Duke besides your education might seem, from your perspective, a clear disadvantage. You, or your parents, are paying a great deal of money to have you come to Duke; even (or perhaps, especially) if you are on financial aid, you and your parents are working hard to provide your own contribution to Duke's costs. It's easy, therefore, to see Duke as a consumption good, like coming to a hotel and expecting everyone who works here to be dedicated solely to providing you with prompt and courteous service, fluffy towels, a heated pool and sauna, and good food in the restaurant.

As you discovered the moment you saw your dormitory room, nobody is going to mistake Duke for a luxury hotel; and you'll have to make up your own mind about the food. But it's important to realize that what you undertake in coming to Duke is different from anything else you've ever done. A Duke education is not just a consumption good; it's a life-transforming experience, a partnership in which you should take a leading role. For you to get the most out of this experience, to make it most deeply rewarding for you for the rest of your life, it is important to think now—and then again occasionally across the years—about what Duke can most advantageously do for you and to you.

First and foremost, remember that you have come here to get an education. That sounds obvious, but it is not so simple as you might think. Some sort of education will happen to you at Duke, whether you want it to or not. Your stay in this powerful environment at a crucial time in your life will inevitably shape you in many different ways. Even as soon as the time you first go home for fall break or Thanksgiving, you will be, in some ways a different person.

But you don't want to be different just in some random or casual way. It should be your responsibility, and your privilege, to be as conscious as you can of how you are being educated, and how much you are taking advantage of this experience for good.

By saying that you have come here to get an education, I do not mean that you have come to Duke just to take classes and exams. However, it is important to remember that the core of your educational experience should happen in the classroom. Many other things will contribute to your education—I'll speculate in a moment about what some of those will be. But many of those things could happen almost as well if you were somewhere else. The unique aspect of your education that can only happen in a great university, the essence of your experience, ought to be the courses that you choose, the books you read, the laboratory experiments you run, the seminar discussions in which you take part, the great lectures you will hear.

Take advantage of the people who are ready to advise you in making your first choices about courses, and be intellectually bold and adventurous. If you stick entirely to subjects you already know something about and feel you will do well in, you'll miss the opportunity to discover whole new ways of looking at the world. You will be like an explorer who chickens out just before the big voyage and decides, instead of traveling up the Amazon or trying to get to Mars, to play it safe and visit the town next door instead. If you don't play it too cautiously, you will be richly rewarded with discoveries you cannot now envision. You may find your major subject, indeed your whole life's vocation, in a subject that you can't even pronounce at this point. And don't spend too much time worrying about whether you are going to get into graduate school.

If I can borrow some terminology from our distinguished medical center, I would say that the biggest cancer on an undergraduate education is worrying too early and too much about what you are going to do afterwards. That kind of worry consumes your time and energies, redirects your vital juices in perverse directions, and slowly drives out more healthy intellectual impulses.

You've worked hard in the past few years to get into college. You've thought a lot about it, directed your courses and extracurricular activities towards that end. Now you are here. You are at Duke. You are beginning a new life. Savor it. Don't move too quickly past it to think about how this is going to help you get somewhere else. It's terrible to live your whole life that way, always seeing your present activities as instrumental to what happens next, never paying single-minded attention to what you are actually doing until you're old and tired and it's too late.

So choose your courses wisely, but choose them with a spirit of adventure, playfully as well as carefully, not seeing them just as a route to med school or law school or business school but as a set of intellectual voyages of discovery that will shape in profound ways the kind of person you are and how you will live your life.

Over the decades of your life you will spend a lot of time with many different people—family, friends, colleagues—but the person you will spend most time with is yourself. One of your major purposes at Duke should be preparing yourself to be an interesting person to spend time with. This has a double advantage: first, that you will enjoy your own company in solitude, when you either choose to be alone or find yourself in circumstances where you are alone; and secondly, that you will be a more interesting person for other people to spend time with, so that friends will seek you out for your wit and conversation, not avoid you as an airhead or a pompous bore.

To become a more interesting person to spend time with, both for yourself and others, ought to be one of the primary purposes of your education—which reinforces the wisdom of being intellectually adventurous in framing your education rather than too cautious or sterile. One of my favorite authors, one whom I hope many of you will discover for yourself, is Michel de Montaigne, a sixteenth-century Frenchman who wrote a book for which he coined a new title that has become a common noun: *Essais*. The French root of this word means to try, to experiment, to give things a chance and see what happens. And this is what he did in his book, providing accounts of his explorations of the world, both the world outside (he was an inveterate traveler) and the world within himself.

Montaigne's favorite place to write was the tower library on his estate, to which he climbed by a series of narrow stairs reaching the very top of his domain, with a view of the vineyards and grainfields, a ceiling carved with some of his favorite quotations, and lines of books around the shelves. When you go to France you can still see that library and understand vividly what his life was like more than four hundred years ago. Here Montaigne would retreat each day he was at home to think and write his essays.

Montaigne hit upon a lovely image that I commend to you: the image of the "backroom of the mind." He thought of his own mind as a kind of tower library to which he could retreat even when he was far away from home, filled with quotations from wise people and experimental thoughts and jokes and anecdotes, where he could keep company with himself. He suggested that we all have such backrooms in our minds, and that the most valuable and attractive people we know tend to be people who have rich and fascinating intellectual furniture in those spaces rather than a void between their ears.

You might think of your education first of all as a way of furnishing that back room of your mind. Fortunately, you don't have to complete the job by the time you get your baccalaureate degree. In fact, the most wonderful thing about a worthwhile education is that unlike most consumer goods, it tends to get better the more you use it. It improves rather than depreciates with age. If you use your time here wisely, you will not just complete the required number of courses, but prepare yourself to embark on a lifelong odyssey in which you will keep learning, keep experimenting, remain mentally adventurous, and continually update and redecorate the backroom of your mind.

I promised you that I would mention a few other factors that will contribute to your education, in addition to your specifically intellectual pursuits.

Next in importance will be the people you meet, the friends you make. And here I have an equally strong-minded piece of advice to give you. Don't make friends only among people who look and act just like yourself. That's a very easy temptation. You are new to this place, and novelty is scary; you don't know exactly what is expected of you, and you'll need the comfort of people you know and trust to discuss what is happening. This is perfectly understandable, and of course some of your friends will be (and should be) people with whom you immediately feel at home.

But if you succumb to the temptation to spend all your time at Duke with people who dress and think and talk just like you do, you will be cheating yourself of one of the most significant parts of a good education. You won't learn very much about the world from people who see it pretty much as you do. They will reinforce your notion that the world really is just exactly the way you think it is; but that's a dangerous conceit. One of the splendid advantages of a great university as a place to be educated is that there are many kinds of people here, with many ways of looking at the world. You should take advantage of that to find out what the world looks like to them, in order to broaden and refine your own knowledge of the world.

Since the beginning of recorded human discourse, people have lamented that they could only experience the world from one set of senses, one life course; for people who are curious, it has always seemed a tragedy that you can never know what the world looks like to someone other than yourself. But you can come close, by getting to know people who come from a different country, speak a different language at home, have skin of another color, worship God in a different way. People who have a lot more money than you do or a lot less, whose views on political and moral issues are much more conservative than yours, or much more radical.

To get to know such people, you'll have to take some initiatives, and risk getting rebuffed or blown off, but I can assure you that the rewards are tremendous in terms of your understanding of the world. You will have the most precious advantage of any education: you will have some outside ways of testing what you've always taken for granted in your beliefs about the world—morally, religiously, politically. Some of those beliefs will stand the test of comparison and emerge as true convictions, convictions that define your character and provide a sturdy compass for you for your whole life. Others will be modified and changed, and some will even be discarded, so that over time at Duke your views and beliefs become more nearly your own, rather than just the views and beliefs of your parents or your high school friends.

We talk a lot at Duke about diversity. It's easy to assume that having different kinds of folks around is just a feature of the place that you are expected to tolerate, carefully avoiding being mean or prejudiced. But diversity on a university campus involves much more than that. It is one of the essential sources of your education; you should value diversity and learn from it.

215

In addition to learning from your classes and from your friends and your acquaintances, you will also learn from the various extracurricular activities in which you will engage. This means, of course, the great parties and basketball games for which Duke is justly famous, and it should mean other things as well. You will be barraged with opportunities to join this club or that intramural sport, to try out for a singing group or drama troupe, and you should indeed get engaged in such things to broaden your experiences.

But in addition to this, you should also make sure that you get involved in doing something for someone beyond yourself. More than three-quarters of Duke students do significant community service. They have discovered something you will soon learn as well, if you do not already know it from your own experience. It makes your own life better to help someone else who needs your energy, your optimism, your good ideas. You are pulled out of your own narrow concerns and fretful worries when you try to help someone who is homeless or ill or lonely or in prison or worrying about how she is going to feed her kids. It puts everything else into perspective, and it allows you to strengthen yourself by giving of yourself.

It is no accident that every major world religion enjoins us to feel some degree of responsibility for other members of the human family. This is a core definition of what it means to be civilized, for only thus can civil society survive. And it also brings unexpected personal rewards to those who heed such mandates; you will become a deeper, stronger, more interesting person if you think at least sometimes first of others rather than yourself. A Duke education should build character, as well as intellect. Character depends on subsuming narrow selfishness in a more enlightened, generous, inclusive vision of the world.

Those are weighty pieces of advice: to plan your education in a bold spirit of adventure, to choose your courses and your friends and your extracurricular activities with the deliberate purpose of broadening and deepening your perspective on the world. But I offer this advice with confidence, based as it is on the wisdom and experience of many who have preceded you at Duke.

I look forward greatly to sharing this adventure with you. There will be hard times, but there will also be many joyous times. I hope that these years at Duke will be full and fruitful for you, as you prepare to join the company of educated men and women. The heartiest of welcomes, and good luck to each and all.

Inaugural Address

23 October 1993

Members of the Duke University community, and our very welcome guests: to be invited to lead this splendid institution, at this crucial moment in its history, is a great honor indeed. I shall do my best to merit your faith, and to carry forward our shared vision for Duke.

For my part in this joyful academic feast day, I want to talk with you about the character of our university, both aspects that are common to all universities and some that are unique to Duke.

Last April, Bob and I spent several weeks at a retreat center called Bellagio, on Lake Como in the Italian Alps. My task was to write an essay on "the mission of the research university." In that setting of unparalleled beauty and serenity of spirit, I defined the university in terms that sounded very much like the Bellagian ideal: a company of scholars engaged in discovering and sharing knowledge.

That was exactly what a group of fortunate scholars were doing at Bellagio. Each morning we worked in solitude in our separate studies scattered across the grounds. We gathered for lunch to discuss what we had been doing and then, in the afternoons, we hiked together in the mountains talking about ideas. We presented our work more formally to one another in the evening, after a splendid dinner with good Italian wines.

Memories of like places, including our own National Humanities Center, will resound pleasantly in the minds of many of you today. The ideal of the gathering of scholars, untouched by the ordinary cares and responsibilities of life, freed to concentrate on the shared love of knowledge, has ancient and durable roots. It is a secular and more luxurious version of the monastic ideal of cloistering and concentrating the fellowship of the spirit. Rabelais's Abbey of Thélème . . . Tennyson's Princess Ida . . . the concept has a very powerful appeal.

Such an ideal bears only a passing resemblance to the bustling, complex world of the modern research university, with our hospitals and football fields, our transportation systems and industrial partnerships, our sophisticated laboratories and power plants. How did we get from there to here?

The pure Bellagian ideal is neither self-sustaining nor, for most of us, indefinitely appealing. It is eternally at the heart of what we do; it cannot stand alone. By considering various steps away from this abstract ideal, we can see how the modern research university has been built up around its core.

Note first that someone had to cook all those meals and clean up afterwards. Others had to keep the books and make arrangements for our upkeep, to free us to hike in the mountains and discuss ideas.

The first step away from the pure Bellagian ideal is the awareness that those who are engaged in the purest acts of scholarship are only part of the university. Those who cook the meals and tend the grounds and buildings and make arrangements for our upkeep are essential to what we do, and are part of the university in their own right.

Thus we must expand our definition: a university is a community organized around the conviction that knowledge is a crucial feature of human life. It is a partnership in discovery and exploration that should include those who provide the material support for the voyage.

The benefits of belonging to a community dedicated to advancing knowledge should extend to all its members. This means job training and skills development for workers and staff, encouragement to attend lectures or take course credits, challenging assignments, and opportunities for personal growth through work. It means respect for the dignity of everyone who contributes to the work of the university. All of us should find in the university a place that expands our understanding of the world and provides us with the tools we need to play our part in the common enterprise.

Note next that someone had to pay for all those splendid meals and all that good Italian wine. The second step away from the Bellagian ideal is the recognition that the university exists because of the generous financial support provided by others.

At Bellagio, all the Rockefeller Foundation asked of us was to think and share ideas. In a university community, support comes from several sources—tuition and fees paid by students, families, and patients; government and corporate support for the costs of research; endowment income; and new gifts. Since we accept this support and enjoy its fruits, we have an obligation to ensure that our knowledge will not be sterile or closely held, but used to improve the society of which we are a part.

Providing a sound baccalaureate education for the next generation of citizens, and training skilled professionals to perform the tasks that must be done if society is to flourish, are the most obvious ways that universities improve the human condition. But there are others: disseminating our research results more widely and applying them for the betterment of human life, tackling the causes of diseases, and providing patient care.

Among these forms of service to humanity, it is appropriate that we should think first of research. It is not accidental that Duke is called a "research university." This name calls attention to a distinctive and richly productive aspect of our work. Research is the closest thing in the university to the Bellagian ideal of scholarly exploration. The joys of pure research, which some of us pursue in laboratories, surrounded by graduate students and research associates, or in the world's great libraries, rather than in solitary studies—the joys of pure research can be profound. For many of us, nothing in the world is more exhilarating than a successful research finding, a discovery that works out as the researcher passionately believed it had to be.

Furthermore, the research done on our campuses contributes greatly to human welfare in directly utilitarian ways: advances in medical science, in both diagnostic and therapeutic techniques, and in the prevention of illness; discoveries in engineering and ecology, in protecting our environment; building more effective legal systems, better communication systems, improved public policies and management systems for large enterprises. In the humanities, in art or literature or history, the benefits of scholarly research are less tangible, but equally important, in expanding our knowledge of the intricate dimensions and potentialities in human life.

We should be bolder in reminding governments and taxpayers about all this. We need to make more explicit the connections between specific beneficial outcomes and the more general condition of our universities. The so-called indirect costs of libraries and laboratory equipment are genuine expenses of research, costs that should be borne in part by the society that benefits, not just by the universities through tuition payments or endowment income.

Research is also the surest way to measure the intellectual vigor of faculty members across universities. When peers in their fields find their work provocative and relevant, this is our best guarantee that the members of our faculty are teaching material that is fresh and deeply grounded, rather than reading from yellowing lecture notes honed over the years to produce an undergraduate response of laughter or recognition at just the right dramatic moment.

However, we must also acknowledge that our incentive systems, our rewards both tangible and intangible (in salaries and status alike), our self-definition as professionals, have become heavily bound up with the research part of our enterprise. It is not surprising, therefore, that in the view of many people we do too much research and too little teaching. A number of universities today are taking a closer look at that imbalance; it is difficult for any single university to move against this current all alone.

It would be particularly hard for Duke University to take unilateral steps that might seem to question the importance of research. Several of our departments and schools have recently reached the first rank; others are poised and hungry to do so. We take justified pride in these achievements, and they attract fine faculty members and students to our university.

However, Duke is also well qualified to provide leadership in a national trend towards greater emphasis on teaching in our research universities. Because we are a comparatively small university that grew from a liberal arts college, undergraduate education has always been central to our mission. Duke faculty have prided themselves across the years in their dedication to teaching, and are remembered fondly by alumni for their success. Many Duke faculty today retain this commitment to teaching, and would welcome a climate that provided more encouragement.

Almost all of us find direct rewards in graduate and professional teaching. These students present themselves as apprentices ready to gain mastery; they have cast their lot with those who regard whichever profession it may be—scholarship or medicine or law or engineering or business or divinity—as the most valuable and productive human work. Teaching these students is a direct extension of one's own commitment to one's own profession.

It is in undergraduate teaching that the problems most obviously arise. Yet students who choose to become faculty members, who opt for the academic life, assume that they will teach undergraduates and look forward to that opportunity. They recall great teachers who presented their disciplines with passion and charisma, and inspired their own choice of a vocation. Students also remember dull or distant teachers, and believe with some degree of contempt that they will of course avoid the fate of becoming one. As with any generational transfer, newly minted graduate students are eager to avoid the mistakes of their parents and chart their own course.

Somehow, along the way, this fresh eagerness gets lost. Young faculty members find themselves increasingly frustrated by the twin pressures of teaching and research, drawn to both but uncertain how to do both well, especially when they are raising children and serving on university committees so as to prove themselves good citizens. Small wonder that teaching can cease to be a fresh and lively activity and become yet one more responsibility to fulfill.

Older faculty members too will often become jaded or burned out from years of bringing yet another generation up to speed in the rudiments of a discipline. As more and more of our undergraduates come to us deficient in the basic skills provided in the past by secondary education, teaching introductory material can be onerous. The difficulty of preparing oneself to enter the mind of the uninitiated yet one more time outweighs whatever benefits one can expect.

Yet undergraduate teaching can bring its own significant rewards. This can be true in any discipline, even the most rigorous, when it is taught so as to enhance a sense of wonder and stimulate curiosity, rather than only to instill accepted methodologies. At any stage of one's career, a fresh perspective can jolt one's stagnant preconceptions and suggest whole new ways of looking at the world.

It is surely not beyond our powers to rebuild an intellectual community in which scholars of all ages share in the partnership of learning and feel a responsibility to one another in doing so. We should not see this as an elective opportunity, something to think about when the pressures of other responsibilities allow. It should be a high priority for Duke University today. The cynical tendency that is too often noted on our campuses—students and faculty members entering a tacit unholy alliance: "You leave me alone, and I'll leave you alone"—corrodes the very heart of the university.

Duke attracts some of the brightest high school graduates in this country and the world. Our brochures promise that Duke will be for them a transformative intellectual experience. That happens for some of our students, but by no means all. It is up to all of us to be sure that such an experience becomes the norm.

We have all the raw material: a strong, well-trained faculty in every field of study; a residential campus that allows students to live in close proximity to each other and to the intellectual apparatus of the university; a very diverse student body made up of young people from every kind of background—ethnic, religious, geographic, economic—who are eager as they enter Duke to learn from one another's experiences; interdisciplinary lines of intellectual connection and stimulus across every faculty of the university; habits of discussion and debate that provide rich fora for exploring issues around curriculum, advising, and other aspects of the academic life.

We can stimulate exciting teaching by the use of computer-based instructional technology in every field; by encouraging team teaching across disciplinary boundaries; by constructing a stronger curricular framework that demonstrates how teaching each course conduces to a strong undergraduate education. Perhaps most important, we can take advantage of the unique strengths of a research university by providing many more undergraduate students with challenging experiences in research, allowing them to reap directly the intellectual rewards that it provides. We need only the will to recast our incentive system to support excellent teaching as well as excellent research, and a vision of how much enriched the lives of all of us will be if we succeed.

Yet even a renewed emphasis on teaching, a greater sensitivity to the justified expectations of those who fund us, and an awareness that all of us in the university are partners in this enterprise of learning do not expand our vision far enough beyond the pure Bellagian ideal. The university is open on all sides to the society around us. We are neither an ivory tower nor an academic village. We are a sizable small city-state, and people and money and requests and opportunities and ideas flow incessantly across our borders. We must recognize the impact of what we do here on our neighbors, and on the quality of the society in which we live.

Members of our university community are engaged in many forms of civic service, drawing skills and energies directly from their work as faculty members, students, and staff. Our medical center provides care and healing every day for many people who cannot afford to pay. Universities cannot single-handedly solve all the problems of our society; our resources are limited, and they are mostly given to us for other purposes. But we depend heavily on the quality of life in our region. In partnership with government and business leaders and interested citizens, we can work to develop coordinated programs for addressing some of the most urgent problems in education, housing, public safety, health care, and other areas of direct concern in the city of Durham, our home.

We must also recognize our social obligation to make a Duke education as affordable as possible to bright, ambitious students from every background. We are the stewards of an immensely valuable resource. To ensure that a Duke education is an affordable ambition for all students, we must be vigilant about two things.

First, we must provide need-based financial aid to all matriculating students who demonstrate a need for it, as generously as we can afford. It is my firm conviction that within the next few years a sharp distinction will develop between those universities and colleges that support need-blind admissions policies, and meet the full need of admitted students, and an increasing number that cannot. Those who have the commitment and capacity to sustain need-blind policies will have a tremendous advantage in recruiting a talented, diverse student body. Those who cannot offer such an assurance will find it much harder to attract strong students and will be forced to fill their classes with students who are less well qualified.

Duke must be among those who play from strength. This is a very expensive commitment, but it is essential; we need to plan for it, allocate our resources to make it possible, and persuade alumni, parents, and friends of the university to give generously in support of this priority.

And secondly, we must take great care about how we administer ourselves. Neither Duke nor any other university can afford to do everything well. Our continued viability will require hard choices about where to invest limited resources. We must remember to ask ourselves, "Is this capital investment really necessary to build Duke's strengths? Will this faculty member's appointment extend our reputation for quality and broaden interdisciplinary research and teaching? Will this proposed new program help students in this school acquire the sophisticated and increasingly international perspective they will need for the twenty-first century?"

To expand our capacities to offer a broad-ranging and high-quality education, we must take better advantage of our fortunate location in a region with several strong universities. We shall continue to compete vigorously on the athletic fields and in our recruitment of students and faculty, of course. But we should much more often think collaboratively about innovative programs, the purchasing of equipment and services that can readily be shared, joint hires of specialized faculty and staff, and other ventures that we have only begun to visualize. We should also expand our collaboration with firms in the Research Triangle Park, to design research partnerships that will produce rich benefits.

One of Duke's great strengths today is the extent to which we have retained our roots deep in our region, the South, at the same time that we have become a truly world-class university. The founders of Duke University were careful to speak of our obligations to the people of this region, especially to poor, bright, young people deserving of an education. But they also, from the beginning, affirmed Duke's openness to the larger world, our adherence to strict standards of intellectual rigor and broad-ranging exploration.

For our generation at Duke, we must sustain that balance with a renewed sense of what it means to be of service to this region, our homeland, and a refreshed and enlarged sense of what it means to be an international university. Fortunately, this is made easier by the extent to which the American South has itself become internationally connected—through the immigration of people and businesses and ideas from around the world.

We need to ensure that all our students will have exposure to international ideas and information during their time here. This can be accomplished in a number of ways—by encouraging them to spend time abroad, by increasing the number of students and faculty who come to Duke from other countries, by designing courses and extracurricular programs with an international dimension. Most fundamentally, however, we must cease to think of "international" experiences as exotic, separate from our basic experience each day. We should make international links and contexts an integral part of the way we think and live at Duke; we should work past special enclaves and earmarked programs towards the day when everything we do will be informed by our global consciousness.

Our university is a comparative newcomer to the ranks of the world's great research universities. What had been Trinity College, a small regional college with strong ties to Methodism, was transformed into Duke University in the 1920s by the generosity and vision of James Buchanan Duke and President William Preston Few.

In the founding indenture of the university, James B. Duke asserted his belief that education "is, next to religion, the greatest civilizing influence." His conception of education was practical and robust; he requested that the courses of study in the new institution be chosen and ordered to "develop our resources, increase our wisdom, and promote human happiness." He thus set up this duo—religion and education—as the twin lodestars to which humankind might look for its salvation, spiritual and secular. And his new university took as its motto "Eruditio et Religio."

When I discovered this, after I had already agreed to become Duke's president, I was initially uneasy. The motto has an archaic sound if one provides a literal translation—erudition and religion—and the emphasis on religion seemed hard to square with the restless yearning for discovery, the staunch and fearless commitment to seek for truth wherever truth may be found that is the hallmark of a great university.

It is clear that William Few, as president of the university, found himself wrestling with the contemporary relevance of Duke's motto, just as I have done. In a speech to the graduating class in 1931 he set forth a rich context for understanding what it means: "As I look back over the life of man in the world," said Few, "I think I can trace a long historic conflict that has been waged through all civilization between beauty and fullness of life without a moral meaning, on the one hand, and austerity and barrenness along with religious intensity, on the other."

Pew went on to speculate that it was this unresolved conflict in the human spirit that "has produced that strange ebb and flow so conspicuous in all human history. It has always been difficult for human society to preserve the gains made generation after generation, and any high and enduring civilization still awaits the synthetic power . . . to combine a full and beautiful living with moral energy and enthusiasm for the causes of humanity."

As an example of the two human impulses that are too often in conflict, he mentions the moral impulse to help the poor—and the scientific urge to find the means to destroy the seeds of poverty. We might add the moral impulse to heal the sick and relieve their suffering—and the scientific urge to find the causes of AIDS or cancer or Alzheimer's disease.

In Pew's vision of how these different human impulses might work together in harmony in a great university, he says: "Here stand side by side science and religion—science and scholarship completely given to the full, untrammeled pursuit of the truth and religion with its burning passion for righteousness in the world—and commit the university in its very inception alike to excellence that dwells high among the rocks and to service that goes out to the lowliest."

At a time when all of us in higher education are wrestling to define our mission more clearly in a rapidly changing world this reading of Duke's motto—the harmony between the impulses of science and of moral value—is a promising point of departure. The splendors of scientific research in any field are ultimately barren without the moral impulse to use those findings to help people achieve the good. The moral impulse to help humanity, as an expression of spiritual commitment that transcends solipsistic selfishness, is equally fruitless without the knowledge and discipline that comes from scientific enquiry.

The final step away from the pure Bellagian ideal of the community of scholars in the mountains is the realization that few of us would choose to live all our lives in the rarified atmosphere of pure scholarship, however exhilarating it may be. We would miss the stimuli provided by more heterogeneous companions; and most of us would eventually feel guilty about living a life that involved no service to others, a life ultimately derivative from the work that others do.

There will always be a tension between the striving for objective knowledge and the subjective commitment to moral value, between free speech and human sensitivity. Too often, on university campuses, we try to keep these two impulses separately boxed so that they will not contaminate each other. Our goal should be to make this tension productive, in a new dialectic of achievement for our future.

And in this spirit, we should this day rededicate Duke University to the "full, untrammeled pursuit of the truth," and to the "burning passion for righteousness in the world"; to "excellence that dwells high among the rocks and service that goes out to the lowliest." Armed by this power, informed by this vision, we can be confident that Duke will move from strength to strength among the universities of the world.

The University of the Future

The Forest at Duke Lecture, 16 February 1996

It's a privilege and a pleasure for me to be here with you today. I know that many Duke alumni and parents are residents of the Forest, and that many more of you became Duke loyalists when you moved here and learned about the university and its intellectual, cultural, and athletic riches—which we warmly invite you to enjoy. Some of you have taken courses through one of our special programs like DILR or MALS; and many others have attended Broadway at Duke or Duke Drama Productions, or the wonderful concerts sponsored by the Music Department or the Chamber Arts Society. Several of you attend Duke Chapel regularly, and many of you also follow events in Duke's "other cathedral," Cameron Indoor Stadium.

We hope that most of you cheer regularly for Duke basketball and football on TV, wherever you went to college—and we trust that we've even converted a few folks who grew up with Carolina blue or NC State red in your heritage.

If you do watch much television, for ACC games or other reasons, you're probably aware of a series of commercials that IBM has been running for the past year or so. These ads, typically set in unnamed but easily identifiable European countries, feature characters conversing in their native languages about some aspect of using IBM computers—two wonderful Frenchmen strolling along the Seine talking about the capacity of their newest personal computers, a procession of nuns in an old Czech convent cloister, with Gregorian chants in the background interrupted by the beeper of one of the nuns.

The characters' discussions are thoughtfully subtitled in English for television viewers. Each commercial ends with an optimistic or lighthearted comment made by one of the characters, such as "incroyable!," roughly translated as "cool!"

One of these commercials shows a man and his young adult granddaughter in animated conversation in a sunlit Italian garden, with the grandfather announcing that he just completed his Ph.D. The granddaughter is thrilled, but when her grandfather notes that he did the research for his thesis at Indiana University, she is confused, because she knows that grandfather has never been to the United States at all, much less to Indiana. Grandfather then explains that the university library has been digitized, thanks to IBM, and that he was able to do his research by accessing this digital library through the Internet. He concludes with the optimistic observation, "It's a great time to be alive!"

Well, he's right, of course. It *is* a great time to be alive, and some of the technological advances referred to in these commercials do indeed contribute to the current quality of life that we enjoy. But what I found most interesting in the Italian commercial was that it makes several assumptions about a social institution dear to my heart—the modern university—and about how that institution seems to be evolving.

CHARACTERISTICS OF THE UNIVERSITY OF THE FUTURE

The first such point we might note together is that the grandfather is earning an advanced degree somewhat later in life than has been usual in the past. Yet that is probably the *least* visionary element of the commercial. We are already quite familiar with the trend for older adults to return to school after the responsibilities of family and career have lessened, and there is more time to pursue lifelong ambitions for study or travel. Indeed, the general support for the concept of "lifelong learning" is clearly an important factor in the happiness and satisfaction of older adults in our society. Elderhostel, alumni trips, and special programs such as those at Duke attract many people in retirement years with lively minds and curiosity about the world. In fact, these opportunities to expand your horizons make the rest of us quite jealous, and sometimes make busy folks like me really look forward to retirement!

Colleges and universities are responding to this continuing

230

hunger for knowledge in a variety of ways. We are trying to become more flexible in our programming, so as to accommodate students of nontraditional ages, with classes scheduled at different times, or programs in which the knowledge, the skills, or the shared interests of the students are themselves a feature of the program. At Duke, we are very proud of the Duke Institute for Learning in Retirement and the Master of Arts in Liberal Studies programs. And we are also developing new programs for professionals in the mid to later stages of their careers—for business people through executive education programs in the Fuqua School of Business, with similar programs in the schools of law and divinity.

The second interesting point about our developing educational system that comes through in the commercial is the emphasis on its international nature. That grandfather does his research in our country is partly a reflection of the quality of American higher education: this is one of the few fields in which the United States remains unquestionably the world leader. But it is also a reminder that we live in an ever-shrinking world, where geographical and political boundaries present fewer and fewer obstacles to commerce and to communication.

In the coming century, when our nation's leading businesses and industries will all face the challenges of global competitiveness, the graduates of our universities will face similar challenges themselves. That competition will come from graduates of the best universities of other countries, as well as from students from other countries who come here to obtain the benefits of American higher education. If our universities are to retain their dominance on the world educational scene, we will have to make sure that American students leave here well prepared to assume positions of economic, social, scientific, and political leadership, not just at the national but at the global level. This means that our students must have the opportunity to study with students and faculty from other countries, either through study-abroad programs or by increasing the presence of international students and faculty on our home campus. We must also make sure, through outreach programs and by bringing more foreign students to our campuses here, that we continue to offer the same advantages in high-quality education and training to the best students from other lands, so that they can prepare themselves for positions of leadership on the global scene as well.

It's relevant here that the IBM commercial is thoughtfully translated into English, since it's a sure bet that only a subsection of Americans (of Italian origins, or fierce devotees of grand opera) would be able to understand the Italian conversation. It's notable that we Americans take for granted that everything in the world we really need to know will come ready-packaged for us in English, to spare us the difficulty of learning other languages.

And yet—we are also in some sense the prisoners of this privilege. Translation never quite does it as well as knowing the originals; and we are, in this respect, one of the most underprivileged people in the world, with very little access to other cultures through their own languages. This puts Americans at a disadvantage in world politics and world trade, compared with the representatives of other countries who can do potential partners the honor of speaking their own language, and also understand far better the nuances of a complex discussion or negotiation, which rarely come through in translation.

We're trying to remedy this in our renewed focus on language instruction on campus, to make sure that the United States will be a better place in the future to participate in this increasingly global world. This growing focus on international education is one of the most distinctive—and most crucial—aspects of the "university of the future."

And this brings me readily to a third point: the important role that new technology, particularly information technology, will play in the university of the future. It's extraordinarily important in language instruction, to name just one area—think of how much benefit we gain, in teaching languages, from labs where people can hear and repeat the language and go through necessary drills that would wear out the most dedicated instructor, until they get it right. The computer doesn't give up or get angry if you miss the answer three times—it just patiently tells you, in print or through its distinctive metallic voice, that you haven't got it right yet, here's the problem with your answer, and please try again.

Beyond this, the computer is, with bewildering rapidity, giving us access to "virtual" reality in ways that offer almost unimaginable educational benefits. Students can now have at their fingertips, on CD-ROMs, whole literatures that would only a few years ago have required many feet of library space and many hours of laborious searching to find just the correct reference—which now takes only the click of a well-guided mouse.

Even more impressive, there are computer discs that you can insert in an ordinary personal computer and that will take you on magical journeys to any of the great museums of the world, or allow you to roam archaeological sites and view the ruins in three dimensions, turn over the major artifacts, learn more about the society and culture of the region, hear commentary or background music—everything but the distinctive smells, and that will surely come next if we want it!

E-mail, on-line databases, CD-ROMs, and web pages are an established fact of life at universities today. The students and faculty members who are most excited about their work are in close communication outside the classroom as well as within it, through "newsgroups" that have sprung up in an increasing number of our classes—e-mail systems that continue seminar discussions late into the night, virtual office hours that allow students to ask a question at 2 a.m. and a faculty member to answer it at 7 a.m.—with different generational habits here, the other party to the conversation is likely to be in bed when the question is asked or the response occurs.

There's a story about the head of a Hollywood studio, who upon his first viewing of a motion picture with the amazing new feature of recorded sound, sagely pronounced, "It's going to be big." That type of understatement may seem to us something less than insightful, until we recall that there were some studio executives who considered sound a needless distraction, and predicted that audiences would grow tired of it once the novelty wore off.

In considering how information technology applies to the university of the future, I fear we are at the point where we cannot realistically say much more than "It's going to be big." Information technology is advancing at such a rapid pace, when we are already straining to assimilate the gains made to date. At first, some institutions approached these innovations with suspicious reluctance, partly because of the tremendous expense associated with acquiring the new technology, but also because the benefits and applications were not always quickly apparent in the world of education, and they were even seen as threatening to the precious relationship between teacher and student.

Despite the widespread view that campuses are hotbeds of radicalism, universities are by nature rather conservative and traditional places, not necessarily in the nature of our academic subject matter or the views on social issues held by faculty and students—these range broadly across the spectrum—but in our approach to the process of learning. We are still finding ways to apply this latest wave of technological advances to make learning easier for students and help faculty be more effective teachers and researchers. We are adopting these new techniques with caution, experimentally, pragmatically. But the more we learn, the more it is clear that many promising possibilities lie ahead for technology in learning, which at the moment we can only envision dimly, if at all.

CHALLENGES TO THE UNIVERSITY OF THE FUTURE

We have so far considered three important characteristics of the university of the future: it will offer learning opportunities suitable and accessible to people throughout their lives; it will be international, both extending its programs to other nations and bringing international students, faculty, and issues to its home campus; and it will integrate the most modern technological advances into its curriculum and into the educational process itself.

However, no matter how desirable we may find these characteristics of our university of the future, we must be careful not to assume that all changes will be positive, that they will be easily achieved, or that all universities will or should adopt them in the same way.

Let's look at the issue of lifelong learning—an issue on which I hope some of you will offer your ideas and comments during the discussion period that will follow this talk.

A stock story for newspapers every May is the feature on the sixty-six-year-old grandmother of eight who is earning her bachelor's degree, preferably from the same institution where one of her grandchildren is enrolled. Our public affairs office at Duke each year receives calls from reporters asking about the oldest person in the graduating class. These reporters usually don't find much to write about, for our oldest undergraduate degree recipient each year is almost invariably in his or her twenties.

The situation is very different for community colleges and large public universities, where publicly supported tuitions and different student recruitment strategies make it more common for students to do their undergraduate work later in life. But the fact is that our nation's best universities, Duke included, focus their recruiting efforts on the very brightest high school graduates, and since competition for the limited number of spaces in these universities is keen, we have little problem filling each entering class with students from this relatively select pool.

What should we conclude from this observation? That to diversify our student body and accept the wisdom of lifelong learning, Duke should radically change its undergraduate student body to appeal to people across their lifetime who wish to earn baccalaureates? I think not. To me, it seems more sensible to achieve the desirable goal of lifelong learning in more complex ways. Each university has a different niche, a different mission—and one of Duke's central missions is residential education for undergraduates from around the country and around the world. We bring these young people together in a diverse and potent mix, and I doubt that most of us at fifty-five or sixty-five or seventy-five or eighty-five would want to live in the residence halls and pursue the lifestyles that attend this particular form of undergraduate education. But it is a wonderful and clearly successful mode.

That our undergraduates lack diversity by age, and that in this one respect we are not serving people throughout their lives, is not a major issue if we realize that other institutions are eagerly offering baccalaureate degrees to people who live at home and commute, and doing a good job of this. And that diversity by age at a strong research university should come through *all* our programs—not just the B.A., but the advanced degrees, which are often taken by people in their middle or later years, and the executive education and lifelong learning programs that are specifically designed to serve mature learners, and would be totally lost on undergraduates.

What we should do more of in the university of the future is create opportunities for people of these different age groups—undergraduates, professional and graduate students, lifelong learners—to mix together occasionally, in varied and stimulating settings, so that they can learn from each other and enrich the entire educational experience, rather than keep them tightly categorized in separate educational boxes.

In the second place, it is clear that the universities of the future will need to educate leaders who can think globally, who are prepared to lead in an increasingly interdependent world, economically, culturally, politically. But we should keep in mind that despite the obvious attractions and advantages of internationalism, it is not an unmixed good. If we focus only on becoming global, we risk losing other good things that have been distinctive and precious to American universities.

In the more international world of the future, human beings will continue to need manageable political and economic units and distinctive cultures and societies. Nobody can live purely globally. Therefore the university of the future will still need to train leaders and citizens for specific polities, each with its own laws and practices, and not just provide an undifferentiated education for citizens of the world. We want people to be able to think and act globally; but we must recognize that most of the time they have to think and act locally, as the saying goes. Leadership must begin and focus on the neighborhood, the town, the state, the firm, the region, the country, rather than leap immediately into some purely global realm.

The impulses towards parochialism in the human spirit are not all bad. They are also a source of much that is good in our lives and our universities. There is a strong sense of place in human consciousness.

That sense of place has meaning for our universities, because it is *place* that partly defines what a university *is*. Of course the most important element of a Duke education is the ability to study with our outstanding faculty, but that in itself does not fully define the Duke experience. Most leading universities today offer certain programs and courses in other countries, taught by the same faculty who teach those courses back home on the main campus, and these experiences bring rich dimensions of international educa-

236

tion. Yet a course taught right here on campus also offers rich ancillary benefits that the same course taught by the same professor in another country cannot replicate. These benefits are also absent even in the best "virtual" education through pure technological modes.

Our grandfather in the IBM commercial may have done his research at Indiana University by Internet, but he surely did not enjoy the same experience as a student who used the same library resources and did her research on campus. The Indiana University experience includes more than just access to its splendid library. It also includes the City of Bloomington, Bryan Hall, the IMU, and, for better or worse, Bobby Knight. For universities truly to come to terms with the implications of being international, we must admit that place *does* make a difference, and we should treasure that, at the same time as we open up our horizons to the world. In the education of undergraduates especially, the intimate fellowship of the familiar cluster of faculty and students working together over time will be essential.

Thus there are some clear downsides to establishing a purely international university without any home campus or sense of place. Furthermore, it would be naïve in the extreme to assume that the world in general is ready for true global openness or a spirit of international exchange. While parochialism is not all bad, it is easily carried to undesirable extremes, and this is not something that happened only in the past. The vivid resurgence of tribalism and nationalism—in Chechnya and other former states of the Soviet Union, in Bosnia, and in Rwanda—makes it clear that such aspects of the human spirit are more deeply rooted than we might have thought. A story this month in the *Wall Street Journal* detailed the great lengths to which China is going to ensure that while its scholars and researchers have access to the Internet, the content of available subject material is tightly controlled, and dangerous foreign ideas are kept inaccessible. This may, in the long run, be a losing battle; but at least for now, it will clearly hamper the efforts of folks in China to communicate with their counterparts elsewhere, and makes a mockery of the notion of a "global" university. If we are to be realistic, we must acknowledge the presence of powerful forces that will work against the drive towards internationalization.

We reach now the complicated topic of advances in information technology, which is without doubt a two-edged sword, although that's a point you seldom hear discussed. Certainly computers and other technological advances—especially the Internet—have made communication easier, and offer a wide range of opportunities for improving education and scholarship. But for all their advantages, these technological advances also present some potential drawbacks for the university of the future.

Ironically, the wonders of e-mail and teleconferences and satellite hookups may make it *less* likely that people in the future will actually assemble. For the foreseeable future, we are unlikely to have ways of moving people around instantaneously, and the expenses and inconveniences of human travel are likely to remain significant. Why risk airline cancellations and jet lag if you can sit in your own study and communicate with your counterparts in Florence or Tokyo? And why should it matter, as long as we are all in touch?

It does matter, however. Closely allied to the human need for a sense of place is the need for a sense of presence. It is quite different to be in touch through a fax machine or e-mail and to be physically present alongside a counterpart in another land, with the ambience of immersion into another culture. Paradoxically, advances in information technology may actually distance us from one another in some important ways, rather than bring us meaningfully together. We shall have the electronic illusion of being in touch without the essential sensual reality.

Consider one scenario, not at all unlikely. Computers, upon which we already depend for so much of the work of higher education, will soon have the capacity to translate immediately anything we might say in our native language and send it to a correspondent in a different language. In some ways this will be a wonderful boon to international scholarship, but in other ways it will not. Being able to communicate instantaneously through a machine that translates for you makes it unnecessary to learn any other language than your own to keep up with scholarly work in your field, or to carry on most other political or commercial activities. With this motive for learning languages removed, people are less likely to take on the task as part of their education. Yet as we know, learning a language is an essential entry point into truly understanding another culture. And understanding at least one other culture is deeply important to one's sense of identity, and to understanding what culture itself is all about. I commented earlier on the disadvantages that Americans suffer from not having to understand someone else's language. If we are not careful, the wonders of information technology will extend that disadvantage to everyone in the world.

It would be sad indeed if the technologies upon which we are depending so heavily to bring us all closer together end up doing so in ways that are mainly illusory, while forcing us apart in the ways that really matter.

THE FUTURE OF UNIVERSITIES

At this point, having drawn a somewhat grim picture of the various attributes of the university of the future, I want to strike a more optimistic note. I am, in truth, quite bullish on the wonderful possibilities of the "university of the future," and I believe that the potential advantages far outweigh the downsides.

Not only will the instruments by which knowledge is communicated become more sophisticated in the twenty-first century, we have every reason to believe that knowledge itself will become more complex. If things continue as they are moving now and have moved for decades, there will be an indefinite burgeoning of knowledge in the century ahead. We will recover more from the past, as our ability to decipher the records of millennia is enhanced. We will learn more about civilizations and species as we discover lost manuscripts, new fossil records, buried cities, along with more sophisticated dating and interpretive techniques. And we will expand our knowledge of what we now call nature, by ventures in all the sciences of which we only dream, including ventures far beyond our planet. If we are careful to use science and technology responsibly—and I know this is a big "if"—we can expect to improve and lengthen human life, at the same time that we learn how to live more sensibly together on this earth.

This explosion of knowledge can be overwhelming—or it can help us to refocus our view of what we want from education. The human brain is one of the most fascinating of creations, but there is a limit to the number of sheer facts and ideas that any single brain can hold, even with every technological aid we might devise. In a world in which the amount of knowledge will far exceed the capacity of anyone to grasp, it will become increasingly important to think more carefully about what education really needs to accomplish, at every stage.

In its true form, education is not simply the hoarding of the most relevant sets of facts. Education is in reality an activity, a dialogue, a process. The goal of the university, then, should be to help people think, to find the answers to their questions, and to stimulate and fix the native curiosity that leads us to want to know.

In that respect, the university of the future will, I hope, closely resemble the best universities of today, and indeed the best universities throughout history. I want to stress that point in closing—the point of continuity, of our linkage with our predecessors across the centuries. In our best moments, universities have always had the same lofty goals for the intellectual lives of our students and faculty.

If we can live up to the best impulses and ambitions of our predecessors in this wonderful human activity that we call education, at the same time as we draw wisely and skillfully on new aids to learning of which they could not even have dreamed in their wildest fantasies, we shall indeed prove worthy heirs of their dreams and faith. We shall have as much as is within our power the obligation to educate our students to face the world they will be called upon to lead—a world which will be for them, as it is for every generation, uncertain, challenging, full of unforeseen dangers and rich possibilities. We cannot figure out in advance what all those dangers and possibilities will be. All we can do, in this or any other generation—in the university past, present, and future—is to prepare them as well as we can, in mind, spirit, and character, to deal wisely with what they will encounter in the years ahead.

Address to the Faculty

25 October 2001

Before the 11th of September, I had been trying to frame some thoughts about the humanities and social sciences at Duke.

I am an enthusiastic advocate of our strategic investments in science and engineering; I'm convinced that they are essential for Duke to become a truly world-class university, and even to remain a player in these crucial areas of human knowledge. But the provost, the deans, and I surely do not want the humanities and the social sciences, which include fields that are already world-class at Duke, to lose hard-won excellence so that other disciplines might be brought to prominence.

You will not be surprised to hear how difficult it proved to say anything of substance in fifteen or twenty minutes about two entire divisions' worth of disciplines that countless scholars have spent their lifetimes studying and teaching, with several of the best of them in the audience. As I contemplated the task I had set myself, I felt rather like the man who survived the notorious Johnstown flood in Pennsylvania, and dined out on stories about it all his life. He died and went to heaven and St. Peter told him that the rules of the place allowed each newcomer to address the assembled host on the first night in residence. So of course, the guy said, "I'll talk about my experiences in the Johnstown flood." St. Peter replied: "Do what you like, but do remember that Noah will be in the audience."

However, recent events have given my topic a clear focus, and a new urgency. Thus, to an audience liberally populated with Noahs, I'm going to talk about the humanities and the social sciences in light of what happened on September 11, 2001, and in the weeks that have followed

Let's think first about the questions that have engaged all of us in the wake of those attacks. Some are in the province of the physical sciences and engineering, to be sure: Why did the buildings implode, and would it even be possible to design buildings that would withstand this particular kind of attack? How does anthrax work on the human body, and what are the most effective ways to cure it?

But there is an entirely different range of questions we have been asking, with particular insistence, and all too frequently with despair.

Our deepest needs are for solace and comfort; in trying to come to terms with September 11, our first impulse was to reach out to the people we love. Some found refuge in religious faith, others in music or literature or art. Some found useful lessons in the history of the past, others in the works of a favorite philosopher.

And then there are the questions. Why would anyone act as the terrorists are acting? What leads them to hate us so much? How are their activities organized, directed, and financed? How should we respond most effectively as a nation? How can we prevent similar horrors from happening again?

In all these ways, we move instinctively onto the terrains of the humanities and social sciences. For those who are not familiar with the way either type of discipline actually does its work, let me step back for a moment to provide a context.

In the late 1970s, I served on a commission on the humanities in American life, chaired by Richard Lyman, former president of Stanford and president of the Rockefeller Foundation. I recommend the first chapter of the report of that commission as still one of the best concise descriptions of what humanists aspire to do.

Let me quote just a few passages: "The humanities presume particular methods of expression and inquiry—language, dialogue, reflection, imagination and metaphor. In the humanities the aims of these activities of mind are not geometric proof and quantitative measure, but rather insight, perspective, critical understanding and discrimination."

And again: "The humanities are an important measure of the values and aspirations of any society. Intensity and breadth in the perception of life and power and richness in the works of the imagination betoken a people alive as moral and aesthetic beings, citi-

242

zens in the fullest sense. . . . They are sensitive to beauty and aware of their cultural heritage. They can approach questions of value, no matter how complex, with intelligence and goodwill. They can use their scientific and technical achievements responsibly because they see the connections among science, technology and humanity."

And finally: "Study of the humanities makes distinctive marks on the mind: through history, the ability to disentangle and interpret complex human events; through literature and the arts, the ability to distinguish the deeply felt, the well wrought, and the continually engrossing from the shallow, the imitative, and the monotonous; through philosophy, the sharpening of criteria for moral decision and warrantable belief."

At this time we turn to history for some understanding of comparable patterns that might shed light on these events, even though the parallels are never perfect. Though no philosopher can fully explain why anyone would want to ram a jet full of people into a building and bring a horrible death to thousands of other people, philosophers can help us think more carefully about how moral decisions can and should be made, even in such difficult times.

Over the centuries those who profess other parts of the humanities have sustained a rich reservoir of works that now provide solace, engagement, perspectives on our world. These scholars have not only conserved these works, they have over time subjected them to the kind of critical attention that means we can turn to a few particularly excellent, or particularly well-beloved, works in troubled times. We do not have to sift back through several millennia of the products of the human mind to find those that have proved themselves of enduring value.

Of course the "canon" thus constructed is not infallible. One of the most intriguing aspects of the humanities is the way the canon is continually refreshed, renewed, re-envisioned with each generation. But there are clearly works that are more richly crafted, more deeply felt, more continually engrossing from any period of human history, any part of our globe, and these are the works the humanists preserve, interpret, and keep vigorous.

Languages, literature, history, the classics, religious studies, and philosophy are the core of the humanities as traditionally defined;

music and the visual and performing arts are crucial humanistic pursuits as well. For some of us, music is particularly powerful at times of great emotion and complexity. Anyone who was fortunate enough to hear the stirring performance of Mozart's *Requiem* and the serene *Adagio for Strings* of Samuel Barber in Duke Chapel on 30 September can certainly attest to that.

On 15 September an essay appeared in the *New York Times* by Bernard Holland, reflecting on how oddly comforting it had been to come across a performance of a beloved Brahms symphony while channel surfing on Tuesday the 11th. It was not, Holland made clear, that music represents good as against evil—too many people who brought clear evil into the world have been connoisseurs of great music, as of art. It was more that "for a moment," the Brahms symphony "fundamentally rearranged our minds," because of the beautiful and powerful ordering that it brought in an immensely disordered time.

For others, favorite poems or plays or works of art serve the same purpose. Your chairman, Peter Burian, drew upon the familiar story of Oedipus in his deeply touching remarks at the community-wide vigil on 12 September. At times such as these, we are made mindful of how much we owe our colleagues in the humanities and the arts, for creating, preserving, interpreting, and teaching us these varied forms of human expression, efforts to capture meaning and find truth.

The Rockefeller commission back in the 1970s was prompted by "a profound disquiet about the state of the humanities in our culture." The disquiet stemmed from uncertain financial support, diminishing interest among students in colleges and universities, eroding commitments to the humanities in secondary schools, and a lack of clear focus for the path ahead. Yet as the director of the National Humanities Center, Bob Connor, points out in a recent essay, "Ironically, federal support for the humanities [through the National Endowment of the Humanities] peaked just as the Lyman report was being prepared for publication," and it's been downhill ever since, in real dollars.

The proportion of students who enroll in both the natural sciences and the humanities has continued to decline on many campuses, as students turn increasingly to majors that are perceived to have a higher career payoff. In that same twenty-year period, the humanities have also been engaged in some fierce culture wars, or canon wars, that have generally produced more heat than light.

Yet there are hopeful signs. We seem to have come through the culture wars with a truce if not a clear victory on any side, and humanists are guardedly optimistic about a period ahead that will offer opportunities for new theories, new paths of exploration. Support from a few private sources, including preeminently the Mellon Foundation and the Lilly Endowment, has given some cautious renewed hope on the funding front as well, although the situation is very far from that in the sciences and engineering.

At Duke, it is a particularly auspicious time for the humanities. The John Hope Franklin Institute is only the most visible of several initiatives that have given a new sense of purpose and optimism to these fields. The institute sponsors a series of interdisciplinary, year-long topical seminars bringing together both scholars from Duke and visitors, along with graduate students.

As articulated by Dean Karla Holloway and Vice Provost Cathy Davidson, the Franklin Institute's purpose is to "make humanities central once again to intellectual life in the American academy and to America in general." The strategy for doing this is to bridge the gap between those humanists who believe that the purpose of the humanities is "knowledge for its own sake" and those who believe in "knowledge for a social purpose," by synthesizing them in vigorous conversation. As they put it, "We want the most pressing, urgent, timely issues [such as race, religion and globalization] to be addressed from the deepest and fullest historical, comparative, and theoretical perspectives—in other words, from a humanities perspective." They go on to say: "In moments of rupture and change [including moments of great scientific and technological advancement, as well as ruptures such as September 11], one needs the humanities as a reminder of how to understand events, how to define ourselves as human." This thematic interdisciplinary emphasis reflects and builds upon some of the most exciting trends in the humanities not only at Duke but elsewhere.

Surely fluency in language, and familiarity with other cultures, have never been more important than they are today. These are areas where Duke has much to offer. Desperate calls have gone out from our government for people who can speak the languages of those who have become our opponents or our uneasy allies; one hopes that the renewed visibility of language and culture will inspire students to take courses in these areas, and see them as intriguing opportunities for their own careers.

The library, in many ways the home of the humanities and humanists at Duke as on any university campus, is flourishing, and has ambitious plans for renovation and expansion that will make it even more welcoming, and more useful, to scholars of all ages and disciplines. Our active participation in the programs of the National Humanities Center right next door in the Research Triangle Park provides yet another dimension of creative opportunity for humanists at Duke. It is also a good time for the arts at Duke, with the Nasher Museum on the immediate horizon, and exciting ideas for expanding our capacities in the visual and performing arts.

The university will depend on, and must support, excellence in all these disciplines, in order to have within our grasp the interpretive frameworks that allow us to understand ourselves and others more deeply.

And what of the social sciences? The social sciences are contested terrain even in describing what it is that distinguishes them from other disciplines. The best succinct definition I have seen is from a book called *Science and the Social Order*, published in 1952. Even this definition was cautious about not presuming too much. "One essential characteristic of the social sciences," it claims, "is that they deal with the social relations between human beings, that is, with those relationships between human beings in which they interact with one another, not as physical objects merely, but on the basis of mutually attributed meanings." Or from Karl Popper, a preeminent theorist by anybody's accounting, in 1948: "It is the main task of the theoretical social sciences to trace the unintended social repercussions of intentional human actions." Or more recently, from *A New Dictionary of the Social Sciences* (1979): "in the strict sense [social science] refers to the application of scientific methods to the study of the intricate and complex network of human relationships and the forms of organization designed to enable peoples to live together in societies."

And yet each of these definitions would be rejected by some

scholars who are clear in their own mind that they are surely social scientists. The line dividing C. P. Snow's "two cultures" runs right through the middle of the social sciences. They are all subdivided into humanistic or scientific disciplines; there is no single separate "social science" methodology that can be identified as such. In each of the fields that we call by that name—anthropology, psychology, economics, sociology, political science, and parts of history and philosophy as well—many aspire to something like the quantitative rigor and lawlike inferences of the natural sciences, and others practice an art of interpretation and narrative much closer to the humanities.

In some disciplines, such as economics, the great majority of adherents identify with the methods and habits of mind of the natural sciences, especially mathematics and physics; in others, such as anthropology, interpretation and narrative are recognized as central, and quantitative methods and the search for laws have less prominence. My own discipline of political science is roughly evenly divided along this fault line, and the intellectual battles that ensue are fierce indeed.

The most useful way to define the social sciences is not by our methods but by the problem areas we have taken as our own. In general, social scientists study, and attempt to explain, social relationships among human beings—whether through valid conditional inferences, historical or textual exegesis, game theory, empirical generalizations, or any one of several forms of interpretation. The different disciplines attend to different types of relationships—based in power, ceremony, exchange, scarce resources, kinship ties, regimes, or legal systems—and there is a good deal of overlapping of territory and mutual borrowing. Even those whose research is focused on the individual—psychologists, for example—study the development of the particular person in a world in which social relationships are crucial to that development; those who study cognitive functioning in the sense of brain science are much closer to the natural scientists, with whom they keep increasingly close company.

Thus it is to social scientists that we turn with our most pressing questions in the aftermath of September 11. What features of the lives of the terrorists—their religious belief systems, psychological characteristics, economic deprivation, bonds of comradeship—led them to undertake these acts? What kind of social or political system fosters or supports this sort of behavior, and how can systems be built that will be more effective and more humane? How can we use our own governmental apparatus and control of force, along with those of our allies and the United Nations, to forestall further attacks? And how can we do this without catalyzing a powerful backlash that will undercut our efforts and lead to the deaths of thousands more, both here and abroad?

What kind of international system could be built that would render such events less likely? Under what kind of legal system, and in what kinds of courts, could the perpetrators be brought to justice? How do we balance appropriate security measures in our own country with due preservation of the civil liberties that we rightly hold so dear?

As faculty in the Sanford Institute know well, social science is both abstract and applied, both objective and normative. We need to use contemporary events as crucibles to refine our theories about politics, our understanding of human psychology, of how religious faith can be deformed into fanaticism, of the geopolitical balance of power, and of the consequences of having a vastly unequal distribution of economic goods around the world. We need to learn more now about how people use technology, communications patterns, kinship ties in traditional societies—dozens of the things that social scientists make it their business to try to understand.

With even greater urgency, we need some good immediate applications of what we already know, in government policies that serve the public interest. However contested our methods may be, however imperfect our knowledge, social scientists are nonetheless the best equipped of all of us to shed useful light on these complex events, and help avert new disasters.

At Duke, we have expertise in all the areas I have outlined above. There are ambitious plans under way to capture even more effectively the fine work that is being done in different departments and disciplines across the university. Interdisciplinary collaboration is robust in many areas, including globalization and democracy, environmental solutions, child and family policy, capital markets, gender, race, and class, Americas studies, cognitive psychology, demographic studies, and many more. As the forums that have been held in several schools of the university in the wake of September 11 have made clear, understanding such phenomena requires transcending any single discipline. Quite a few of our most exciting current endeavors bridge both the social sciences and the humanities, to bring to bear our best possible collective thinking on issues that are crucial to our lives.

No social scientist could have "predicted" September 11 in detail, in the sense that a good natural scientist tests a hypothesis by making a prediction that is or is not borne out in experimentation. There is no way to experiment, to go back and change the conditions before we replay the tape, to see what factors were most obviously responsible. Human events of this kind are extraordinarily complex and, in the most basic sense, unique. But despite the enormous difficulties of analysis in any of these fields, it is imperative that we at Duke and elsewhere do the intellectual work we call the social sciences as well as we possibly can, for the sake of our whole future.

Threats to Academic Freedom

Excerpted from Address to the Faculty 2003

I worry about threats to academic freedom, from both outside and inside our institution. The freedom to write, teach, speak our minds, as faculty members and students, is fundamental to institutions like Duke.

At a time when our nation is engaged in a new kind of war against a different kind of enemy—terrorism at home and abroad— the threats to academic freedom from outside the institution are increasingly intense. Freedom must always have boundaries; freedom and chaos or anarchy are not the same. Some constraints on the publication of research on sensitive security subjects may be essential, and we all need to accept this. Some heightened vigilance about visitors to our country, their goals and whereabouts, may also be required to protect us against terrorism.

But the boundaries must be cautiously erected and carefully observed. The threat of terrorism should not be used to rule out certain types of speech or arguments on campuses like this. We have seen recently an increase in outside criticisms of Duke's allowing a platform for people whose views are anathema to some observers, including views as disparate as those of Laura Whitehorn and David Horowitz. We are asked by these observers to exercise close vigilance over invitations to outside speakers, whether issued by faculty members or students or administrators, and to bar from our campus anyone whose views strike them as dangerous or offensive. This is a classic case of misunderstanding what free speech is all about.

We believe, with ample historical evidence, that the best way to challenge speech that you don't like or disagree with is not to silence it but to counter it with more speech. Duke has more organizations that provide programming than any other institution I've ever known, and a very active set of student publications. Somebody will always provide the counterargument to a speaker who puts forward a controversial position. Not allowing the speech to occur in the first place is a very different proposition.

As many of you know, Duke has a proud history of protecting free speech. This year we celebrate the one hundredth anniversary of the Bassett affair, a landmark academic freedom case involving Trinity College and the historian John Spencer Bassett. Bassett wrote that Booker T. Washington and Robert E. Lee were the greatest southerners of the nineteenth century, creating a firestorm across the state and demands that the trustees fire Bassett. President Few and the board refused, and thereby established this institution as a place that staunchly defends academic freedom.

I am not, therefore, worried about whether Duke faculty, trustees, and administrative leaders will protect freedom of speech against outside attacks; I have every confidence that we will do so. But I do think we need to pay more attention to explaining the crucial importance of free speech to those outside our walls, in op-ed pieces, in essays, in talks to alumni and civic groups, and in the education of our students.

There are also some threats against academic freedom right here on campus that concern me. This is a very complex issue, and I want to choose my words with special care so that I will not be misunderstood. As I noted above, freedom is not boundless. Any freedom worth the name must be exercised responsibly, within the constraints of basic civility, if society is to continue to foster freedom. In campus discourse, this responsibility translates into a willingness to allow others to be heard as a fair recompense for allowing you to speak out with your own views as well.

Civility requires respect for others, being willing to listen to what they have to say, not trying to silence them or dehumanize them with belittling stereotypes. But there is a fine line here. Civility does not require that everybody feel comfortable all the time. I worry about a tendency by our students to assume too often that the norm is one in which nobody gets very passionate about what they believe, or states it in a way that might bring offense to somebody else. Strongly held views are indeed sometimes offensive to those who do not share them, especially those who believe the opposite. But this is no good grounds for preventing the expression of those views.

As faculty members, we have a special obligation to make sure that our classrooms are places where students can express strongly held views and disagree ardently with us or with their classmates within the bounds of civility. We should discourage cheap shots and ignorant contentions, but we should also encourage the students themselves to counter such tactics. They will learn much more than they will if everyone agrees with everyone else on all occasions. If you need an intellectual answer to students who find this disagreeable, suggest that they read John Stuart Mill's *On Liberty*—still, to my mind, the best defense of freedom of speech ever written, and very pertinent today. Open dialogue between human beings about issues that are subjects of conflict or misunderstanding is the only sure avenue to better understanding, and to truth.

Over the years I have often heard people at Duke claim that we can move faster and with greater agility than our peers because we are a young, hungry, entrepreneurial, innovative university. That theme is sometimes overstated around here, as anyone who has bumped up against inertia, lethargy, or stubborn bureaucracy can unfortunately attest. But there is enough truth in it to give all of us confidence that Duke will, in the years ahead, justify James B. Duke's faith in this institution as "a place of real leadership in the educational world."

These are very difficult problems, and none of us has all the answers. Knowing the faculty and administration of this university as I do, I have no doubt that Duke will continue to be one of the places where the problems are forthrightly identified and discussed, and one of the places where solutions will be found.

Founders' Day Address

2 October 2003

It is an exceptional honor to be invited to give this Founders' Day address, and to reflect back on that sunny autumn day when I stood in front of this Chapel to be inaugurated as the eighth president of Duke University.

The main West Quadrangle looked then virtually as it does now. There have been many internal renovations, and the trees have been pruned so that the original vista from Davison to Clocktower once again pleases the eye. But a visitor today will see what the audience saw on 23 October 1993, sitting in front of the Chapel or watching from nearby windows or parapets.

Yet a great deal has changed. Anyone who has been away for awhile can confirm, with a mixture of awe and frustration, that even the roads have refused to remain in place. Most of us would celebrate these changes, and others that are still only a gleam in the eye of outrageously ambitious officers and deans who will keep construction firms in solid business for years to come.

Among the small but lovely innovations of the past decade are the banners on the Duke lampposts down Chapel Drive and Campus Drive, celebrating each new first-year class and then, four years later, honoring their graduation. The seniors when I was inaugurated will be back for their tenth reunion in April. Almost all the graduate students in 1993 have moved on to careers after Duke, although I have no doubt that at least a few who were here that day are still working on their dissertations. We wish them well!

Many of you have been part of these full and fruitful years, making your distinctive contributions to the life and work of this institution. Much has happened in our lives, joy and sadness, tribulations and triumphs; but the commitment to one another, and to Duke, has been powerfully sustained.

Other good friends and colleagues are no longer with us. The pictures of the inaugural ceremony highlight President Emeritus Terry Sanford sitting beside me with a thoughtful, appropriately avuncular expression. I learned much from Terry, and was fortunate to have his wise counsel. And we miss others of equal importance in helping me steer this ship in the early days—Tommy Langford, Charles Putman, Wes Magat, and many others.

In a recent interview, I was asked about the greatest accomplishment of my presidency; I responded without hesitation, building an exceptionally talented administrative team. One of my strongest sentiments is the grateful awareness that there is nothing I could have done alone. I've had to resist the temptation today to thank all the people who made this decade possible, in the spirit of the standard Oscar speech. If I started doing that, we'd be here late into the night. So I will not mention by name any of my partners on this journey—trustees, administrators, faculty, employees, student leaders, even my own senior officers. You know who you are, and you know what we have done together. You will know exactly when, in this speech, you hear the unspoken thank-you.

In 1993 my inaugural address began with the image of scholars at a retreat center called Bellagio. Next fall Bob and I will pursue our scholarship not on the shores of Lake Como but by the more uncertain waters of Lake Lagunita, in the Stanford Hills, not the Italian Alps. Our intellectual home will be the Center for Advanced Study in the Behavioral Sciences, a place very like Bellagio in many respects, with the added good fortune that one is in residence for nine months rather than a few short weeks.

My inaugural address moved outward from the collaborative pursuit of knowledge to the international mission of Duke. Today, as I prepare to make the journey back to the scholar's study, I will briefly replay the tape in the opposite direction.

DUKE IN OUR CITY, OUR REGION, AND OUR WORLD

One of the commitments I made in October 1993 was to lead our institution to a more certain awareness of "what it means to be an international university." I believe we have made good on that.

Duke has a stronger and more deliberately focused international presence, and the world is more fully respected in our campus every day.

There are robust new Duke clubs from Hong Kong to Santiago, and despite the complexities of travel in the wake of September 11, 2001, the number of international applicants for study at Duke in every school has grown substantially. These international students and faculty members greatly enrich our institution with the perspectives they provide in the classroom and in our cultural activities.

But of course there is still much work to be done. The occasional sighting of kids in Duke t-shirts from Beijing to Buenos Aires is no substitute for the instant brand recognition that a few institutions of higher education in the United States enjoy abroad. We're making progress; Duke programs on every continent, Duke alums in leadership in major cities, Duke experts consulted and cited on many issues around the world. But we are still notably behind some of our older colleagues in international visibility. I have no doubt that this effort will continue to be one of Duke's priorities in the years ahead.

During these ten years we have also, by design, put great emphasis on "a renewed sense of what it means to be of service to this region, our homeland." We have significantly expanded collaborations with our university neighbors in every direction. The Robertson Express that connects Duke and UNC Chapel Hill is only the most visible sign of that deepened sense of joint enterprise. Countless other collaborations have been launched and sustained, not only with Chapel Hill but also with State and Central, with Durham Tech and other institutions across our region from Georgia to Tennessee. Students and faculty members can now, with much greater assurance, take advantage of the marvelous proximity of several top-notch institutions to enhance their own scholarly endeavors.

Yet one of my few regrets is that we have missed opportunities for partnership between our universities, businesses in our region, and state government. Ten years ago I hoped this might be a decade that historians would regard as they did the 1930s, when our libraries undertook the bold venture of near full integration, or the 1950s, when visionary leaders from all sectors came together to create the Research Triangle Park, putting North Carolina on the map. Such descriptions, alas, will not be part of the historical account.

This is no time for complacency about the economic future of North Carolina. Our historic industries—tobacco, furniture, textiles—are under siege, declining or moving elsewhere. They could and must be replaced by new industries that arise from advances in genomics, photonics, informatics, marine sciences, medical care, and financial management, all areas that are well represented in the campuses of the Triangle, including ours.

States that have in the past looked to us as a model are rapidly outstripping us in this innovation. We have fallen behind Maryland and Georgia, Virginia and Texas, which have made this interinstitutional collaboration a high priority. These states have included as full partners private universities like Johns Hopkins and Emory and Rice. All of them are reaping rich rewards. It will not be easy to make up the ground we have lost, but I believe that doing so is imperative for the next generation of leadership.

In 1993 I pointed out that a university is "neither an ivory tower nor an academic village. We are a sizable small city-state, and people and money and requests and opportunities and ideas flow incessantly across our borders." As a result, I said, "we must recognize the impact of what we do here on our neighbors, and on the quality of the society in which we live."

Not all the impact has been positive, as our neighbors near East Campus on the first weekend of school made clear. But the Neighborhood Partnership Initiative has been one of the best aspects of our outreach as a university. In a focused and systematic way we have, together, made some fundamental difference for good in the lives of our neighbors on all sides. In schools and churches, clinics, neighborhood centers, and renovated housing, Duke people are out there every day working *with* our neighbors as partners.

We are also involved with our city and county as partners in improving "the quality of the society in which we live." One of my colleagues is fond of reminding folks that Duke isn't going to be moving anywhere else. And I have no doubt that we will continue to be part of the solution to problems we face, and join in celebrating the many advantages of this vibrant region.

As we move back on campus in this imaginary journey from our international horizons to the scholar's study, we should be mindful of the crucial contributions to the work of the university made by tens of thousands of people who are not themselves scholars by trade or training.

These contributions include financial resources as well as time, energy, and talent. Here the decade has indeed been fruitful, and there are many reasons for celebration at this anniversary mark. Ten years ago $750 million was a stretch fund-raising goal for Duke. We are now approaching the $2.2 billion mark, with three months left to go in the campaign. This is a tremendous achievement for any university, and a transformative expression of faith in Duke and our future.

Equally transformative, in a different way, have been the contributions of skill and love and labor by Duke people everywhere in this institution. Ten years ago, I noted that those who engaged directly in scholarship are only part of the university, that "those who cook the meals and tend the grounds and make arrangements for our upkeep are essential to what we do, and part of the university in their own right." I urged us, therefore, to recognize the university as a "partnership in discovery and exploration that must include those who provide the material support for the voyage." With the benefit of ten more years of experience, I would underscore this point even more strongly.

One of the things I have enjoyed most about this job has been getting to know and work with many people, in all the different jobs and pursuits that together define this immensely complex institution. When I am wrestling with one of the thorny dilemmas that cross a president's desk, the best tonic is to get out of my office, stopping to say hello to the housekeepers or the men planting flowers by the front door; then head over to Duke Hospital and watch the intricate and compassionate pursuits of the whole patient care team; or walk into the cool sanctuary of Duke Chapel to listen to somebody playing the organ and enjoy the light from the stained-glass windows on the stonework; or steal a few moments in Duke Gardens, watching children feed the ducks or a gardener

257

planting chrysanthemums. These too are Duke, and without them this would be a sterile place indeed. In fact, it would never be any "place" at all.

When you stop to think about it, it is amazing how many different complicated pieces go into making and sustaining a university, every minute of every day. Around the core scholarly enterprise thousands of people are facilitating, enriching, strengthening. The people in information technology, in student affairs and residence life, in research support and tech services, in athletics and the arts, at the nursing station and in the police cars, the library and the secretarial staff—all contribute to life here in ways that many of us too often take for granted.

And they find aspects of working at a university that nourish them as well. For many, Duke is not just a job but a way of life that extends across the generations of their family. Mindful of our own Duke "family values," in the past decade we've provided more opportunities for people to take steps in their professional development, and included all of the community in events on campus. We've let Duke managers know that it is important to respect everybody in the workforce, as individuals with ideas and distinctive contributions. We've been mindful of the need for more support for those who are trying to juggle careers and family demands, especially in recent months, through the work of the Women's Initiative. But there's still plenty of work to be done to push the values we extol at the top of the hierarchy down through the institution, and extend the advantages of a community of teachers and learners across the university.

In my inaugural address, I noted that we owe several things to the people who pay tuition and provide generous gifts to the university. Among them was that we "take great care about how we administer ourselves." Duke has made great progress in these past few years in improving the efficiency of its administration while holding administrative budgets flat, through imaginative procurement strategies, careful monitoring of building projects and administrative programs, and mergers of redundant activities.

We have also been exemplary in the sophisticated nature of our strategic planning, linking priorities with resources in a way that makes it much easier to keep our eyes on our major goals and hold people accountable for reaching them. It's true that we haven't gored many oxen, and there isn't a lot of blood on the floor. But those of us in senior leadership positions in the Allen Building, the Green Zone, and every dean's office say no to people with excellent ideas in the student body, the faculty, and the administration, every day of our lives.

Yet there is still reason to be worried about the inexorably rising costs in higher education. If we truly wish to be "one of the handful of institutions that define what is best in higher education," as we say in our strategic plan, we should do so not just by adding new programs and building new facilities, but also by figuring out how to provide the best more efficiently. That too will be one of the most significant challenges we will face in the years ahead.

THE CORE SCHOLARLY ENTERPRISE

Yet all this is a means to an end: the core scholarly enterprise that is the heart and soul of the university. Teaching and learning, pushing back the boundaries of knowledge, and exploring new terrain that we call "research" are what this is all about. All the services, all the infrastructure, all the support functions, all the extracurricular activities surround and undergird the central work we do, which is undoubtedly some of the most exciting, rewarding, and deeply meaningful work done anywhere.

If you ask why universities survive and flourish for centuries in many disparate cultures, despite incredible challenges and changes; why the students and teachers in Iraq are still dedicated to their enterprise amid bombed-out and looted classrooms; why girls and women in Afghanistan rushed to take advantage of the education that had so long been denied them—the answer has to be that universities are places where we pursue and nurture a fundamental human passion.

This passionate spirit is captured in the best rhetoric of the strongest leaders of higher education. It inspired William Preston Few to celebrate the "full, untrammeled pursuit of the truth" through "excellence that dwells high among the rocks and service that goes out to the lowliest." It led one of Wellesley's early presidents, Alice Freeman Palmer, to say, when someone asked, "Why

259

go to college?": "We go to college to know, assured that knowledge is sweet and powerful, that it emancipates the mind and makes us citizens of the world."

This passion for knowledge is as deep and hungry as any other human passion, and it shows itself in comparable ways. Athletes are driven by a passion to excel, to know the thrill of victory or the deep reward of the "personal best." They know that to get there means pushing your body beyond its limits, and that the rewards make all the long hours of practice, the punishing physical demands, the soreness and tiredness well worthwhile. Artists are driven by a passion to create, and may undergo enormous deprivations to succeed at this, living in the proverbial garrets, abandoning home and family, exploring bizarre regimens, and undergoing rigorous training to find the perfect way to express their passion through paint or music or poetry or sculpture.

Scholarship, when you love it and give yourself to its demands, is like that. It offers moments of exhilarating discovery when you finally hit on the evidence to confirm an insight you knew had to be true, or come across something that you could not possibly have known that all of a sudden transforms your world. To describe that experience, the only helpful analogies are to other powerful human passions. Scholarship in those moments is like the pure sharp love of parents for the newborn child, or the thrill of an explorer finding a new continent or planet. It was Keats who reminded us that intellectual discovery can be like contemplating the Pacific after a long and arduous journey, "Silent, upon a peak in Darien."

Yet like all worthwhile human enterprises, like athletics or art or parenting or exploring, scholarship also includes long periods of hard work, tedium, and bone-tiredness, wrong turns and false starts, losses and disappointments. Knowledge comes not easily, but through wrestling with an idea or a problem until things come into focus and you can see the world from an angle you never saw before. The sweetness and the power come from a well-crafted argument or an elegant equation, from a long day in the laboratory or the library, knowing something that in a real sense no one has ever known before, because no one has ever put things together in precisely the same way.

As with athletics or art or parenting or travel, sometimes the best experiences are enhanced by being shared. Sometimes the passion is collaborative, as in a laboratory where the work of the whole team comes together, or a seminar where the ideas that emerge are better than any single member could have ever thought alone. At other times, the work is rigorously solitary, the scholar in the library or the study, thinking hard and long, finding an answer on a walk on the beach or a run through the forest.

Such passionate experiences, such deep rewards, happen to scholars of all ages, from the first-year undergraduates who suddenly see the world from a whole different perspective to the emeritus professors who finally find the words for something they have been wanting to say for a long time. Such experiences are different from the feeling that you get when you score an easy point in a debate, or get a good grade on a paper on which you haven't really worked very hard. These deeply rewarding experiences come from stretching yourself mentally, taking intellectual risks, putting in the long hours and intense energy that are required to know.

For those of us who have chosen scholarship as a profession and dedicated our lives to its distinctive requirements and rewards, there is an element of faith and fervor here that started us out and keeps us going. This sustains us through all the messiness of petty faculty quarrels and bureaucratic red tape and students or colleagues who just don't get it—or worse, don't care. Occasionally we need to remind ourselves, and each other, that this is what it's all about.

Teaching transforms lives and carries our civilization forward; research saves and improves lives everywhere; scholarship can mean providing service that goes out to the lowliest, acting responsibly as a citizen of the world. But most fundamentally, the love of learning is an end in itself, one of the few human enterprises that truly deserve that honorable standing.

I think about the deep rewards of this vocation each commencement when I salute the bachelors of science, art, and engineering. As I welcome them to the company of educated men and women, I always hope that a goodly portion of them have caught the fever and will spend the rest of their lives pursuing *philosophia*. I also hope that many of those who have chosen other professions and vocations will nonetheless experience something of this passion here at Duke, and that the sweetness and power of knowledge will enrich their lives in the decades to come in ways they could never have foreseen.

And it is very much in my mind as I welcome our newly minted Ph.D.'s, doctors of the love of learning, as they join the company of scholars—past, present, and future—in our continuing search for truth.

In a few months I will return happily to the scholar's study, to rediscover my intellectual roots in the great works of political philosophy. I'll attempt to distill some of what I've learned in the past ten years into insights and nuggets that will make sense to others and help advance our common goals. I know that it will not be easy; being a university president is a demanding job, but no harder, in the end, than sitting down before a blank computer screen to begin to craft what you want to say about a subject of great importance to you and to the world, to say it wisely and powerfully. But I look forward greatly to that stage of my journey.

And I look forward as well to following with deep and affectionate interest the future course of this great university I have been fortunate to lead. Duke is extraordinarily blessed in the deep loyalty of many people who care about this special place—alumni, students, faculty members, administrators, trustees, and employees. I have no doubt that because of that loyalty, and the restless visionary passion that has always inspired this institution, Duke will continue to move from strength to strength among the universities of the world.

Notes

1 This conviction is not shared by all leaders in higher education; a recent essay by Martin Trow begins by citing three presidents of major universities who have expressed doubt about whether universities will continue to exist in recognizable forms in the years ahead. "From Mass Higher Education to Universal Access: The American Advantage," *Minerva* 37 (spring 2000): 303.

2 These quotations are from my inaugural address at Duke in October 1993; I emphasized the same theme in the Founders Day speech in October 2003, designed as a "bookend" to that first address, in which I noted that "it is amazing how many different complicated pieces go into making and sustaining a university, every minute of the day."

3 From "The American Campus: From Colonial Seminary to Global Multiversity"; see also the first section of the Tate Lecture in 1995, "Pro Bono Publico"—both included in this volume.

4 Harvill Eaton, provost of Drexel University, reflects on this image in his "State of Academics Address," 11 March 2003, available on line from the Drexel home page.

5 Donald Kennedy, *Academic Duty* (Cambridge: Harvard University Press, 1997).

6 "Of Solitude," *The Complete Essays of Montaigne*, trans. Donald M. Frame (Stanford: Stanford University Press, 1958), 177.

7 As one of my predecessors as president of Wellesley, Alice Freeman Palmer, put it in 1882 when someone asked "Why go to college?": "We go to college to know, assured that knowledge is sweet and powerful, that it emancipates the mind and makes us citizens of the world."

8 This address, "The Public Role of the University" is not reprinted in this collection, but much of it was included in "When Should a College President Use the Bully Pulpit?"

9 Martin Trow's article in *Minerva*, cited in note 1, above, provides an overview of this tendency not only in the United States but also, in different forms, in European universities.

10   William G. Bowen, Martin A. Kurzweil, and Eugene M. Tobin, in their recent study *Equity and Excellence in American Higher Education* (Charlottesville: University of Virginia Press, 2005), provide the essential data on this subject, as well as careful argument and eloquent advocacy. One of their major themes is "that the continued *successful* pursuit of excellence in American higher education depends on opening the gates of opportunity wider" (161; their emphasis). Indeed, they argue for the "essential complementarity of equity and excellence goals all over the world" (258). On socioeconomic status, see especially chapter 7, "Broadening the Quest for Equity at the Institutional Level."

11   The Atwell Lecture (2000), in this volume.

12   Frank H. T. Rhodes provides an eloquent affirmation of this in his essay "The University and Its Critics," *Universities and their Leadership*, ed. William G. Bowen and Harold T. Shapiro (Princeton: Princeton University Press, 1998). As he puts it (9): "I believe teaching has a moral dimension because of its impact not just on the mind but on the character and will."

13   For example, in his introduction to *A Free and Ordered Space: The Real World of the University* (New York: W. W. Norton, 1988), Bart Giamatti notes that families and religious institutions are the proper places to teach "moral values" and that when the university does this it "*acts as an institution*, by its institutional behavior" (his emphasis), not by teaching moral doctrine in the classroom. Yet to judge from many of the speeches reprinted in his collection, Giamatti clearly believes that universities have an obligation to educate the "whole person"; that a liberal education is "inextricably intertwined" with preparation for "a life elevated by dignity, decency and moral progress"; that "education is a matter involving character as well as intellect"; and that good education should have a "civic goal" (109, 123, 127, 136).

14   Gutmann, "How Can Universities Teach Professional Ethics," *Universities and Their Leadership*, ed. Bowen and Shapiro, 157.

15   The essay, entitled "Aim High: A Response to Stanley Fish," was prompted by several articles by Fish in the *Chronicle of Higher Education* and the *New York Times*.

16   I quoted this passage in several speeches, including the Tate Lecture (1990), "Moral Education in the Modern University" (1996), and the Atwell Lecture (2000). In preparing this book we have omitted it everywhere except in "Moral Education" to avoid repetition.

17   "Corporatization of the University: Seeking Conceptual Clarity," *Annals of the American Academy of Political and Social Sciences* 585 (January 2003): 66–83.

18 In an excellent essay called "The 'Crisis' Crisis in Higher Education," Robert Birnbaum and Frank Shushok Jr. provide ample evidence —including a quotation from 1865 and a review of the literature between 1970 and 1994 that yields "593 citations containing 797 references to specific crises"—of "a long-standing tendency to claim that higher education is in crisis." *In Defense of Higher Education*, ed. Philip G. Altbach, Patricia J. Gumport, and D. Bruce Johnstone (Baltimore: Johns Hopkins University Press, 2001), 61–62.

19 Steck, 68.

20 A more comprehensive and nuanced account of this concern about commercialization, and some suggested remedies for dealing with it, are provided by Derek Bok in *Universities in the Marketplace* (Princeton: Princeton University Press, 2003).

21 This governance model is sketched out in "More Power to the President?," in this volume; the Faculty Address of 1997 is not included here, since much of it was specific to its time and place.

22 This topic is given particular attention in my Opening Convocation Address in 1993 and in the essays "The Mission of the Research University" and "The Liberal Arts and the Role of Higher Education."

23 An illuminating and unusually balanced treatment of this vexed topic is D. Bruce Johnstone, "Higher Education and Those 'Out-of-Control Costs,'" *In Defense of Higher Education*, ed. Altbach, Gumport, and Johnstone, 144–78.

24 On this topic, see the sections "American Egalitarianism" in the Atwell Lecture and "What Kind of an Élite?" in "The Liberal Arts and the Role of Élite Higher Education." The recent leadership on this issue demonstrated by several university presidents, notably Shirley Tilghman and Lawrence Summers, is heartening.

25 Charles Vest showed admirable courage in the early 1990s in defending, against the misguided opposition of the Justice Department, MIT and the consortium of institutions that had long cooperated to ensure the dedication of scarce financial aid funds to needy students rather than its diversion for use in "bidding wars." In the end, his position prevailed in the courts; but much had been lost, as has been amply demonstrated by subsequent events.

26 In March 1994 the chair of the faculty at UNC, Chapel Hill, invited me to address my colleagues on its neighboring campus. This was one of my key priorities as president of Duke, and I was fortunate to have counterparts in Chapel Hill who shared this view. But for some alumni, students, and faculty on both campuses, such collaboration was an incomprehensibly perverse endeavor.

27 Included in *From Max Weber: Essays in Sociology*, ed. and trans. H. H. Gerth and C. Wright Mills (New York: Oxford University Press, 1958), 128.

28 "Science as a Vocation," *From Max Weber: Essays in Sociology*, ed. and trans. Gerth and Mills, 135.

29 "Science as a Vocation," 145.

30 On this topic, and more generally on the qualities that are useful in leading, see N. O. Keohane, "On Leadership," *Perspectives on Politics* 3, no. 4 (2005): 705–22.

31 Giamatti, *A Free and Ordered Space*, 17.

32 Robert Birnbaum, *How Colleges Work: The Cybernetics of Academic Organization and Leadership* (San Francisco: Jossey-Bass, 1988), offers thoughtful insights on this and other issues facing academic leaders in varied situations. On page 200 he notes that a significant part of wisdom in leadership in higher education involves (on the model of iatrogenic illnesses) preventing "what might be termed Caesargenic problems—that is, institutional problems created by the unnecessary interventions of leaders."

33 As Henry Rosovsky describes this transition from faculty member to administrator: "Governance is a form of class treason, a leap from 'we' to 'they,' and a betrayal of our primary mission—teaching and research." For this reason, "Colleagues will offer condolences (congratulations would be a breach of manners)." Nonetheless, he describes the alternative—relying on professionally trained managers to handle academic administrative jobs—as "a prescription for disaster. The technical skills of the executive . . . are trivialities compared with understanding the fundamental nature of the university." *The University: An Owner's Manual* (New York: W. W. Norton, 1990), 243–45.

34 *Republic*, book VII, 514a–518c.

35 *Republic*, book VI, 488b–489c; Birnbaum, *How Colleges Work*, chapter 9, describes "cybernetic leadership" on campus as a blend of other forms, including bureaucratic, political, collegial, and symbolic.

36 "Governance," *In Defense of Higher Education*, ed. Altbach, Gumport, and Johnstone, 313.

37 "Collaboration and Leadership: Are They in Conflict?," reprinted here, was originally an address to the New England Regional Assembly of the College Board in February 1985.

38 "More Power to the President?" (1998). Donald E. Walker, *The Effective Administrator: A Practical Approach to Problem Solving, Decision Making, and Campus Leadership* (San Francisco: Jossey-Bass, 1979), 12–

23, develops a similar model at greater length. Walker's book contains trenchant analysis and valuable advice for administrators in higher education. There is a handy list of maxims at the end, distilled from the chapters of the book (194–95).

39 In the fifth edition of *The Uses of the University* (Cambridge: Harvard University Press, 2001), Clark Kerr continues his custom of adding a new chapter reflecting his current perspective on the future, following the initial views expressed in 1963. In this newest edition, he professes himself troubled and baffled by what he sees ahead. His chapter on the future speaks of "The 'City of Intellect' in a Century for the Foxes," picking up on Isaiah Berlin's famous distinction between the fox and the hedgehog. This quote is from the preface (vii). Fortunately he retains his characteristic optimism, noting (212): "higher education has been very resilient in turning fears into triumphs. I expect that this will continue."

40 Kerr, *The Uses of the University*, 201. Although Kerr is widely, and rightly, admired for his foresight, he may be glossing over the difficulties that most other people felt about predicting the future back in 1963. It is not only in 2005 that the future is hard to fathom.

41 Jack M. Wilson, "The Technological Revolution: Reflections on the Proper Role of Technology in Higher Education," *In Defense of Higher Education*, ed. Altbach, Gumport and Johnstone, 202–26, offers a thoughtful perspective on this cluster of issues which differs from my own, although our basic conclusions are quite similar. See also Martin Trow's essay "The Development of Information Technology in American Higher Education," *Daedalus* 126, no. 4 (fall 1997): 293–314.

42 The notable rapidity of developments in this area is one of the factors that makes prediction so difficult; as Trow puts it in his essay in *Daedalus* (293): "anything older than three months is pre-history, anything further ahead than ten years is science fiction."

43 From "The University of the Future," the Forest at Duke Lecture 1996, in this volume. I refer to *The Tempest* in "You Say You Want a Revolution? Well . . ."

44 Woolf, *Three Guineas* (Orlando: Harcourt Brace, 1966 [1938]). In her case this meant a "love of England dropped into a child's ears by the cawing of rooks in an elm tree, by the splash of waves on a beach, or by English voices murmuring nursery rhymes" (109).

45 From "The University of the Future," in this volume.

46 From "You Say You Want a Revolution? Well . . .," in this volume.

47 From "The University in the Twenty-First Century," Stanford Centennial 1987, in this volume.

48 From "The University of the Future," in this volume.

49 Among the significant exceptions to this generalization was the consortium of Pacific Rim universities formed under the leadership of Steven Sample of the University of Southern California.

50 The *Chronicle of Higher Education* has done a good job of tracking developments in this area; the quotation is from Burton Bollag's article "Enrollment of Foreign Students Drops in the US," 19 November 2004. He goes on to note that the figure is nonetheless an improvement when compared with the previous year, when the drop for the same graduate institutions was 10 percent, and with the 28-percent drop in applications from foreign graduate students in spring 2004. The same issue of the *Chronicle* includes data on the overall drop in foreign student enrollment in the United States, the percentage changes in students for the top twenty countries, and the distribution of students in the United States. Across the board, Bollag reports: "The number of foreign students on American campuses declined last year by 2.4 percent—the first drop in enrollments of students from abroad since the 1972–73 academic year."

51 Michele Diament, "Associations Urge Foreigner Access," *Chronicle of Higher Education*, 27 May 2005.

52 Bollag, "Enrollment of Foreign Students Drops in the US": "Other English-speaking countries, especially Australia, Britain and Canada, have been vigorously recruiting international students. And data suggest that they are succeeding in attracting students who in previous years might have gone to the United States. In addition, some countries that traditionally send many students to the United States have been building up their own higher-education capacity in recent years." Kerr (*The Uses of the University*, 225) notes this among five possible "wild cards" that could create challenges for college and universities; as he puts it, "The American university may no longer be supreme." The other "wild cards" on his list are uncertainties about "increases in productivity," "fluctuations in returns to higher education," possible "new episodes of student unrest," and "how various battles within the professoriate will turn out."

53 "The Aims of Education," September 1987, in the book by the same name published by the University Publications Office for the College of the University of Chicago, 69.

54 Published in the Raleigh, N.C., *News and Observer*, 14 October 2001; omitted from the version of the address printed in this volume.

1   Association of Governing Boards of Universities and Colleges, *Presidents Make a Difference: Strengthening Leadership in Colleges and Universities*, report of the Commission on Strengthening Presidential Leadership (Washington, 1984).

2   James L. Fisher, *Power of the Presidency* (New York: ACE / Macmillan, 1984).

3   Fisher, *Power of the Presidency*, 135.

4   Michael D. Cohen and James G. March, *Leadership and Ambiguity*, report prepared for the Carnegie Commission on Higher Education (New York: McGraw-Hill, 1974), 3, 91, 209.

5   George Keller, *Academic Strategy: The Management Revolution in American Higher Education* (Baltimore: Johns Hopkins University Press, 1983), 148–49.

6   Max Weber, "Politics as a Vocation," *Essays in Sociology*, ed. H. H. Gerth and C. Wright Mills (New York: Oxford University Press, 1958), 127–28.

THE MISSION OF THE RESEARCH UNIVERSITY

1   Roberto Michels, *Political Parties*, trans. Eden and Cedar Paul (New York: Hearst's International Library, 1915), pt. vi:4, 405.

2   James A. Perkins, *The University in Transition* (Princeton: Princeton University Press, 1966), 7–16.

3   Harold Perkin, "The Historic Perspective," *Perspectives on Higher Education: Eight Disciplinary and Comparative Views*, ed. Burton R. Clark (Berkeley: University of California Press, 1984), 23–39, provides another good overview of the development of universities, and cites several useful sources.

4   Jaroslav Pelikan, *The Idea of the University: A Re-examination* (New Haven: Yale University Press, 1992), includes some especially valuable reflections on this theme; see especially 57–61. See also A. Bartlett Giamatti, *A Free and Ordered Space: the Real World of the University* (New York: W. W. Norton, 1976), 33–46.

5   Charles W. Anderson, *Prescribing the Life of the Mind* (Madison: University of Wisconsin Press, 1993), 41, takes the Aristotelian position that among the "natural associations" created by human beings, there is a need for those that provide "shared methods of deliberative inquiry," of which the modern university is an example. Perkin, "The Historic Perspective," 20, asserts that "all civilized societies need in-

stitutions of higher learning to meet their need for esoteric knowledge and its keepers and practitioners."

6 To paraphrase Aristotle, from *Politics*, trans. Ernest Barker (Oxford: Clarendon, 1946), 1281b: Feasts to which many contribute are better than those with a single host. Those who prefer a dinner neatly orchestrated by a single connoisseur to a potluck supper may question whether the illustration works as well in culinary enterprises as in intellectual ones, but the basic argument remains persuasive.

7 Derek Bok, *Higher Learning* (Cambridge: Harvard University Press, 1986), 35–36.

8 Discussions of this topic often generate more heat than light; a useful exception is Charles Taylor, *Multiculturalism and "the Politics of Recognition"* (Princeton: Princeton University Press, 1992), especially the Introduction by Amy Gutmann, ed.

9 Anderson, *Prescribing the Life of the Mind*, 42, speaks of education as the "public purpose of the university," and includes activities such as these in the "cultivation of practical reason" that is part of our educational program. He argues that the university should be "implicated in the affairs of the world" rather than attempt to remain aloof. The university "will scrutinize, and try to improve upon, the practices of the state, business, the arts, medicine, the media, our conceptions of the proper use of arms and the proper stewardship of the earth, and all of this in close collaboration with the practitioners and professionals in these various endeavors" (99).

10 Bok, *Higher Learning*, refers to the growing threat of competition from abroad, and argues that given our economic situation and supply of raw materials, we Americans will have to live by our wits, innovative technology, and imaginative problem solving. "Of all our national assets," he asserts, "a trained intelligence and a capacity for innovation and discovery seem destined to be the most important" (5).

11 Eugene Skolnikoff's essay in this volume provides a good overview of the dilemmas posed in each of these areas.

PRO BONO PUBLICO

1 Alexis de Tocqueville, *Democracy in America* (New York: Alfred A. Knopf, 1945), vol. 2, book 2, chapter 2, 104.

2 *Democracy in America*, vol. 2, book 2, chapter 5, 114.

3 *Democracy in America*, vol. 2, book 4, chapter 6, 336.

4 James A. Joseph, *Remaking America: How the Benevolent Traditions*

of Many Cultures Are Transforming our National Life (San Francisco: Jossey-Bass, 1995).

5 Robert N. Bellah et al., *Habits of the Heart: Individualism and Commitment in American Life* (Berkeley: University of California Press, 1985), 277.

6 Bellah et al., *Habits of the Heart*, 84.

MORAL EDUCATION IN THE MODERN UNIVERSITY

1 *General Education in a Free Society (Report of the Harvard Committee)* (Cambridge: Harvard University Press: 1945), 43.

2 *General Education in a Free Society*, 46–47.

3 *General Education in a Free Society*, 77.

4 In *Democracy and Disagreement* (Cambridge: Harvard University Press, 1996), 53, Amy Gutmann and Dennis Thompson distinguish three principles for the resolution of conflict among citizens: prudence, reciprocity, and impartiality. Civic virtue, in the sense in which I use it here, falls between simple prudence and full reciprocity. It requires a generous view of one's own self-interest, including a predisposition to collaborate to achieve goods that no single person can accomplish. It does not require that the outcomes of the deliberation be mutually justifiable to each participant according to other moral principles that they might hold.

5 The discussion that follows focuses primarily on residential colleges and universities. Much of what I say holds true, however, for community colleges and large "commuter" institutions, which may also offer their own distinctive ways to achieve the general goals I have in mind.

6 Benjamin Barber, in *An Aristocracy of Everyone: The Politics of Education and the Future of America* (New York: Ballantine, 1992), chapter 7, has an especially good discussion of the importance of community service and "service learning" in training citizens in our democracy.

7 On this point, I am particularly indebted to conversations with Professor Elizabeth Kiss, director of the Kenan Ethics Program at Duke.

8 "On Racial Integration," *Dissent*, summer 1996, 47–52 [special issue, "Embattled Minorities around the Globe"].

9 David A. Hollinger, *Post-Ethnic America: Beyond Multiculturalism* (New York: Basic Books, 1995), has a particularly thoughtful conception of a true "cosmopolitanism" that moves beyond the separatist tendencies of contemporary pluralism; see especially chapters 4 and 5.

10 Alexis de Tocqueville, *Democracy in America* (New York: Alfred A. Knopf, 1945), vol. 2, book 2, chapter 2, 104.

11 Tocqueville, *Democracy in America*, vol. 2, book 2, chapter 8, 131.

12 The literature on this topic in contemporary social analysis is large and growing. The best-known work in the field is by Robert Putnam; see especially "Bowling Alone: The Decline of Social Capital in America," *Journal of Democracy* 6, no. 1 (1995).

13 Tocqueville, *Democracy in America*, vol. 2, book 2, chapter 8, 132.

MORE POWER TO THE PRESIDENT?

1 Hanna Gray, "On the History of Giants," *Universities and Their Leadership*, ed. William G. Bowen and Harold T. Shapiro (Princeton: Princeton University Press, 1998), 106.

2 James A. Perkins, *The University in Transition* (Princeton: Princeton University Press, 1966), 31–59.

3 Alexander Hamilton, James Madison, and John Jay, *The Federalist Papers* [1787–1788] (New York: New American Library, 1961), no. 51, 325.

4 Hamilton, Madison, and Jay, no. 70, 423.

5 Donald Kennedy, *Academic Duty* (Cambridge: Harvard University Press, 1997), 2.

6 Frank H. T. Rhodes, "The Art of the Presidency," *Presidency* 1, no. 1 (spring 1998): 12–18.

7 Hamilton, Madison, and Jay, no. 1, 33.

FROM COLONIAL SEMINARY TO GLOBAL MULTIVERSITY

1 U.S. Department of Education, National Center for Education Statistics, *Digest of Education Statistics, 1997*, NCES 98-015 (Washington, 1997); A. Levine, "How the Academic Profession Is Changing," *Daedalus* 126 (1997): 4, 1–20.

2 M. Trow, "Federalism in American Higher Education," *Higher Learning in America, 1980–2000*, ed. A. Levine (Baltimore: Johns Hopkins University Press, 1993). Trow's chapter provides an especially good brief overview of the development of higher education in the United States.

3 H. Perkin, "The Historical Perspective," *Perspectives on Higher Education*, ed. B. Clark (Berkeley: University of California Press, 1984).

4 J. Kauffman, "Governing Boards," *Higher Learning in America, 1980–2000*.

5   J. B. McLaughlin and D. Riesman, "The President: A Precarious Perch," *Higher Learning in America, 1980–2000*, 180.

6   A. de Tocqueville, *Democracy in America,* vol. 1 (New York: Alfred A. Knopf, 1945).

7   M. Trow, "Federalism in American Higher Education," *Higher Learning in America, 1980–2000*.

8   Perkin, "The Historical Perspective."

9   McLaughlin and Riesman, "The President."

10   Trow, "The Development of Information Technology," *Daedalus* 126 (1997): 4, 293–314.

11   C. E. Finn Jr., "Today's Academic Market Requires a New Taxonomy of Colleges," *Chronicle of Higher Education*, 9 January 1998, § B, 4–5.

12   M. Trow, "Aspects of Diversity in American Higher Education," *On the Making of Americans: Essays in Honor of David Riesman*, ed. H. Gans et al. (Philadelphia: University of Pennsylvania Press, 1979).

13   P. G. Altbach, "An International Academic Crisis?," *Daedalus* 126 (1997): 4, 315–38.

THE ATWELL LECTURE

1   Alexis de Tocqueville, *Democracy in America* (New York: Alfred A. Knopf, 1945), vol. 1, chapter 3, 48–60.

2   According to the World Bank.

3   Robert H. Frank, "Higher Education: The Ultimate Winner-Take-All Market?" Paper presented at the Forum for the Future of Higher Education, Aspen, Colo., 27 September 1999.

4   *Democracy in America*, vol. 2, book 2, chapter 20, 171.

5   *Democracy in America*, vol. 2, book 1, chapter 9, 39–40.

6   Robert H. Frank and Philip J. Cook, *The Winner-Take-All Society* (New York: Free Press, 1995).

7   10 March 2000.

8   Democracy in America, vol. 1, chapter 18, 414, 450.

9   Derek C. Bok and William G. Bowen, *The Shape of the River* (Princeton: Princeton University Press, 1998).

10   *Democracy in America*, vol. 1, chapter 18, 370, 373.

11   *Democracy in America*, vol. 2, book 2, chapter 5.

12   Robert D. Putnam, "Bowling Alone: America's Declining Social Capital," *Journal of Democracy* 6, no. 1 (1995): 65–78.

13   *Democracy in America*, vol. 2, book 3, chapter 15, 235.

14 *Democracy in America*, vol. 2, book 1, chapter 10, 46.

15 *Democracy in America*, vol. 2, book 1, chapter 8, 35.

16 *Democracy in America*, vol. 2, book 1, chapter 10, 48.

17 *Democracy in America*, vol. 2, book 1, chapter 9, 40.

LIBERAL ARTS AND ÉLITE HIGHER EDUCATION

1 C. Clotfelter, "The Familiar but Curious Economics of Higher Education: Introduction to a Symposium," *Journal of Economic Perspectives* 13, no. 1 (winter 1999): 3–12.

2 W. Cronon, "Only Connect," *Liberal Education* 85 (winter 1999): 6–12.

3 R. B. Graber, *Valuing Useless Knowledge: An Anthropological Inquiry into the Meaning of Liberal Education* (Kirksville, Mo.: Thomas Jefferson University Press, 1995).

4 B. Giamatti, *A Free and Ordered Space: The Real World of the University* (New York: W. W. Norton, 1988).

5 B. Barber, *An Aristocracy of Everyone: The Politics of Education and the Future of America* (New York: Ballantine, 1992).

6 H. T. Shapiro, "Liberal Education, Moral Education," *Princeton Alumni Weekly*, 27 January 1999.

7 M. S. McPherson and M. O. Schapiro, *The Student Aid Game: Meeting Need and Rewarding Talent in American Higher Education* (Princeton: Princeton University Press, 1998).

8 D. Bok and W. G. Bowen, *The Shape of the River: Long-term Consequences of Considering Race in College and University Admissions* (Princeton: Princeton University Press, 1998).

9 A. W. Astin, "How the Liberal Arts College Affects Students," *Daedalus* 128, no. 1 (winter 1999): 77–100.

10 F. H. T. Rhodes, "The Place of Teaching in the Research University," *The Research University in a Time of Discontent*, ed. J. R. Cole, E. G. Barber, and S. R. Graubard (Baltimore: Johns Hopkins University Press, 1994).

11 W. P. Few, "Duke University Architecture Discussed by President W. P. Few," *Duke University Alumni Register* 17, no. 6 (June 1931): 195–97.

"YOU SAY YOU WANT A REVOLUTION?" WELL . . .

1 Clayton Christensen, *The Innovator's Dilemma* (Cambridge: Harvard University Press, 1997).

1 Londa Schiebinger, Barbara D. Finberg Director of the Institute for Research on Women and Gender.

2 Susan G. Bell and Karen M. Offen, *Women, the Family, and Freedom: The Debate in the Documents, 1750–1880*, vol. 1 (Stanford: Stanford University Press, 1983).

Index

academic freedom, 250–52
academic leadership and governance, 1, 58, 112–19, 183; authority and, 41–42; board of trustees and, 112, 115–18; characteristics of, 20–25; collaboration and, 24–25, 37–51, 118–19; decision making and, 41; defining, 38–40; in early American college system, 122–23; entrepreneurial model of, 115; faculty members and, 115–18; Hamiltonian model of, 25, 114–17; Jeffersonian model of, 25, 114–15; loneliness of, 40–41; Machiavelli–St. Simeon model of leadership and, 42–45, 48; Madisonian checks and balances and, 13–14, 25, 113, 116–17; making things happen and, 47–49; in nineteenth-century America, 127–28; passion and perspective in, 50–51; political theorists and, 31–32; problem solving and, 46–47; taking a stand and, 49–51; as Wizard of Oz, 41–42. *See also* universities and colleges; university presidents
Academic Strategy, Leadership and Ambiguity (Keller), 32, 45
access to education, 8, 15, 57–58, 128; government threats to, 131–32, 165–66; inequality of, 143–46; in liberal arts, 165–68; women and, 195–96

affirmative action, 148, 166
alumni programs, 75
American society: associations and, 32, 89–91, 149–50; collaboration and, 85–88, 90–91, 96; diversity in, 146–49; education and, 156; egalitarianism in, 141–46; enlightened self-interest and, 88–90, 96, 109–10; fragmentation of, 109–10, 147; immigrants in, 146; individualism and, 88–92, 96, 141, 149–51; lessons of the frontier and, 85–87, 90; loosening of social bonds and, 87–88; on Nantucket, 84–86; pragmatism in, 152–56; privilege in, 143–46; slavery and, 142, 148–49; Tocqueville on, 11–12, 88–92, 109–10, 124, 141–55; as "winner-take-all society," 144, 166. *See also* September 11; universities and colleges
Anderson, Charles, 32
Aristotle, 32, 47
associations, 32, 89–91, 149–50
athletics, 14
"Attending, The" (Chappell), 33–34
Atwell, Bob, 140, 155

Bacon, Francis, 95
Bassett, John Spencer, 251
Beatles, 178
Bellagian ideal, 218–20, 224
Bellah, Robert, 95–96

13; diversity at, 215, 223, 235; East Campus of, 209–10; as employer, 257–58; ethical education and, 216; financial resources of, 13–14, 257; GEMBA program of, 137–38; humanities and social sciences at, 245–49; interinstitutional collaboration by, 19, 225; as international university, 226, 254–55; John Hope Franklin Institute at, 245; Kenan Institute for Ethics at, 11; language instruction at, 232, 246; lifelong learning at, 234–36; motto of, 226–28; as neighbor, 256; need-blind admissions at, 224–25; Ph.D. training at, 137; principled intolerance and, 108–9; privileged students at, 137; research at, 220–21, 224, 259; rising costs at, 137, 259; Southern roots of, 225–26; teaching at, 210, 221–24; UNC collaboration with, 19, 255; undergraduate education at, 210–17; women's initiative at, 196, 198–203, 258. *See also* Trinity College

Education Act (1972), 129
Eliot, Charles W., 127
élite universities, 8–9, 136–37
Emory University, 256
Essais (Montaigne), 7, 213
ethical education, 71–72, 91–111, 150; diversity and, 104–7; Duke University and, 216; faculty members and, 102–4; Kenan Institute for Ethics, 11; liberal arts education and, 163–64; objectivity in classroom and, 103–4; obstacles to, 102–4; principled intolerance and, 108–9; teaching

and, 73. *See also* moral purpose, of universities and colleges
Euben, Peter, 11

faculty members, 2, 6, 133–34; burnout of, 170, 176, 222; ethical education and, 102–4; governance and, 115–18; limiting tenure and, 132; preserving community and, 184–85; in nineteenth-century America, 127–28. *See also* teaching
Federalist Papers, 113, 119
Few, William Preston, 176, 226–27, 251, 259
Field, James, 39
financial aid: Education Act and, 129; need-blind, 148, 184, 224–25; for poorer students, 17, 143, 165–66
Fisher, James L., 42–45, 48–49
Five Colleges of the Connecticut Valley, 18
for-profit institutions, 131
foreign languages, 26–27; as lingua franca of internet, 139; reluctance to learn, 139, 232, 238–39; September 11 and, 246
foreign students, 77; declining enrollment of, 30–31, 139; funding and, 77–78; in nineteenth-century America, 127. *See also* students
Fourier, Charles, 195
Frank, Bob, 144

Garfield, James A., 6
GEMBA (Global Executive MBA) program, 137–38
Genovese, Kitty, 88
German universities, 60, 126; Johns Hopkins inspired by, 5

Perkins, James A., 60, 117
Ph.D. training, 137; information
  technology and, 181–82
"Planetarium" (Rich), 204
Plato, 4, 22
political correctness, 94, 100,
  250–52
Political Parties (Michels), 60
"Politics as a Vocation" (Weber),
  20, 50
Popper, Karl, 246
Power of the Presidency (Fisher),
  42–45
pragmatism, 152–56
Prescribing the Life of the Mind
  (Anderson), 32
Prince, The (Machiavelli), 44
privilege: in American society, 143–
  46; Duke University and, 137;
  élite universities and, 8–9, 136–
  37; financial aid and, 165–66;
  stress and, 145
Putman, Charles, 254
Putnam, Robert, 149, 183

racial integration, 105–7. *See also*
  diversity
"Red Book" (Harvard Committee
  on the Objectives of a General
  Education in a Free Society
  Report), 99–100
Remaking America (Joseph), 94
research universities, 1; as community, 218–20; corporate funding
  of, 80–81, 153; economics of, 16;
  German model and, 60, 126; government funding of, 80, 129–32,
  221; human condition improved
  by, 3–5, 67, 76–83, 220–21; hybrid model and, 61; knowledge
  discovery and sharing at, 2, 60;
  land-grant universities and, 126;

liberal arts universities vs., 169;
  mission of, 2, 59–83; nationalism
  and, 78–80; Oxford and Cambridge as models for, 61, 121;
  Ph.D. training at, 137; productivity of, 171; teaching at, 169–73,
  220–21; teaching vs., 63–68, 221.
  See also Duke University; universities and colleges
Research Triangle Park, 80, 225, 256
residential education: diversity
  and, 56–58, 104–7; durability of,
  54–55, 134–35, 180–82; ethical
  education and, 94, 101, 149; virtual education vs., 54, 134–35,
  138, 154–55, 174, 181–82, 237–39
Rhodes, Frank, 118
Rice, Condoleeza, 30
Rice University, 256
Rich, Adrienne, 204
Rockefeller Foundation, 244
Rosaldo, Shelly, 192
Roth, Susan, 199
Rousseau, Jean-Jacques, 32
Rukeyser, Muriel, 205

Sanford, Terry, 254
Schmidt, Benno, 52
"Science as a Vocation" (Weber), 20
September 11, 33; humanities and
  social sciences and, 241–49; lan-
  guage learning and, 246. *See also*
  American society
Shape of the River, The (Bok and
  Bowen), 148, 168
Silber, John, 114
Silicon Valley, 80
slavery, 142, 148–49
Snow, C. P., 247
social sciences. *See* humanities and
  social sciences
St. Simeon the Stylite (Saint), 43;

Machiavelli–St. Simeon model of leadership, 42–45
Stafford Little Lectures, 60
Stanford University, 52, 125, 135; German model and, 126; IRWG at, 192–94, 198, 204
state universities, 127, 135
Steck, Henry, 12–13
students. *See* foreign students; graduate students; student-teacher relationships; undergraduate students
student-teacher relationships, 6, 54–55; at élite universities, 136–37
Swarthmore College, 39
sweatshops, 189–90

teaching, 1; burnout and, 170, 176, 222; ethics and, 73; of graduate students, 65; by graduate assistants, 72, 137, 175; incentive structure and, 171–72, 221; information technology and, 133–34, 174, 223–24; lecture system and, 18; research vs., 63–68, 221; research productivity and, 171; at research universities, 169–73, 220–21; team, 175; of undergraduate students, 66–74, 210, 220–23. *See also* faculty members
technical schools, 8
terrorism, 250
Thomas, M. Cary, 127
Three Guineas (Woolf), 27
Tocqueville, Alexis de, 88–90, 109–11, 141–55
Trinity College, 125, 209–10, 226. *See also* Duke University
Trow, Martin, 121, 136

UNC Chapel Hill, 19, 255
undergraduate students, 6–7; apa-

thy of, 176; changing composition of, 6, 57; consumerist mentality of, 2, 6, 114, 131, 166; deficiency in basic skills of, 222; distribution requirements for, 160–61; at Duke, 210–17; GI Bill and, 128; obligations to, 68–71, 173; older, 6, 26, 57, 74, 128, 133, 230–31, 234–36; student-teacher relationships and, 6, 54–55, 136–37; teaching of, 66–74, 210, 220–23. *See also* foreign students; universities and colleges
universities and colleges: access to, 8, 12, 57–58; alumni groups and, 95; challenges to, 2, 12–15; class bias of, 57–58; coeducation at, 124–25; in colonial times, 121–23; community service and, 95, 150–51, 185, 216; as company of scholars, 218–20; complacency of, 29–30; consumerist mentality and, 131; contemporary relevance of, 93–97; as "convenience" institutions, 135; corporatization of, 2, 9–15, 146; dire predictions about, 178–81; diversity and, 9, 146–49; durability of, 181–86; ethical education and, 11, 71–72, 91–111, 150; European, 1–2, 5; expense of, 133; financing of, 57–58; foreign students at, 30–31, 127, 139; freed slaves at, 125; future of, 25–34, 52–58, 132–35, 230–40; German, 5, 60, 126; GI Bill and, 128; goals of, 2–7; government funding and, 129–32; historical overview of, 120–39; increasing practicality of, 133; inequality and, 144–46; intergenerational partnership and, 2–3; international, 30–31;

283

NANNERL O. KEOHANE was president of Duke University from 1993 to 2004, where she also held the position of professor of political science. Before coming to Duke she was the president of Wellesley College and taught political theory at Stanford University, Swarthmore College, and the University of Pennsylvania. She is the author of *Philosophy and the State in France: The Renaissance to the Enlightenment* and co-editor of *Feminist Theory: A Critique of Ideology*. Keohane is currently the Laurance S. Rockefeller Distinguished Visiting Professor of Public Affairs and the University Center for Human Values at Princeton University.

Several of the pieces in this collection have been previously published. Publication information for these pieces is as follows: "Collaboration and Leadership: Are They in Conflict?," *College Board Review* 135 (spring 1985): 101–25, © 1993 American Academy of Arts and Sciences, reprinted with permission; "The Mission of the Research University," *Daedalus* 122, no. 4 (fall 1993); "Moral Education in the Modern University," *Proceedings of the American Philosophical Society* 142, no. 2 (1998), reprinted with the permission of the American Philosophical Association; "More Power to the President?," *The Presidency* (fall 1998); "The American Campus: From Colonial Seminary to Global Multiversity," *The Idea of a University*, ed. David Smith and Anne Karin Langslow (London: Jessica Kingsley, 1999), reprinted with permission; "The Liberal Arts and the Role of Elite Higher Education," *In Defense of American Higher Education*, ed. Philip G. Altback, Patricia J. Gumport, and D. Bruce Johnstone (Baltimore: Johns Hopkins University Press, 2001), reprinted with permission; " 'You Say You Want a Revolution?' Well . . .," *Proceedings of the Association of American Universities International Convocation* (2001); "When Should a College President Use the Bully Pulpit?," *Chronicle of Higher Education*, 7 February 2003, § B, 20.